THEATRICAL TOURING AND FOUNDING IN NORTH AMERICA

Edited by L. W. CONOLLY

Foreword by MICHAEL SIDNELL

Contributions in Drama and Theatre Studies, Number 5

G
P

GREENWOOD PRESS
Westport, Connecticut • London, England

D0068959

Library of Congress Cataloging in Publication Data
Main entry under title:
Theatrical touring and founding in North America.

   (Contributions in drama and theatre studies,
ISSN 0163-3821; no. 5)
   Bibliography: p.
   Includes index.
   1. Theater—North America—History—19th century—
Addresses, essays, lectures. 2. Theater—North America
—History—20th century—Addresses, essays, lectures.
I. Conolly, L. W. (Leonard W.) II. Series.
PN2219.5.T5   792'.097   81-23766
ISBN 0-313-22595-8 (lib. bdg.)   AACR2

Copyright © 1982 by L. W. Conolly

Library of Congress Catalog Card Number: 81–23766
ISBN: 0–313–22595–8
ISSN: 0163–3821

First published in 1982

Greenwood Press
A division of Congressional Information Service, Inc.
88 Post Road West
Westport, Connecticut 06881

Printed in the United States of America

10 9 8 7 6 5 4 3 2 1

Copyright Acknowledgment
Quotations from Susan Glaspell's *The Road to the
Temple* (1926) are reprinted by permission of the
publisher, Ernest Benn.

THEATRICAL TOURING AND FOUNDING IN NORTH AMERICA

Contributions in Drama and Theatre Studies
Series Editor: Joseph Donohue

American Popular Entertainment: Papers and Proceedings of the Conference on the History of American Popular Entertainment
Myron Matlaw, editor

George Frederick Cooke: Machiavel of the Stage
Don B. Wilmeth

Greek Theatre Practice
J. Michael Walton

Gordon Craig's Moscow *Hamlet*: A Reconstruction
Laurence Senelick

Contents

Illustrations

Foreword

In inviting the International Federation for Theatre Research to hold its Executive and Plenary Sessions in Toronto in 1979, we, the Canadian members, had two main motives: first, to make a contribution to the work of the IFTR; and second to heighten interest in the study of the theatre in Canada; that is to say, in the discipline generally and in its application to the Canadian theatre. The subject of the conference that accompanied the meeting was intended to be of interest from many angles of vision and to engage participants from many countries in fruitful discussion. And so it proved. We were delighted that so many members of the IFTR came—from Austria, Britain, Czechoslovakia, Denmark, the German Democratic Republic, Korea, the Netherlands, Norway, Switzerland, the United States, Ghana, Yugoslavia, Italy, Poland, and from all over Canada—and that they found the meeting and conference useful and, apparently, enjoyable.

Somehow, one of the bulletins carrying a notice of the conference transmogrified its title into "Theatrical Touring and *Fund*ing in the *United States*," an interesting pair of Freudian slips. Well, from *found*ing to *fund*ing is a short step (mentally) and the United States *is* a very important part of North America, but the conference certainly made clear that there is more to founding than cash and that the theatre in Canada has its distinctness. In fact, nobody said much about money and there was a considerable interest in the Canadian theatre. Happily we were able to take our visitors to a couple of performances and on a tour of the Stratford Shakespearean Festival Theatre archives; so all of them got at least a taste of the thing itself as well as discourse on it. Those who were visiting Canada for the first time went away with a clear sense, I believe, of our theatrical and general identity; very likely a clearer, if less complex, sense than we have ourselves.

Readers of this collection of essays cannot share the pleasure of the theatre trips, the social occasions, and the discussions. You do have before you most of the papers that were given, however, and six additional essays, and the book is, in its own manner, a congress of minds, nations, and people.

On this occasion, I must make the thank-yous brief, but they are no less cordial for that: to the IFTR for coming to Toronto; to the Social Sciences and Humanities Research Council of Canada for help with funding (and thus with laying some foundations!); and to the Association for Canadian Theatre History and the four host universities: Alberta, Dalhousie, Toronto, and York. Certain individuals I cannot help but thank by name even though many helpers are not thus singled out: Tom Lawrenson, our man in the IFTR; Alan Andrews and Ann Saddlemyer, two sure guides and active workers; Leonard Conolly, the editor of this volume, who assembled the speakers and was our conference chairman; Derrick deKerckhove who was responsible for the logistics and a most resourceful, elegant host; and Pia Kleber, Françoise Mignault, and Carmen Sayers, the conference assistants, whose laborious and precise preparation, gifts of tongues, and amiability resulted in the smooth execution of most of our plans and the enhancement of the aleatory elements of an occasion of which this book is one of the results.

Michael Sidnell
Graduate Centre for the Study of Drama
University of Toronto

Introduction _____

Of the thirteen essays included in this book, seven—those by Mary Brown, Helen Krich Chinoy, Robertson Davies, Jean-Cléo Godin, Richard Moody, Andrew Parkin, and Arnold Rood—were read as papers at a conference held at the University of Toronto in August 1979 in conjunction with the executive and plenary committee meetings of the International Federation for Theatre Research. The subject of the conference, "Theatrical Touring and Founding in North America," has been retained as the title for this book, though the conference papers have been supplemented by six further papers—by Marvin Carlson, Douglas McDermott and Robert K. Sarlós, Ann Saddlemyer, Ross Stuart, Don B. Wilmeth, and Alan Woods. Two other papers delivered at the conference by François Kourilsky and Mavor Moore are not printed here. [Mavor Moore's paper, "Founding: Transplant, Native Plant or Mutation?" is printed under a slightly different title in *Canadian Theatre Review*, 25 (Winter 1980):10–16.]

Theatrical touring and founding in North America is a subject that might well be said to encompass the continent's entire theatrical history, but the essays here deal mainly with one century of that history, from the early 1880s to the present, and only with particular features of it. Between the triumphs and the failures of Ernesto Rossi's first American tour of 1881–82 (the subject of Marvin Carlson's essay) and the vigorous debates over the role of Ontario's Stratford Festival Theatre in the 1960s and 1970s (discussed by Ross Stuart), theatrical developments were many and varied, and thirteen books, let alone thirteen essays, could hardly hope to treat them adequately. What these essays do trace, however, is one vital development of those one hundred years: the transition from a theatre of commerce to a theatre of art. If these essays have a theme, that is it.

Qualifications are immediately necessary. Of course Irving cared about theatrical art, and the Stratford Festival, heaven knows, cares about making money. Naturally enough, Rossi worried about his artistic reputation, and John Martin-Harvey, whose tours are recalled by Robertson Davies, was deeply committed to his art, as undoubtedly were the other major touring stars and companies Professor Davies had the good fortune to see in Ontario in the period between the wars. Having said that, however, one cannot help but be impressed, or sometimes depressed, by the commercial aspects of the touring era. The publicity, the hectic itineraries, the encouragement of the star system, the power of the impresarios and syndicates, all focused on commercial success, which inevitably militated against artistic achievement and artistic seriousness. Robertson Davies remembers some touring shows that resembled those given by the King and the Duke in *Huckleberry Finn.* Now the same reproof could not be levelled against, say, Frank Benson's Stratford (England) Company, which toured Canada in 1913, but even the best-intentioned of actors and companies felt, and sometimes succumbed to, commercial pressure. As Arnold Rood's essay on Irving shows, one important measure, perhaps the most important measure, of the success of an Irving tour was the final balance sheet. Irving needed money and he came to North America to get it. As Rossi ruefully remarked, "Dramatic art has become a matter of business only and principally of advertising."

There are three essays in this volume that usefully divert our attention away from the major foreign touring stars like Rossi, Irving, and Martin-Harvey and the big towns and theatres in which they normally (though not exclusively) played. Alan Woods assesses the career of provincial Shakespearean actor Thomas W. Keene; Douglas McDermott and Robert Sarlós give a detailed analysis of a typical season at a minor Californian touring house; and Mary Brown describes the small-town Ontario circuit controlled by impresario Ambrose Small. Here again, commercialism is evident, in some instances even rampant. Professor Woods comments, for example, on Keene's advertising techniques, "the luridly colored posters . . . posters which, in size, color, and design, were more reminiscent of circus billboards than Shakespearean grandeur." In Woodland, California, similar principles applied. The theatre existed for profit, and it could stay in the black by giving audiences what they wanted—a regular and predictable diet of "song, dance, humor and thrills," to quote Professors McDermott and Sarlós. The profits made in Woodland were negligible, however, compared to the fortune accumulated by Ambrose Small in Ontario. Worth some two million dollars when he mysteriously disappeared in 1919 (never to be traced), Small applied ruthless business procedures to theatre. "Ambrose Small's business was theatre as Molson's was ale," Mary Brown tells us. Canada's answer to the American syndicate giants, Small cared not a jot for the artistic worth of what went on in his theatres. Actors and plays, like bottles of beer, were commodities to be exploited for purely commercial ends.

However, the commercialism of the touring era cannot be dismissed, nor should it be, quite so easily. Professors Carlson, Rood, Woods, Davies, McDermott, Sarlós, and Brown write in praise more than in sorrow, and they have good reason for doing so. In a presubsidy age, the North American theatre reverberated with an enviable vigor, a truly splendid vitality, and it did so through the box office, not government grants. Robertson Davies mourns the loss of "the flair, the theatrical radiance" of the touring shows; Mary Brown credits Ambrose Small with having maintained "the continuity of the Canadian theatrical tradition"; and Alan Woods rates

Keene's as "the last period during which North America possessed a vitally alive theatre across the entire continent." Reaction against commercialism, whether the commercialism came from abroad or from Broadway, was inevitable, right, and proper; but at least the stars, the impresarios, the publicity writers, and the hundreds of humdrum performers who took to the road made sure there was a living theatre to react against.

Two essays, Andrew Parkin's and Jean-Cléo Godin's, begin to suggest the nature of the transition from touring to founding. In British Columbia, Professor Parkin argues, there is a relatively smooth and untroubled continuity from early British nautical theatre, through later American road shows, to the founding of indigenous amateur drama groups and professional companies. In Quebec, the situation is different, with a rather less harmonious connection between the touring and founding elements of the province's theatre history. In the face of strong opposition from the Roman Catholic Church, the theatre in Quebec was able to survive at least in part because of the frequent visits of touring companies, francophone and anglophone. Professor Godin's essay shows how necessary such visits were to the very existence of theatre in that province. Professor Godin also makes us aware, however, of the negative effects of foreign dominance, and the second part of his essay charts mid-twentieth century reaction by Quebecois actors, designers, and directors against foreign intrusion. In Quebec's case, it was not so much an objection to commercial crassness that prompted the reaction; it was, rather, an urgent concern that so long as influences and standards emanated from Paris or New York or London, the development of Quebec talent and ambition would be stunted. This brings us directly to the five specifically "founding" essays in this collection, those by Richard Moody, Helen Krich Chinoy, Don B. Wilmeth, Ross Stuart, and Ann Saddlemyer.

Dissatisfaction with the values and standards of the commercial theatre, on tour or on Broadway, arose partly from artistic and partly from nationalistic causes. Perhaps one can speak of an artistic nationalism, that fervent blend of aesthetics and politics that inspired the founders of the Abbey Theatre. It is interesting that Ann Saddlemyer finds such compelling parallels between the early history of the Abbey and Canada's emerging theatrical identity. Only intermittently has Canada's best-known theatre, the Stratford Festival Theatre, experienced the Abbey-like energy and clear sense of purpose that characterize many other Canadian theatres; consequently, as Professor Stuart shows, Stratford has frequently been at loggerheads with the rest of the country's theatrical community. In the end, Canada's expensive picnic theatre may come to be regarded merely as an irrelevant hiccup in the development of a genuinely Canadian theatrical tradition.

The Abbey, and other great national theatres like the Moscow Art Theatre (MAT), have been a source of inspiration in the United States as well. What had been achieved in Russia and Ireland could be achieved in America, but not in the commercial theatre. Both Richard Moody and Helen

Krich Chinoy recognize a commitment to the founding of theatres as thoroughly American as MAT was Russian and the Abbey Irish: Professor Moody in his essay on the "incredible decade" of the Little Theatre, 1909–1919, and Professor Chinoy in hers on the Group Theatre, whose members "thought of themselves as uniquely American. . . . their whole reason for existing was to respond to what was happening to America and to themselves in the early years of the Great Depression." This nationalistic stimulus is seen too in the work of the redoubtable Margo Jones in Dallas, where, Don Wilmeth calculates, some 70 percent of the plays produced under her management at the Margo Jones Theatre were new.

The Little Theatres, the Group Theatre, and regional and college theatres all gave opportunities to scores of gifted American and Canadian playwrights, directors, actors, designers, and technicians for whom there was no place in the commercial theatre. The "rhinoceros-hided magnates" (to borrow Maurice Browne's phrase) of the commercial theatre could not afford to take risks. In the noncommercial theatres there was artistic freedom— freedom to experiment, to be imaginative, to be inventive; freedom to be eccentric; freedom to fail—and the likes of Browne, Winthrop Ames, Cheryl Crawford, Harold Clurman, Lee Strasberg, Emile Legault, John Coulter, and many others thrived on the risks this freedom entailed. The risks paid off (artistically speaking, that is), and they are still paying off.

The commercial theatre in North America has long been dying; in Canada, it is virtually extinct already. Likewise, the independent Art Theatres, which flourished in the first half of the twentieth century, are gone, replaced by government-subsidized theatres, large and small. The distinctions between commerce and art have become more blurred. It now behooves most theatres to extract the best from both traditions, to eschew artistic iconoclasm as much as blatant commercialism, and to strive for artistic excellence while keeping a wary eye on the box office. Thus it is that artistic directors have about as much job security as do Italian prime ministers.

The essays collected in this volume each have their individual value, but they amount to more, I believe, than a miscellaneous collection of pieces on North American theatre. Collectively, they explore, albeit from different perspectives and with some inevitable gaps, two key aspects of a century of North American theatre history. They cannot pretend to resolve what seems to me to be still a fundamental dilemma of all theatre—the dilemma of commercialism versus art—but they serve the valuable function of putting that dilemma into a sharper, more intelligible perspective.

L. W. Conolly

THEATRICAL TOURING
AND FOUNDING
IN NORTH AMERICA

Marvin Carlson   1

Ernesto Rossi in America———————

By the beginning of the 1880s, the touring foreign star had become a fairly common phenomenon in the American theatre, and the American public had come to expect that the leading actors of Europe, despite the language barrier, would inevitably seek to display their talents in the new world as well. According to a pattern established with the first American tour of Adelaide Ristori in 1866–67, major stars would spend an entire season in America, arriving in the fall after their advance managers had spent several months carefully building public anticipation by extensive publicity campaigns. Thus, during the summer of 1881, the newspapers in the leading cities of America carried a series of stories acquainting their readers with the career and achievements of the Italian actor, Ernesto Rossi, who was scheduled to perform for the first time in the United States during the coming fall.

Carlo Chizzola, the entrepreneur who supervised most of the publicity and arranged the advance bookings for Rossi, was by this time an experienced organizer of such tours, having performed a similar service for the earlier American tours of Ristori and Tommaso Salvini. Advance publicity for foreign stars followed a fairly predictable pattern, predictable enough, indeed, to stimulate occasional mockery. One critic, deploring the fact that Rossi had been "preceded and accompanied by as noisy a crowd of gong-beaters as those who made the name of Sarah Bernhardt odious to quiet theatre-goers," cited a series of spurious anecdotes about Rossi as an inevitable part of such gong-beating:

Story showing the valor of Rossi. Being challenged by a gentleman whom he had bidden, from the stage, to be silent, the actor fought him at a hotel in the dark, guided only by the light of a cigar, and wounded him severely in the shoulder.

Story showing the fascination of Rossi. Having gained the affections of a confectioner's daughter at Pistoia, he was shut up in an oven by the girl's father and not released till his person was thoroughly heated and his passion entirely cooled.

Story showing the disinterestedness of Rossi. Being led by a king into a sumptuous apartment and being told that all it contained should be his if he would remain as the king's dramatic instructor, he replied: "No, your majesty, I cannot accept the flattering position. I am a bird that is mute when caged; I can sing only when I am free."[1]

Equally predictable, but somewhat more informative, were articles containing biographical information, selected quotations from the coming actor on his art, and comparisons with other stars. A major article usually appeared in August containing these elements, and that for Rossi was printed by several papers on 7 August 1881. The most complete version appeared in the *New York Tribune*, where it filled three and a half columns. After some preliminary remarks on the extent of Rossi's previous touring (to France, Germany, Spain, England, and South America), and his fame in Europe (where he was considered the peer of Salvini, a star already known and much admired in America), the article proceeded with a fairly detailed biography. Rossi was born, the article noted, in 1829, the same year as Joseph Jefferson, and after some difficult years with a strolling company, began touring with the great Gustavo Modena, who had also instructed Ristori and Salvini.

One of the features of the acting of these great Italian stars most commented upon was its realism, a feature which, as we shall see in the case of Rossi, aroused both positive and negative reaction. Clearly, much of this was inspired by Modena, under whose guidance, according to the article, Rossi

discarded the desiccated classicism and teapot style of the old school, and breathed the breath of life into whatever he touched. Under the teachings of Modena, who never shackled his pupils with traditions, and never exacted even the copying of himself, he had been trained to be natural in his own way, and this was a development in the spontaneous direction of his mind. All the pupils of Modena, who have been heard of at all, have exemplified the master's wisdom in one notable way—they have kept their distinct individuality and advanced in pathways of their own.

Thus, while Rossi "ruffled the pedants, he won the hearts of the people."[2]

By 1855, Rossi had become a member of the leading Italian theatre troupe of the period, the Royal Sardinian Company, playing leading roles opposite Ristori. That year they appeared in Paris at the International Exposition, achieving a dazzling and unexpected success. Ristori was widely and favorably compared with the reigning French actress Rachel, and though this comparison dominated critical reaction, Rossi also drew the warmest praise. He and Ristori were even approached by members of the Comédie Française who asked them to consider remaining in France, learning the language, and becoming pensioners of that famous company. The triumph of 1855, important as it was for the careers of Rossi and Ristori, was equally important in the history of the Italian theatre, since it demonstrated that Italy, regarded for generations as productive only in opera, possessed major talents in the spoken theatre as well. The age of the international Italian stars had begun.

For Rossi, the 1855 tour provided another benefit. In Paris, he saw his first production of Shakespeare—James Wallack of the London Marylebone Theatre, appearing as Macbeth, Shylock, and in other roles. Although the *Tribune* biography did not mention it, Rossi did not return to Italy with the rest of the company, but went on to London, specifically to acquaint himself more thoroughly with the English theatre. To his disappointment, because of the system of long runs, he was able to see Charles Kean in only a single Shakespearean role—Richard III—but he made Kean's acquaintance, discussed acting and Shakespeare with him in broken French, and received from Kean copies of Garrick's acting versions of *Othello* and *Hamlet* to take back to Italy.[3]

At this time, Shakespeare had still never been offered successfully in Italy. Only a few isolated attempts had been made, one of them by Modena himself in Milan in 1843. On that occasion the audience, accustomed to the neoclassic approach of Alfieri and the French, were so outraged by the unconventional opening scene of *Othello* that they did not even allow Modena to appear. Still, the efforts of Manzoni and the romantics had at least introduced Shakespeare to the reading public—Rossi himself developed his love for the English dramatist as a child, from readings by his godmother—and upon his return from Paris, Rossi felt the time had come to make a new attempt at production. The *Tribune* article quoted a letter from him to a friend, reporting the results:

There was reason, of course, to fear that our public, ignorant of the Shakespearean moulds and style—which are better adapted to the pensive and reticent character of the northern nations, than to the tumultuous and demonstrative people of Italy— would be repelled rather than attracted by this novelty. I did not hesitate, though, to make the experiment. I brought out "Hamlet", "Othello", "Macbeth", "Coriolanus", and "King Lear" in rapid succession, and I rejoice to say that all these sublime creations were accepted with delight.[4]

Actually, Rossi first offered *Hamlet* and *Othello* in 1856, *Macbeth* and *King Lear* in 1858, and *Coriolanus* in 1861, by which time he had also presented *Romeo and Juliet*, *Julius Caesar*, and *The Merchant of Venice*. Thus, this "rapid succession" of plays in fact covered five years, but during these years the Italian public's enthusiasm for Shakespeare grew steadily, and much of the credit for this clearly was due to Rossi. Soon after Rossi's *Hamlet* and *Othello* in Milan, Salvini successfully offered the same two plays in Vicenza. Although Salvini came to be regarded as the greatest Othello of his time, Rossi's fame as Hamlet was, at least in Europe, almost as great, and Rossi's repertoire, unlike Salvini's, was always composed almost entirely of Shakespearean works. The *Tribune* called Rossi "the Booth of Europe as Salvini is the Forrest," and concluded its lengthy article by citing numerous decorations and honors given Rossi in various European and Latin American countries, by a physical description of the actor, and by the observation that the arrival of an artist of such stature would unquestionably prove an event of high magnitude.

Rossi at last arrived in New York on 30 September 1881, and the following day met his supporting company for the first time. Ristori and Salvini on their first American tours had brought with them companies of their countrymen which they had assembled themselves, but the year before Rossi's tour a different arrangement had been inaugurated for Salvini by Chizzola and the Boston theatre manager John Stetson, the same entrepreneurs now sponsoring Rossi. Stetson, one of the most colorful of the American impresarios in a period remembered for flamboyant figures, was notorious for his blunt speech and apparent indifference to artistic and literary concerns. Nevertheless, he was a remarkably shrewd businessman who made a fortune in theatre management. It was apparently his idea to tour European stars not with their own troupes but with companies assembled for them in America. Aside from the obvious financial advantages of such an arrangement, it would, Stetson hoped, make the work more accessible to English-speaking audiences, or, at the very least, attract attention as an experiment.

The mechanical and artistic problems of a performance with a leading actor speaking a different language from his fellows were, typically, ignored by Stetson entirely. Salvini, at first scarcely able to believe that this was a serious proposal, finally accepted the challenge, and offered America its first tour of bilingual Shakespeare in 1880–81. It was financially a great success, though the strain upon the leading player was great. In an interview in Cincinnati midway through the tour, Salvini was asked for his reaction to this arrangement. "I am the first artist who has engaged in a long series of bilingual performances," he replied, "and I think I shall be the last."[5] The strain on the star, he felt, was simply unacceptably great. Stetson, looking only at the profits from the tour, understandably had quite a different opinion, and before Salvini had even left America, preliminary arrangements had been made for Rossi to follow in the next season.

Some impresarios believed in surrounding visiting stars with companies of no distinction whatever, but Stetson and Chizzola were not miserly on this score. They provided both Salvini and Rossi with solid, established supporting players, and for the major supporting roles, with actors and actresses of significant reputation. Louise Muldener, who appeared with both actors, had performed with Wallack and Jefferson and toured with Booth in some of the same roles she played with Rossi—Ophelia, Desdemona, Cordelia, and Juliet. Many years later, she observed that no other actor had ever lifted her to such emotional heights as did Rossi with his portrayal of Hamlet.[6] Milnes Levick, who played Iago, Edgar, and Mercutio for Rossi, had served as a leading man for Barnum and Laura Keene and in the tours of Mary Anderson. Mercutio was his particular specialty, and no American actor of the period was better known for this role.

Rossi had only a single rehearsal with his new companions in New York and one more in Boston before the opening. The company had been rehearsing together for several weeks before his arrival, however, and he was pleased to find them already comfortable in their roles without a prompter, a situation rarely found in Italian companies of the period. The major problem then was surely that of cueing, since Rossi understood not a word of what his fellow actors were saying. Probably, like Salvini, he simply numbered his lines and recited them in sequence. These few days before the opening must have been extremely stressful ones, made more so for Rossi by the fact that President Garfield had been assassinated only a few days before. Thus, the announcements of Rossi's forthcoming appearances in New York and Boston appeared in black-bordered newspapers. Rossi was not a strongly superstitious man, but only a year before, he had been left stranded with his company in Russia by the assassination of Czar Alexander, and his uneasiness at the possibility of another such calamity can surely be understood.

Nevertheless, the black-bordered pages gave enthusiastic coverage to his arrival, and the Boston opening on 3 October with *King Lear* was a great success. Correspondents were present from every major New York paper, from Cincinnati, Chicago, even San Francisco for the event. Rossi was given several curtain calls at the end of each act, and Longfellow, a warm supporter of Italian culture, appeared backstage after the fourth act to offer his personal congratulations. *Hamlet*, which followed, was equally well received, and was called by the *Boston Globe* "one of the finest that this country has ever seen." The reviewer reported that some persons had speculated that such "Northern" characters as Lear and Hamlet were not accessible to Italian actors, but concluded that Rossi had magnificently refuted this assumption, and that indeed he enjoyed a distinct advantage over English interpreters by the "superior mobility of countenance and flexibility of person characteristic of the Latin race."[7]

Despite this warm praise, the suggestion of the incompatibility of the Latin temperament to some of the major roles of Rossi's repertoire was ominous, for it was a problem that dogged Rossi throughout his career. In Barcelona, he had silenced such criticism by giving a public lecture on Hamlet (subsequently published) to demonstrate his intellectual grasp of the character, and in London he had been driven by continual adverse criticism on this point to plead for his right to depart from English tradition in an open letter to the *Times*. Inevitably, the same charges were made in America, though the enthusiasm of the Boston reviews kept them muted temporarily.

1. Ernesto Rossi as Hamlet, 1881. From *The Critic*, 1881.

A much more serious problem in Boston was the unexpected indifference of the general public to the new star. The "cream of Boston society" appeared, at least for the opening performances, but despite highly favorable reviews, the rest of society did not follow. The *Globe*, which compared Rossi regularly to Salvini, and almost invariably to Rossi's advantage, found it "difficult to understand" why the same city that had given Salvini his most cordial welcome in America should show itself so cool to Rossi. Perhaps, the reviewer speculated, it was simply a result of scheduling these tours in too close proximity: "It is undoubtedly true that the Italian-English style of dramatic representation was very fully exemplified during the Salvini engagements, and probably the public was not altogether disposed to welcome so soon its revival. But it is not creditable to our community, nor does it maintain Boston's reputation as quick to recognize genius, that Rossi should have been so neglected."[8]

Rossi followed the Boston engagement with two weeks of one- and two-night stands in various New England cities, then arrived in New York on 31 October. He appeared at Booth's Theatre, one of the largest and best equipped in the city, which Stetson had purchased and refurbished the previous summer. The critical response in New England had generally followed the Boston lead, calling Rossi one of the greatest artists of the contemporary stage, but a significant contrasting note was struck in *The Critic* of 22 October 1881, which suggested that Rossi's proper domain was romantic drama, since he lacked the "breadth of conception and largeness of execution" necessary for tragedy. Unfortunately, he had elected to base his repertoire on Shakespeare, but "not the Shakespeare that Americans, Englishmen and Germans either know, or are likely to accept; it is the warm, glowing, passionate Shakespeare which alone is to the liking of the Latin races. As Lear, Hamlet, Romeo, he must here be judged by tests which it is hardly fair to apply."[9]

The New York critics divided sharply on this issue. George Edgar Montgomery, the reviewer of the *New York Times*, repeated the praise of the Boston critics and took issue specifically with the article in *The Critic*. "Men like Salvini and Rossi," he wrote, "tell us more about Shakespeare than all the commentators tell us. They aim at life, not at abstract conceptions."[10] Far from agreeing that only the English, Americans, or Germans could properly interpret Shakespeare, Montgomery called the Othellos of Sonnenthal, Irving, Booth, and McCullough all inferior to those of Rossi and Salvini. In this, admittedly Salvini's greatest role, Rossi had less intensity, but compensated for it in his pathos. Nor did Montgomery subscribe to the compromise position which allowed an "Italian" interpretation of Othello, but not of Hamlet or Lear. Having seen all of these, plus Rossi's Romeo, Montgomery judged him "one of the greatest artists and actors of the time," and "of all living tragic artists, the most flexible, versatile, and gifted."[11]

A sharply opposed position was taken by William Winter, the highly respected critic of the *New York Tribune*. Winter had little love for *Othello* in any case, a play with a "dreadful theme" that he felt normally left its audiences in "unmitigated affliction," but Salvini and Rossi, he thought, emphasized the most unattractive elements in the play. Both stressed "the animal over the ideal" and prose over poetry. It was not to Irving and Booth that Winter looked for comparisons with Rossi but to J. B. Studley, Joseph Proctor, and L. R. Shewell, minor actors associated with a rather plodding realistic approach. Clearly, Winter's antagonism to the new interest in realism then appearing in the theatre contributed in no small measure to his antagonism toward Rossi, for he concluded, "He will undoubtedly find adherents, however, among those who advocate the application of prose methods—colloquialism and the like, what they call 'nature'—to the poetic drama of the English stage."[12]

Reinforcing this antagonism toward Rossi's style was an aesthetic chauvinism, clearly manifested in Winter's review of *Hamlet*, which concluded:

These and the other great Shakespearean works exist in their integrity nowhere outside of the English language—unless, perhaps, in the German. The English ideals of them are the right ideals of them, and the English method of acting them is the right method. The foreign actors who come here ought to deal with what they really understand, and give the great works of their own literature, with companies speaking their own language.[13]

The strong endorsement of Montgomery doubtless helped Rossi in New York, for Montgomery's opinion was highly respected, Montgomery being well known for his objective and honest reviewing, but equally certainly the negative opinion of Winter was damaging, since Winter was at this time the city's most influential critic. Reading mixed reviews, the New York theatre public, which like Boston had given Salvini an enthusiastic reception the previous season, proved now equally unwilling to renew that enthusiasm for the new Italian star. Even Montgomery had to admit ruefully that Rossi was not attracting in New York the audiences he deserved.

After these New York performances, Stetson's active participation in the tour ended, and Chizzola took over the management of bookings elsewhere. The unexpectedly weak reception Rossi had received in New York and Boston concerned the entrepreneur greatly, and he attempted to protect his venture by scheduling Rossi for a far more exhausting tour than had been arranged the previous season for Salvini. Salvini had normally performed only three nights a week, but Rossi performed six, often with a matinée as well. To this was added the strain of travel; following the New York engagement, Rossi, within a space of two weeks, appeared in London, Hamilton, and Montreal in Canada, and in Buffalo, Troy, Rochester, Syracuse, Utica, and Albany, New York.

Not until he reached Philadelphia early in December did he enjoy an extended stay—two weeks in a single theatre—though he continued to give seven performances a week. Here his critical reception was more unanimously positive than it had been in New York, but the audiences remained small. So far in America Rossi had offered only Shakespeare. Now, in an attempt to broaden his appeal, he added two romantic plays which had been quite successful for him in Europe, Casimir Delavigne's *Louis XI* and Dumas père's *Edmund Kean*. Charles Kean played Louis XI on his 1865 American tour and it was occasionally repeated thereafter, but it was not widely known, and *Edmund Kean* was a new work for Americans, so unfamiliar that Rossi's advance publicity was able to claim, quite falsely, that Dumas had created the work expressly for him (in fact, the work had been inspired by the great French romantic actor Frédérick Lemaître).

Louis XI aroused so little interest that, after its single performance in Philadelphia, Rossi offered it only once more, in Chicago, but *Edmund Kean* proved much more attractive. By the end of Rossi's two weeks in Philadelphia, he was giving nothing else. During the remainder of the tour, Rossi would usually offer *Lear* or *Hamlet* in cities where he was appearing only once, but for longer engagements, *Kean* now became the basis of the repertoire. Thus, for example, during his week in St. Louis, he played *Hamlet* on Monday, *Lear* on Wednesday, *Othello* on Friday, and *Kean* on Tuesday, Thursday, and Saturday.

After Philadelphia, Chizzola booked Rossi into a series of Southern cities where for the first time he would not have to compete with memories of previous touring Italian stars. Salvini had not toured the deep South at all, and Ristori had visited only Memphis, New Orleans, and Mobile. Rossi's tour took him to Richmond, Charleston, Savannah, and Atlanta during the latter half of December. The pattern of his reception established in the North continued. Reviews were almost without exception strongly favorable— the *Charleston News and Courier*, for example, called his *Hamlet* "warmer, softer, and more genuine than that of any other major actor"[14]—but the general public was not enthusiastic. Clearly, the problem was not, or not entirely, one of audiences sated with Italian stars. If anything, Rossi did less well in cities that had not been visited by Ristori or Salvini. In the South he was forced for the first time to cancel performances because attendance was too small. This seems to have been the real reason for cancellation of an evening performance of *Othello* in Charleston and a matinée in Savannah. The announced reason was indisposition of the star, but the newspapers hinted that advance sales had been a major cause of this illness. The opening performance in Atlanta, of *Hamlet*, was unambiguously announced as cancelled due to inadequate advance sale.

Striking out into territory where he would find audiences unacquainted with Salvini clearly had not solved Rossi's difficulties, so he tried another, somewhat more desperate experiment, introducing English sections into his parts. On 21 December, playing King Lear in Charleston, he startled the audience by suddenly crying out in English "Every inch a king" in the fourth act, then continuing in Italian. The effect was enormous, the audience stopping the performance with applause. Encouraged by this enthusiastic response, Rossi added more and more English lines as he appeared in Baltimore and Washington in early January. When he reopened in *King Lear* at the Academy of Music in New York on 17 January 1882, he was able to present the entire final act in English.

Although the two weeks Rossi now spent in New York still did not attain the level of Salvini's success, they were a striking improvement over the November performances, and it began to appear that the actor was at last beginning to win over the American public. *Kean*, not offered by Rossi in New York before, was this time given for half of his performances, and was very well received. William Winter was as determinedly unenthusiastic as ever, calling the play a "dreary, rambling, platitudinous production" and remarking that "it scarcely need be added that no sort of the idea of the man that Edmund Kean really was is to be derived either from the play or from Signor Rossi." Nevertheless, even Winter was forced to admit that Rossi seemed to possess a "distinctive and exceptional excellence" at least in this style of play and that the applause was "frequent and warm."[15]

The English passages that Rossi now interpolated into his Shakespearean roles also proved attractive, though the audiences seem to have come more out of curiosity and applauded more in encouragement of the artist's attempt than from any aesthetic enthusiasm. Most reviewers found Rossi's English understandable and distinct, but somewhat labored. He tended to speak slowly and to divide long words into individual syllables as if he did not quite understand them himself. He possessed a mellifluous stage voice, and the softness and pleasantness that always characterized his delivery remained, but the *New York Herald* remarked that when he "abandoned his mother tongue for the harsher language of his audience there was a discordance in it that made it indeed like the sound of 'sweet bells jangled out of tune.'" Nevertheless, the attempt met with "hearty and admiring response" from an audience "fairly electrified by a patriotic or egotistical enthusiasm."[16]

Unhappily, when Rossi once again left New York, this time to go west to St. Louis, Minneapolis, St. Paul, and Chicago, he again encountered the familiar and frustrating pattern of highly favorable reviews and sparse audiences. McVicker's Theatre in Chicago was the usual stopping place for visiting stars, but its owner, concerned over Rossi's record so far, refused to book his theatre to Chizzola for the normal percentage of the profits, insisting instead on a flat fee of $2,000 a week. The prudence of this arrangement was soon demonstrated, for at the end of the Italian star's first week, the *Chicago Tribune* reported that "despite good weather, liberal advertising, and the undivided judgement of the newspapers in favor of the actor" only McVicker's of the major Chicago theatres was doing poor business. The second week saw no improvement, and a local manager commented in the *Tribune* on that perplexing question, how an actor "unanimously praised to the skies by the local papers" could not attract a public. He suggested that the American people had been so sold on Salvini that swerving them enough to interest them in any other Italian star was now extremely difficult. He suggested, however, that if Rossi could return later to Chicago as he did to New York, word of his excellence would doubtless spread and he could anticipate a better reception.[17]

Rossi had no opportunity to test this hypothesis. Chizzola was near the end of his resources, both financial and managerial. The company appeared briefly in Milwaukee and Toledo, then, upon reaching Detroit, had to be disbanded for lack of funds. The actors made their way individually back to New York, and Rossi, who had planned on a tour lasting into the spring, cast about for some engagements to fill the remainder of his time. He managed to arrange a week of performances of *Kean* in Philadelphia which at least supported him through March.

While in Philadelphia he was interviewed about his experiences in America, leading him inevitably to discuss why the success he had achieved throughout Europe had eluded him in America. He had suffered most, he felt, from a widespread unwillingness to accept Shakespearean interpretations that differed from the conventional approaches to these roles. "There are many methods in art," he said, "and why all should follow one method, or be judged by the merit of that one way, or be abused when they do otherwise, I do not see. Many have spoken of my Hamlet as if it should not be different from others, but it is my conception of what I believe is true."[18] Unquestionably, this was a serious problem for Rossi. Those critics who attacked him, led by William Winter, invariably based their attacks on his unfaithfulness to the Shakespearean "tradition" created by English and American actors. Of course, Salvini had achieved a triumph as an unorthodox Othello, but many critics were willing to tolerate an "Italianate" Moor of Venice, but never an "Italianate" Hamlet, Rossi's particular speciality, or Lear.

Rossi felt also that he had suffered from the American reliance upon publicity: "Dramatic art has become a matter of business only and principally of advertising. The one who advertises most succeeds best." A number of critics, in fact, remarked on Chizzola's failure to "sell" the public adequately on the new star before his arrival. Rossi did receive an advance campaign, with billboards, notices in the newspapers, reporting of engaging anecdotes, and so on, very similar to that mounted for Salvini the previous season. Salvini, however, was a star already known in America, and less promotion was necessary. Indeed, the tendency of Stetson and Chizzola to generally repeat for Rossi the main features of the previous year's successful advertising for Salvini seems to have had on the whole a more negative than positive effect, encouraging the public to consider Rossi not as a major star in his own right but merely as another, lesser Italian actor in the Salvini tradition.

Finally, Rossi admitted that his own performances in America had not been up to his usual standard. "I cannot act with credit six times in the week," he complained. "I did not do it until I came to this country. Since I came I have been nowhere but from the hotel to the theatre, then back to the hotel, and off to the depot. Acting requires inspiration, and inspiration does not come from either the hotel, theatre, or depot."[19]

Before returning to Europe, Rossi played one final American engagement which must have convinced him, were he not convinced before, that fate was set against his success on this tour. He was invited by Thomas Maguire, San Francisco's most famous theatre manager, to perform for two weeks in April at the Baldwin Theatre there. The reputation of both manager and theatre was great, and on the face of it, this offer seemed a godsend. Ristori had appeared at the Baldwin in 1875 with success, but Salvini had not yet been seen in California, so Rossi need not fear that comparison. What he did not know was that the famous Maguire was now on the brink of bankruptcy, having never recovered from the crash of 1877, and that this engagement was a last desperate attempt to salvage a sinking venture. The 1881–82 season had been one of constant decline; audiences remained away and Maguire's unpaid actors deserted him. David Belasco, then Maguire's playwright-in-residence, remained faithful, but he often received neither salary nor royalties, and he found himself serving as stage manager, painting scenery, helping in the box office, arranging advertising, playing minor roles, and even borrowing money for Maguire.[20] It was at this point that Maguire invited the unsuspecting Rossi and his stage manager to appear at the Baldwin, with results that can well be imagined.

Since the Baldwin had practically ceased paying salaries, the only actors on hand were amateurs willing to perform for nothing or even to pay for the opportunity of public exposure. A few more qualified performers were now attracted by the hope that Rossi's arrival would make some wages available. According to his contract, he was to keep half of the box office receipts, while other expenses and salaries were to come from the rest. The opening performances of *Hamlet* and *Othello* each produced a total of about ninety dollars, dashing any hopes of significant financial success. The actors and musicians began to leave, so that by 21 April the combined French and English armies in *King Lear* numbered only four persons.[21] Rossi, undaunted, was preparing *Romeo and Juliet* to open his second week, but "Lucky" Baldwin, the owner of the theatre, had had enough. His lawyer notified Maguire that the theatre was being put up for lease on 24 April, thus ending both the Rossi engagement and the Maguire administration.

Rossi returned to New York and sailed for Europe, exhausted and dispirited by his reception in America. Where Ristori and Salvini had found unprecedented fame and financial success, he had encountered only frustration and almost impossible demands. The charges that he lacked an intellectual grasp of Shakespeare were surely among his greatest irritations, spurring him to write extensive commentaries on the plays in *Studi drammatici e*

Lettere autobiografiche (Florence, 1885) and in *Quaranta anni di vita artistica* (Florence, 1887–89). He continued to tour widely in Europe, where his reputation as a major Shakespearean actor was secure, and even appeared successfully in bilingual productions there, most notably in 1886 with the famous company of the Duke of Saxe-Meiningen, which supported him in *Othello, Hamlet,* and *King Lear.* However, although Salvini returned twice more to America, in 1885 and 1889, Rossi never again attempted to achieve there the success that had eluded him on his first tour and of which he was assured elsewhere.

Notes

   1. P. M. Potter, "Ernesto Rossi," *The Critic,* 1 (1881), 286.
   2. *New York Tribune,* 7 August 1881, p. 5.
   3. Ernesto Rossi, *Studi drammatici e Lettere autobiografiche* (Florence, 1885), p. 127.
   4. *New York Tribune,* 7 August 1881, p. 5.
   5. *New Orleans Times-Picayune,* 13 February 1881, p. 6.
   6. Louise Muldener obituary, *New York Times,* 11 May 1938, p. 19.
   7. *Boston Globe,* 7 October 1881, p. 9.
   8. *Boston Globe,* 18 October 1881, p. 10.
   9. Potter, p. 286.
  10. *New York Times,* 6 November 1881, p. 4.
  11. *New York Times,* 13 November 1881, p. 9.
  12. *New York Tribune,* 1 November 1881, p. 5.
  13. *New York Tribune,* 6 November 1881, p. 7.
  14. *Charleston News and Courier,* 21 December 1881, p. 4.
  15. *New York Tribune,* 19 January 1882, p. 4.
  16. *New York Herald,* 18 January 1882, p. 6.
  17. *Chicago Tribune,* 19 February 1882, p. 9.
  18. *New York Times,* 17 March 1882, p. 1.
  19. *New York Times,* 17 March 1882, p. 1.
  20. William Winter, *The Life of David Belasco* (New York, 1918), I, 253.
  21. *San Francisco Examiner,* 22 April 1882, p. 6.

2

Henry Irving's Tours
of North America _____

Early in his renowned management of the Lyceum Theatre, Henry Irving came to know Joseph Hatton, the London correspondent for the *New York Tribune*, through whom favorable reports of Irving's work reached New York.[1] In the summer of 1882 William Winter, the already important and distinguished American dramatic critic, went to London with Lawrence Barrett (Irving, p. 418). After seeing Irving play Romeo at the Lyceum, Winter became his staunch friend, and took part in fruitful discussions about an American tour. Winter strongly recommended *The Bells* for the opening night which was to take place in New York. " 'I shall act on my friend's counsel,' said Irving. 'He says that I shall be under great excitement on that night, that my audience will be much excited; that it is best to take advantage of the agitation of that time, and above all to avoid comparison with any established favourite. I shall act Mathias!' " (Irving, p. 419).

To further assure his success in America, Irving sent the journalist Austin Brereton ahead as advance man; L. F. Austin was to remain behind and supervise the Lyceum; Joseph Hatton, on leave from the *Tribune*, was to travel with Irving throughout the entire tour (Irving, p. 419). Thus fortified, Henry Irving's first American tour was launched.

Ellen Terry left Liverpool on 11 October 1883 convinced she would never return because of the "unknown dangers of the Atlantic and of a savage, barbarous land. Our farewell performances in London had cheered me up a little—though I wept copiously at every one—by showing us that we should be missed."[2] Among those who came to Liverpool to bid farewell to the Lyceum company were Lily Langtry and Oscar Wilde; he wore "curly hair to match the curly teeth" (Terry, p. 253).

The *Brittanic* arrived in New York harbor and anchored off Staten Island on 21 October 1883. Coming to meet her was the *Blackbird*, on board of which was Henry Abbey, the impresario who had booked the tour, and some reporters. Accompanying the *Blackbird* was the *Yosemite*, a steam yacht that had been borrowed by Lawrence Barrett who wanted to be the first to greet Ellen Terry and Henry Irving. He was accompanied by Irving's champion, William Winter (Irving, p. 419).

The tour had been preceded by reports of the size of the company and the amount of scenery to be utilized. When asked about this, Irving replied that he wanted "to do justice to himself, to the theatre, and to the American public" (Irving, p. 420). On this first tour, as well as on the seven to follow, it should be remembered, too, as Sir John Martin-Harvey pointed out, "that every play in the various repertoires which Irving took on his tours, was mounted to precisely the same elaborate extent as at the Lyceum: i.e., of course, wherever the stages on the route permitted. There was no economy in any single detail of production. . . . Every 'flat,' every 'cloth,' every step, every platform, every costume used in the Lyceum production, aggregating hundreds of tons, was carried."[3] Martin-Harvey goes on to say about this first trip to America that "before Irving took his company to New York, nothing to compare with the completeness of the *ensemble* and the artistic harmony of his productions had been seen there" (Martin-Harvey, p. 77).

When they disembarked from the *Britannic*, Irving was driven to Brevoort House on lower Fifth Avenue, while Ellen Terry was taken to the Hotel Dam near Union Square and the Star Theatre where they were to perform.[4] At that time, the Star Theatre was no longer in the center of the theatre district which had moved farther uptown. Despite this, the theatre still had a quite impressive auditorium, although the backstage areas were inferior to what the company was accustomed to in London (Terry, p. 257).

In the week between the company's arrival and the opening on 29 October, seven plays had to be set up and rehearsed: *The Bells*, *Charles I*, *The Belle's Stratagem*, *Richard III*, *The Lyons Mail*, *Louis XI*, and *The Merchant of Venice*. With *Hamlet*, which was not presented in New York, these plays constituted the repertoire for the first tour.[5]

The premiere in New York on Monday, 29 October 1883, featured *The Bells*, in which Irving played Mathias. The audience reaction to his first appearance was reflected in the *Sun* the following morning: "When Irving came upon the stage he was received with an outburst of feeling so warm, spontaneous, demonstrative in character as to be fairly deafening. People rose to their feet and shouted their welcome at him as if they would never tire of it. The reception was, perhaps, the most enthusiastic that any stranger ever enjoyed at our hands" (Brereton, *Life*, p. 19). The conclusion of the play brought an even greater response from the audience, the *Herald* saying:

An audience notable even in the house which is foremost in the traditions of fashion, an attention persistent and polite, and enthusiasm yielded with spontaneity of sincerity, and caution of good judgment, welcomed Henry Irving last night to the American stage. The curtain which rose at the Star Theatre on an artist fresh from the adulation of cultured people, but yet uncertain of the favour which a strange public might accord to manners and methods hitherto untried before them, went

2. "It is I!" The first words spoken by Henry Irving before an American audience when, as Mathias in *The Bells*, he appeared on the stage of the Star Theatre, New York, 29 October 1883. From the collection of Arnold Rood.

down upon him at the finish assured of their acceptation by the testimony of intoxicating homage (Brereton, *Life*, p. 17).

Ellen Terry, who made her American debut in *Charles I*, was received with equal warmth,[6] and box office receipts during this first New York appearance reflected the growing popularity of Irving and his leading lady, rising from $15,000 to $22,000 in the four-week engagement (Irving, p. 424). The critics, however, seem to have been divided into three factions: "Those, headed by Winter, who hailed his genius with measured eulogies; those who, though conscious of his mannerisms and critical of his eccentricities, were swept away against their better judgment by his manifest power; and those, a small voice in the din of general acclamation, who found him and his company altogether unacceptable" (Irving, pp. 424–25). Then there were those who claimed that "the Americans did not like Henry Irving as an actor, and that they only accepted him as a manager—that he triumphed in New York as he had done in London, through his lavish spectacular effects." "This," says Ellen Terry, "is all moonshine. Henry made his first appearance in *The Bells*, his second in *Charles I*, his third in *Louis XI*. By that time he had conquered [New York], and without the aid of anything at all notable in the mounting of the plays. It was not until we did *The Merchant of Venice* that he gave the Americans anything of a 'production' " (Terry, p. 274).

On the last night of the season in New York, a potpourri was presented consisting of the first act of *Richard III*, *The Belle's Stratagem* in two acts, and a reading of the poem, *The Dream of Eugene Aram* (Brereton, *Life*, p. 30). And then the long haul began.

The four-week stay in New York ended on Saturday, 24 November 1883, and the company opened on Monday, 26 November, at the Chestnut Street Opera House in Philadelphia. During the course of the journey from New York to Philadelphia, Irving recognized the impracticality of moving what Laurence Irving calls "the vast impedimenta" of sets around the country. Consequently, he sent much of the equipment back to New York and henceforth relied more on local scene painters and carpenters. This meant, as Laurence Irving says, that "New York and Philadelphia alone . . . saw the Lyceum productions in their entirety . . . the favourable verdict of the other cities was won more by the company's acting than by scenic spectacle" (Irving, pp. 427–28).

In addition to the seven plays seen in New York, Irving added *Hamlet* to the Philadelphia repertoire. At first, the audience was puzzled by Irving's interpretation because, for two acts, he did not observe the points and artificialities to which they were used, but with the play scene they "were swept off their feet . . . and thereafter sustained the actor with their rapt attention and applause" (Irving, p. 426). Of course, Irving's Hamlet was compared to Booth's but not necessarily to the former's disadvantage,[7] so much so that at a breakfast in his honor at the Clove Club he was presented with Edwin Forrest's silver watch, perhaps a symbol of the unification of the English-speaking stages (Irving, p. 427).

At the conclusion of two successful weeks in Philadelphia, the company moved on to Boston for a two-week season beginning on 10 December at the Boston Theatre (Brereton, *Life*, p. 43). Not only was *Hamlet* given a warm reception but so were the other plays. For example, the *Transcript* said that "in Mr. Irving's Charles I one recognizes the man in whom, as Matthew Arnold might say, the instinct for beauty transfuses and informs the instinct for conduct. With the historical exactness of the character we have for the moment nothing to do; we look upon it simply as a wonderfully well-rounded and incomparably well-realized dramatic conception" (Hiatt, p. 205).

In true trouper tradition, the Lyceum company ran into a blizzard en route to Baltimore from Boston. They reached the city only four hours before the curtain was to rise at the Academy of Music. While the stage was being set, Irving rehearsed the company and at the scheduled time the curtain rose —on a small but enthusiastic audience (Irving, p. 428). From the one-week stand in Baltimore, the company doubled back to Brooklyn for a week and then entrained for a two-week season in Chicago (Brereton, *Life*, p. 43).

During the engagement at Haverley's Theatre in Chicago, Irving's rendition of Shylock proved to be a great success and was contrasted favorably with Booth's. "Booth's rendition brought tears of emotion to the eyes," said the *Tribune*; "Irving's utterance flashed across the brain in the splendour of its naturalness. Booth's cry ('I thank God; I thank God. Is it true? Is it true?') embodied one overmastering passion, Irving's the complex passions of the Hebrew's heart. The former was more melodramatic; the latter was, beyond all question, the more artistic. In a word, Booth recited, while Irving impersonated. Which of these schools of acting will be the school of the future? That question is one which the good taste of the English-speaking world has already answered" (Hiatt, p. 204).

In addition to *The Merchant of Venice*, the repertoire was made up of *The Bells*, *The Belle's Stratagem*, *The Lyons Mail* and *Louis XI*. On the return visit to Chicago for a week, after a week in St. Louis and another in Cincinnati, *Hamlet* was presented. The second visit to Chicago was followed by a split week between Detroit and Toronto.

In Toronto the Lyceum company appeared in four plays in three days, opening with *The Bells*, followed by *The Merchant of Venice*, *Charles I*, and *Louis XI*. About *The Merchant of Venice*, the most spectacular of the plays, the *Mail* (23 February 1884) reported (after commenting at length on the audience):

The production of *The Merchant of Venice*, witnessed last evening, was undoubtedly a grand dramatic representation. Nothing to approach it in completeness, in perfection of arrangements, in beautiful stage setting, in magnificent scenery, in the thorough equipment of every member of the company, in short in everything which would tend to place dramatic art in the position to which it properly belongs, has ever been witnessed in this city before. To many the production was a revelation as to what could be accomplished in dramatic representation. It was the result of a combination of arts, and showed the hand of the scholar, the painter, and designer.

After this short Toronto engagement, Irving played for a week in Boston, before journeying to Washington, where he opened on 3 March 1884 for another week's performances. While in Washington, Irving met President Chester Arthur who entertained him in the White House. The Washington visit was followed by a week in New Haven, Worcester, Springfield, Hartford, and Providence. Return visits were paid to Philadelphia and Brooklyn and a four-week season in New York concluded this triumphant first tour. For the very last performance, 26 April 1884, Irving again presented a potpourri: scenes from *The Merchant of Venice, Louis XI, Charles I,* and *Much Ado About Nothing.*

What was the reaction of the public by the end of this arduous six-month *tournée?* The London *Times* recorded: "Mr. Irving has vindicated for his vocation a definite position among the serious arts. He has been accepted . . . with distinguished honour in virtue of his championship of the right and duty of the dramatic art to be a fine art. The remarkable success he has achieved is a gratifying sign of the willingness of public opinion in America to co-operate with that of England to rescue the stage from the lower level to which it has sometimes sunk."[8] Howard Kyle wrote: "I did not know Henry Irving off the stage, but I saw him in a round of characterizations when he was in America in 1883. The repleteness of his stage mountings and the masterly direction of his casts, apparent in every play he produced, surpassed anything American theatre patrons had ever seen. This was generally acknowledged, and throughout the acting profession here he was hailed as 'a great stage artist'."[9] Ellen Terry, writing of the reaction in America, said:

The American critics . . . at the time of our early visits, were keenly interested, and showed it by their observation of many points which our English critics had passed over. For instance, writing of *Much Ado About Nothing,* one of the Americans said of Henry in the Church Scene that "something of him as a subtle interpreter of doubtful situations was exquisitely shown in the early part of this fine scene by his suspicion of Don John—felt by him alone, and expressed only by a quick covert look, but a look so full of intelligence as to proclaim him a sharer in the secret with his audience."

"Wherein does the superiority lie?" wrote another critic in comparing our productions with those which had been seen in America up to 1884. "Not in the amount of money expended, but in the amount of brains;—in the artistic intelligence and careful and earnest pains with which every detail is studied and worked out." (Terry, p. 263)

The six-month American tour of 1883–84 brought in box office receipts of $400,000. Half of this went to Irving, who after covering company expenses, was still able to place a considerable amount in the Lyceum coffers (Irving, p. 434). To complete the record, it must be noted that the Lyceum

Theatre in London did not remain empty during its tenants' six-month absence. Mary Anderson acted in *Ingomar*, *Pygmalion and Galatea*, and *Comedy and Tragedy* from 1 September 1883 until 5 April 1884. Her company was followed on 12 April by Lawrence Barrett in *Yorick's Love*, an adaptation by William Dean Howells (Brereton, *Lyceum*, pp. 244–45).

Henry Irving's second American tour opened at the Academy of Music in Quebec City on 30 September 1884 with *The Merchant of Venice* (Irving, p. 709). This tour was arranged, as were the succeeding ones, by Irving himself without the intervention of an impresario and was planned so that there was no unnecessary backtracking as had occurred on the first tour. After the opening in Quebec, the company went on to Montreal, London, Hamilton, Toronto, Buffalo, Syracuse, Boston, New York, Philadelphia, Pittsburgh, Cleveland, Detroit, Chicago, and Washington. Return visits to Philadelphia and Boston were followed by an engagement in Brooklyn with the finale occurring in New York. Ending on 4 April 1885, the tour lasted twenty-seven weeks, and the repertoire consisted of *Louis XI*, *The Merchant of Venice*, *Hamlet*, *Twelfth Night*, *Much Ado About Nothing*, *The Bells*, *Eugene Aram*, *Charles I*, and *The Lyons Mail*.

Once again the response from both critics and audiences was enthusiastic and need not be detailed here. Perhaps one of the high points of this tour was that it marked the debut, in a speaking role, of Ellen Terry's son, Gordon Craig. As Christmas 1884 approached, Ellen Terry felt so lonely for her family that she cabled Stephen Coleridge, Craig's guardian, to bring Teddy Craig to America.[10] The Coleridges and Teddy sailed on *The City of Chicago*, arriving on 23 December in New York where Teddy was "pursued by all the little girls in the hotel."[11] They were met by Irving's secretary, L. F. Austin, who accompanied them to Pittsburgh, where they joined the company on Christmas Eve, complete with the Christmas pudding Teddy Craig had carried all the way from England (Terry, p. 275). On 14 January 1885, in Chicago, Craig appeared as Joey, the gardener's boy, in *Eugene Aram* (Craig, *Index*, p. 63). Predictably, his mother was very proud of him.

Was it not a Chicago man who wrote of my boy, tending the roses in the stage garden in *Eugene Aram*, that he was "a most beautiful lad"! "His eyes are full of sparkle, his smile is a ripple over his face, and his laugh is as cheery and natural as a bird's song. . . . His mother has high hopes of this child's dramatic future. He has the instinct and the soul of art in him. Already the theatre is his home. His postures and his playfulness with the gardener, his natural and graceful movements, had been the subject of much drilling, of study and practise. He acquitted himself beautifully and received the wise congratulations of his mother, of Mr. Irving, and of the company." (Terry, p. 280)

Following the conclusion of the tour, but before returning to England, Irving and Terry performed the fourth act of *The Merchant of Venice* at a matinée for the Actors' Fund at the Academy of Music in New York. On 6

April, Irving was tendered a banquet by a group of prominent Americans including Edwin Booth, Oliver Wendell Holmes, Mark Twain, and H. H. Furness (of the Shakespeare Variorum edition). Because of illness, Chester Arthur was replaced in the chair by Senator Evarts. The return to England took place three days later on the *S.S. Arizona* (Irving, p. 454).

Irving's decision to tour under his own management proved to be a fruitful one; the gross receipts amounted to £80,000 with a net profit of £15,000 (Irving, p. 454). In the absence of the company from the Lyceum, the theatre was once again occupied by the American actress, Mary Anderson, from 1 November 1884 through 25 April 1885 with revivals of *Romeo and Juliet* and *The Lady of Lyons; Pygmalion and Galatea* and *Comedy and Tragedy* played on the last evening (Brereton, *Lyceum*, p. 250).

For 1887–88, Irving planned another tour of America under his own aegis. The tour was scheduled for twenty weeks, the shortest Irving was to make in America, and he limited the number of stops to four: New York, Philadelphia, Chicago, and Boston with a return visit to New York (Brereton, *Life*, p. 121). The repertoire consisted of *The Merchant of Venice, Louis XI, Jingle, Olivia, The Lyons Mail, The Bells, Much Ado About Nothing* and, as the new attraction, *Faust*. By limiting the tour to four cities, Irving was able to produce *Faust* as he had at the Lyceum in its very elaborate production. "The consummate stage-craft and the display of so many original technical devices appealed, very naturally, to a public who found novelty for its own sake infinitely entertaining," says Laurence Irving (Irving, p. 487). The play was very well received wherever it was performed. In fact, the Goethe Society of New York invited Irving to speak to them on Goethe's methods of theatrical management, and William Winter praised Irving's performance as superior even to Goethe's conception of Mephistopheles (Irving, p. 488).

During the visit to New York, Ellen Terry managed to see Augustin Daly's company perform. She found it to be "a revelation . . . of the pitch of excellence which American acting had reached" (Terry, p. 293). She was not as impressed with Daly's artistic merits: "The productions of Shakespeare at Daly's were really bad from the pictorial point of view. But what pace and 'ensemble' he got from his company!" (Terry, p. 295).

The consensus seems to have been that the apogee of this third tour took place during the return engagement to New York. On 19 March, Irving cancelled the scheduled performance in order to perform *The Merchant of Venice* at the Military Academy of West Point. Because the playing area was so small, only the company and their costumes, not scenery, went to West Point (Irving, pp. 489–90). The scenic locales were indicated by signs lowered from behind the proscenium of Grant Hall (Brereton, *Life*, p. 121). John Martin-Harvey recorded his reaction to this exceptional performance: "There was no scenery. The entire play was performed against curtains on an improvised stage of about twenty feet square in the Grant Hall. Some four hundred cadets were present. I never heard the play 'go' with such enthusiasm, understanding and responsiveness. At the conclusion every youngster threw his cap into the air with a shout and Irving made one of the happiest hits in his long series of speeches by declaring that 'the joy-bells are ringing in London to-night, because for the first time in history the British have captured West Point' " (Martin-Harvey, p. 97).

The tour ended on 24 March 1888 in New York. Average weekly receipts were £3596 19s. 6d. with the weekly profit being £596 14s 3d., despite unusually high expenses (Brereton, *Life*, p. 125).

During this absence, the Lyceum was occupied for the last time by Mary Anderson who opened on 10 September 1887 with *The Winter's Tale*, which ran for 166 performances, a record for the play. Miss Anderson doubled as Hermione and Perdita (Brereton, *Lyceum*, pp. 264–65). On 2 April 1888, she was followed into the Lyceum by Genevieve Ward for a few performances of *Forget-Me-Not* and *Nance Oldfield*; this was succeeded on 7 April by a new play, *The Loadstone* (Brereton, *Lyceum*, p. 268).

The fourth tour of America, starting on 4 September 1893 and ending on 17 March 1894, was planned to cover a wider territory than ever before; visits were paid to San Francisco, Portland, Tacoma, Seattle, Minneapolis, St. Paul, Chicago, New York, Boston, Philadelphia, Washington, Toronto, Montreal, and return trips to New York and Boston. The repertoire consisted of *The Merchant of Venice, Becket, The Bells, Nance Oldfield, The Lyons Mail, Olivia, Charles I, Louis XI, Henry VIII*, and *Much Ado About Nothing*, though the last two were not included in the West Coast stops (Brereton, *Life*, pp. 186–87).

Although Gordon Craig was scheduled to go on this tour, he withdrew because of his impending marriage. In 1957 he was to recall, "I was not in the company this time. A wife was the reason. H. I. had warned me *before* I married of the possible result—in fact his very wise, kind letter did all it could do to help me—but like a fool I went on. H. I. was right and I was wrong. But having been brought up by women . . . I did not pay attention. H. I. had offered me *parts* and *glory* and *money* . . . but I needed a woman. In consequence I married, which was the wrong thing to do" (Craig, *Index*, p. 148).

The new production of *Becket* had its American premiere in St. Paul, and the Chicago engagement coincided with the World's Fair in the fall of 1893, the resulting enlarged population being reflected in the box office receipts (Irving, p. 562). Despite this success, some members of the company were not happy being in the Windy City. Martin-Harvey found it

. . . very like what one imagines Hell to be. Here one can see what Midas does when his monstrous materialism is allowed to express itself without (what to him would be) the disturbing and irritating influence of the spirit. The height of the buildings; the breadth of the side-walks, worn by the myriad footsteps of those seeking only pelf or gew-gaws; the brutal manners of the pedestrians who regard you with cold, inhuman eyes; these things depressed us as a spectacle of the depths to which a God-given energy can drag those who spurn the sweet fruits of culture and the things of the spirit. (Martin-Harvey, pp. 159–60)

During this fourth tour, 194 performances were presented, bringing into the box office £123,445 3s. 4d. (Brereton, *Life*, p. 186). The Lyceum at home remained dark until the Christmas season when *Cinderella* was produced by Oscar Barrett. It was so successful in London that it was brought to New York at the close of the engagement (Brereton, *Lyceum*, p. 293).

On 16 September 1895, the Lyceum's fifth American tour opened at Montreal's Academy of Music with *Faust* (Irving, p. 709). Stops in cities that had been visited on earlier tours were now augmented by a swing through the southern states. In consecutive order, the company followed the Montreal engagement with visits to Toronto, Boston, New York, Philadelphia, Baltimore, Washington, Richmond, Charleston, Savannah, Atlanta, New Orleans, Memphis, Nashville, Louisville, St. Louis, Cincinnati, Chicago, Indianapolis, Detroit, Cleveland, Buffalo, and Pittsburgh. Return engagements were arranged in Philadelphia, Boston, Providence, Springfield, Hartford, and New Haven, concluding with a return to New York. (Many of these stops were split weeks and one-night stands.) The repertoire included *Macbeth*, *Becket*, *King Arthur* (an immensely popular success), *The Merchant of Venice*, *Much Ado About Nothing*, *Louis XI*, *Charles I*, *Faust*, *The Lyons Mail*, *Nance Oldfield*, *The Bells*, *The Corsican Brothers*, *Don Quixote*, *Journeys End in Lovers Meeting*, and *A Story of Waterloo* (Brereton, *Life*, pp. 246–47). The shorter pieces were combined or augmented by readings or performances of *Godefroi and Yolande* by Irving's son, Laurence, based on a poem by Swinburne (Martin-Harvey, p. 187).

One of Irving's outstanding recollections of this tour was an event that occurred during the Philadelphia engagement where Eleonora Duse was playing at another theatre. She sent Irving a letter "signed by all the Italian members of her company, expressing their gratitude to him and to Ellen Terry 'for having revealed to the minds of aliens, through your great talent, and by the proud flights of your genius, the sweet idioms of Shakespeare' " (Irving, p. 587).

There can be no question of the success of this tour; in seven months 240 performances were presented (Brereton, *Life*, p. 245), yielding gross receipts of £116,516 16s. 9d., of which £75,735 18s. 6d. came to Irving. After deducting expenses, he was left with a profit of £6,614 8s. 4d. (Brereton, *Life*, p. 247). It may be that receipts increased in response to Irving's having been knighted in May 1895, shortly before the tour commenced. During this absence from London, the Lyceum was occupied by Johnston Forbes-Robertson, who opened his season with *Romeo and Juliet*.[12]

After a five-week tour of the provinces early in the autumn of 1899, Irving and his company sailed again for America on the *Marquette* (Brereton,

Life, p. 283). The sixth American tour began on 30 October 1899 with *Robespierre* at the Knickerbocker Theatre in New York. After New York, the company played in Boston, Philadelphia, Washington, Baltimore, Brooklyn, Pittsburgh, Cleveland, Detroit, Toledo, Columbus, Dayton, Indianapolis, Louisville, St. Louis, Chicago, Toronto, Montreal, a return visit to New York, Providence, Springfield, Hartford, New Haven, Albany, Syracuse, Rochester, Buffalo, Cincinnati, Kansas City, St. Joseph, Omaha, a return to Chicago, St. Paul, Minneapolis, Milwaukee, and a return to Philadelphia, with the closing in Harlem on 18 May 1900. The repertoire, somewhat curtailed from former visits, an indication of rising costs, included *Robespierre*, *The Merchant of Venice*, *The Bells*, *The Amber Heart*, *Nance Oldfield*, and *A Story of Waterloo* (Brereton, *Life*, pp. 283–84).

Months before this tour began, on 31 May 1899, Terry was already indicating her concern about her relationship with the Lyceum company. She confided in Bernard Shaw: "In America we only do *Robespierre*, *Merchant of Venice* and *The Bells*. I am engaged to go to America and go I will, *must*! It's a pity, but—" (*Terry and Shaw*, p. 297). To this letter, Shaw replied on 1 June, "I quite endorse the trip to America: it did you ever so much good before. But the point is, do you seriously propose to go back there without H. I. on your own account?" (*Terry and Shaw*, p. 298).

During the tour itself, Irving and Terry discussed the possibility of concluding their professional relationship. She wrote, perhaps thinking he no longer cared for her, "I can only *guess* at it, for he is exactly the same sweet-mannered person he was when I felt so certain Henry loved me. We have not met for years now, except before other people, when my conduct exactly matches his. All my own fault. It is I am changed not he" (Irving, p. 633). The actual separation was not to occur for some time, however.

This sixth tour of America, which included over thirty cities in six months, was also a profitable one. The gross receipts amounted to £111,000 with a profit to Irving of £24,000 as a result of the abbreviated repertoire (Irving, p. 631).

The seventh American engagement opened at the Knickerbocker Theatre in New York on 21 October 1901 with *Charles I* (Irving, p. 709). It continued with stops in Brooklyn, Philadelphia, Chicago, St. Paul, Minneapolis, Omaha, Kansas City, St. Louis, Indianapolis, Columbus, Toledo, Pittsburgh, Cleveland, Buffalo, Rochester, Syracuse, Albany, Springfield, Boston, Providence, Hartford, New Haven, and closed in Harlem on 21 March 1902. The plays presented were *The Merchant of Venice*, *Charles I*, *Louis XI*, *Waterloo*, *The Lyons Mail*, *The Bells*, *Nance Oldfield*, and *Madame Sans-Gêne* in the twenty-nine-week engagement. Once again both critics and public were enthusiastic in their appreciation. Irving's profit amounted to approximately £12,000 (Brereton, *Life*, pp. 296–97).

Possibly the most outstanding feature of this tour was that it was the last time Ellen Terry toured America as a member of the Lyceum company.

Under her own management, she made her last tour of America in 1907, a tour that was "chiefly momentous to me because at Pittsburgh I was married for the third time, and married to an American" (Terry, p. 301). Her new husband was James Carew, the actor, who, she told Shaw, "goes on trying and striving and acts better and better every week. He is a splendid fellow and adores you, *and me!*" (*Terry and Shaw*, p. 397).

Irving's eighth and last tour opened on 26 October 1903 at the Broadway Theatre in New York with *Dante* (Irving, p. 709). This last tour was probably also the most wearing of the eight. The itinerary, following New York, included Philadelphia, Boston, Portland, Worcester, Waterhurst, Springfield, Hartford, New Haven (the last six in one week), Brooklyn, Washington, Trenton, Scranton, Syracuse, Harrisburg, Ithaca, Rochester (the last six also in one week), Pittsburgh, Buffalo, Albany, Montreal, Ottawa, Toronto, Detroit, Chicago, St. Louis, Cincinnati, Indianapolis, Columbus, Dayton, Toledo, and Cleveland, with the close of the tour taking place in Harlem on 25 March 1904 (Brereton, *Life*, pp. 310–11).

In addition to *Dante*, on which Irving had been counting for a huge success, the repertoire included only *The Merchant of Venice*, *The Bells*, *The Lyons Mail*, *Waterloo*, and *Louis XI* (Brereton, *Life*, p. 310). Although *Dante* was not poorly received by the critics, the public did not warm to it and so, after a few performances in New York, Irving was forced to drop it and rely solely on the balance of the plays. Irving found it so much a disappointment that his last great production was not more appreciated that he was only able to plod through the balance of the tour, thirty-three cities in five months (Irving, p. 653). Despite the artistic disappointment, the tour was a financial success, the profit amounting to £32,000.

In Irving's eight tours of the United States and Canada between 29 October 1883 and 25 March 1904, he played for 209 weeks (four years). The total receipts amounted to £711,016 18s. 4d., or $3,441,321.94; the profits were £119,669 12s. 5d., or $579,201.04 (Brereton, *Life*, p. 312), an average profit per tour of $72,400. Artistically, too, the tours must be considered a success. Despite limitations imposed by daunting itineraries, Irving was able to maintain on tour the quality of his Lyceum productions. The discipline he brought to his own performances never faltered, but he saw to it as well that the visual impressiveness of the plays was not compromised, that historical authenticity in setting was adhered to, that rehearsals were consistently thorough—in short, that technical expertise and artistic intelligence remained the hallmark of his productions. For this, the Lyceum coffers were amply rewarded, but in addition the reputation of a remarkable actor and producer was enhanced throughout the continent of North America.

Notes

For their kind cooperation I thank the staffs of the Harvard Theatre Collection and the Theatre Section of the Metropolitan Toronto Library. This is an abbreviated version of the delivered talk.

1. Laurence Irving, *Henry Irving. The Actor and His World* (New York, 1952), p. 418.

2. Ellen Terry, *The Story of My Life* (London, 1908), p. 252.

3. [Sir John Martin-Harvey], *The Autobiography of Sir John Martin-Harvey* (London, 1933), p. 77.

4. Austin Brereton, *The Life of Henry Irving* (London, 1908), II, 11.

5. Irving, p. 421; Brereton, *Life*, p. 43.

6. Joseph Hatton, *Henry Irving's Impressions of America* (London, 1884), pp. 164–65.

7. Charles Hiatt, *Henry Irving. A Record and Review* (London, 1899), p. 203.

8. Austin Brereton, *The Lyceum and Henry Irving* (London, 1903), p. 246.

9. *We Saw Him Act. A Symposium on the Art of Sir Henry Irving*, eds. H. A. Saintsbury and Cecil Palmer (London, 1939), p. 291.

10. Edward Craig, *Gordon Craig. The Story of His Life* (New York, 1968), p. 58.

11. Edward Gordon Craig, *Index to the Story of My Days* (New York, 1957), p. 62.

12. *Ellen Terry and George Bernard Shaw. A Correspondence*, ed. Christopher St. John (New York, 1931), p. 16.

Alan Woods

3

The Survival of Traditional Acting in the Provinces: The Career of Thomas W. Keene _____

When the then-famed tragedian Thomas W. Keene collapsed after a performance as Richelieu in Hamilton, Ontario, on 23 May 1898, there seemed little cause for serious alarm to his company. After all, Keene, then fifty-seven years old, was completing his eighteenth year as a touring star and was, moreover, nearing the end of an arduous season which had begun the previous August in Cumberland, Maryland. Between Cumberland and Hamilton, Keene—supported and managed by Charles B. Hanford, later a minor touring tragedian in his own right—had crisscrossed the North American continent, reaching as far west as the Oklahoma Territory, south into Texas, and north into the Dakotas, Winnipeg, and Ontario.[1]

It soon became apparent that the tragedian needed rest and, accordingly, he returned to his home on Staten Island, New York, by special train. There he died on 1 June 1898; his collapse in Hamilton had been due not to exhaustion and overwork, but to appendicitis.

Thomas W. Keene (born Thomas Eagleson—whether his stage name was intended to honor Laura Keene or was a mistaken appropriation of the English tragedian's name, I have not been able to discover) is now virtually forgotten, but was one of a small band of American actors in the late nineteenth century attempting to keep both the traditional repertoire and its acting style alive, primarily on provincial stages. To a large extent, he succeeded. Even at the end of his career, Keene was still able to attract attention in larger cities as well as in the smaller, less sophisticated, centers that made up the bulk of his tour. Unlike his contemporaries and fellow Shakespearean tragedians, Frederick Warde and Louis James, Keene did not avoid New York City. Indeed, during his final season he met with modest success during a two-week engagement in North America's theatrical capital.

Keene's approach to touring was sharply differentiated from the norm followed by Warde and James in another major aspect of his career. He was the first touring classic actor to exploit modern advertising techniques effectively, at least in his early career. While other tragedians modeled themselves after the understated approach of Edwin Booth, Keene's first years were marked by luridly colored posters touting him as a great tragedian—posters which, in size, color, and design, were more reminiscent of circus billboards than Shakespearean grandeur. Early in his career, Keene scored a major success in *Drink! (L'Assommoir)* for the Boston Theatre Company in Boston and on a nationwide tour in 1879–80. His performance attracted the attention of W. W. Cole, a major circus promoter, who offered Keene a starring tour in classic tragedy. Keene accepted. According to one account, Cole took Keene in hand and "theatrical people were horrified to see lithographs, scores of different kinds and in every color of the rainbow, representing Keene in various Shakespearean roles. The campaign of advertising has never been equalled."[2]

The splash of his first years as a touring star always stained Keene's later career. Although his advertising after 1886 no longer relied on enormous billboards and colorful lithographs, Keene was marked as an actor whose career began with publicity even after his accomplishments should have earned him greater respect. Keene "is not an actor, and . . . lithographic advertising cannot make him one," said the *San Francisco Wasp* during his second tour.[3] Similar comments followed the actor throughout his career.

Keene was marked not only by his flashy beginnings, but by his stubborn maintenance of the classical repertoire as well. Theatrical taste was changing by the early 1890s, at least in major Eastern cities, to a new style drawing heavily upon then-modern Realism. The traditional style had disappeared from the drama, even at the popular level; Nora and Hedda Gabler may not have been accepted by North American audiences, but the Uncle Nate of James A. Herne's *Shore-Acres*, silently ending that play with a Naturalistic silent scene, and the polished urbanity of Bronson Howard were a far cry from the poetic thunderings of Sir Giles Overreach or Bulwer-Lytton's Richelieu. Traditional styles of acting also had changed in New York and other major cities by the late 1880s. Ada Rehan's charm, John Drew's sophistication, Joseph Jefferson's warmth (even in the service of Sheridan)—all were as distant from the Forrests, Booths, Cushmans, and McCulloughs as they themselves would be in future years from Mrs. Fiske, Alla Nazimova, and Arnold Daly.

Thomas W. Keene attempted to forge a career as a traditional classic actor, performing the traditional roles, in this period of transition. Whether he was or was not a good actor is impossible to determine, let alone whether he ever achieved greatness. He toured throughout the continent for nearly two decades, playing thousands of performances in thousands of theatres. Many, if not most, of those performances received some mention in the local newspapers, either through reviews or press releases (and the two are often indistinguishable). It is possible, therefore, to find comments extolling Keene's abilities: "The words of the author were so spoken by the actor as to convey the perfect ideals which the playwright had in mind. Mr. Keene impressed upon his auditors the mind of Shakespeare and the genius of Keene. . . . "[4] It is also equally possible, of course, to find printed reports that state precisely the opposite: "Keene's physical portraiture [as Richelieu] has a tendency to alternate between excessive senility and unnecessary virility. . . . "[5]

Many positive responses can be explained away easily; small town newspapers account for many, and often the press reporter is more anxious to prove that the local citizenry is fully as advanced as that of major metropolitan areas than concerned with critical judgments. It is equally true that reviewers in major cities often used their space to prove their own superiority and higher cultural values; such was clearly the case in Pittsburgh early in Keene's career:

Keene truckles to a vitiated popular taste. He is on too familiar terms with his audience. He values applause more than a conscientious adherence to the highest principles of his art. Some may say in defense of this style of familiar acting that it tends to popularize the classic drama. Nothing of the kind. The effect is to degrade the drama to a low level. Shakespeare can only be popularized by the actor's educating the audience up to the standard of what he plays.[6]

In the final analysis, it matters little what the quality of Keene's acting actually was (if, indeed, an absolute judgment can ever be made about acting talent). To sophisticated critics and audiences, he was an old-fashioned ranter, while to less experienced (or more conservative) viewers he brought excitement and thrills. The majority of Keene's career was spent touring the North American provinces, and there the evidence suggests that he was overwhelmingly regarded as a star of the first order, a worthy successor to the tradition of classic actors running from Cooper and Cooke through the younger Booth. His career deserves analysis, therefore, in order to comprehend further what the touring theatre was like at the end of the nineteenth century, in the last period during which North America possessed a vitally alive theatre across the entire continent.[7]

Keene stayed close to what was considered the classic repertoire of the tragic actor, in contrast to some of his contemporaries who occasionally attempted new plays to increase audience size. In his final season, Keene offered seven plays, enough to provide a different bill at each performance during the week's engagement. Two Shakespearean tragedies (*Richard III* and *The Merchant of Venice*) formed part of his repertoire each year from his first starring tour in 1880, while *Hamlet* and Bulwer-Lytton's *Richelieu* had been offered each season but one. *Othello* was featured in Keene's repertoires for twelve years, while his *Louis XI* had been on the boards each season since he first attempted the role in September 1889. The least performed play from his final tour was *Julius Caesar*; even it was on Keene's bills for at least eight of his eighteen seasons.[8]

These seven pieces were typical of Keene's offerings to the public. Early in his career, he presented non-Shakespearean plays associated with earlier tragedians (*The Corsican Brothers*, one of Charles Kean's great triumphs; *The Fool's Revenge*, *The Lady of Lyons*, and *A New Way to Pay Old Debts*, all frequently acted by Edwin Booth; and *Ingomar the Barbarian*, one of John McCullough's muscular heroes), but settled into the Shakespearean repertoire relatively quickly. While *Richelieu* and *Louis XI* were not by Shakespeare, of course, they formed part of the standard classic repertoire, their nineteenth-century origins effectively masked by their quasi-poetic language and their period settings. Each of the plays provided the starring actor with multiple opportunities to impress his audiences: in common with other touring stars, Keene wasted little money on his supporting casts, preferring to focus audience attention upon himself.

Keene's repertoire was not only traditional, but also conservatively traditional. He did not include "gentlemanly melodrama" in his range of roles, as had Charles Kean, Henry Irving, and so many others before him, despite his own early success in similar plays. Nor did he attempt to have poetic tragedy written for him, as had both Irving and Frederick Warde. Keene's conservatism also apparently extended to his physical productions. Only seldom were they mentioned in reviews, and then either negatively or summarily. Keene's acting of the great roles was the attraction, and nothing was allowed to either detract from him, or distract his audiences from what they had come to see and hear.

Keene was most impressive, by all accounts, in the title roles of *Richard III* and *Louis XI*. As was the practice, he used Colley Cibber's version of Shakespeare's play, which incorporates scenes from *Henry VI, Part III*; Cibber's adaptation held the North American stage until well into the twentieth century. *Louis XI* was originally a French play by Casimer Delavigne, but Keene's version was the product of so many hands that an author designation is impossible. Keene used Henry Irving's version, adapted from the French in five acts by Dion Boucicault, but emended Boucicault's text by collating it with W. R. Markwell's three-act adaptation, which was then further altered for Keene's use by Arden Smith and Edwin Arden. Richard was his single most popular role, one he performed some 2,500 times (Graham, p. 261). In this essay, focus will be upon Keene's performances of *Richard III* and *Louis XI*, although occasional reference will be made to his other classic roles.

Keene relied heavily upon physical characterization in approaching Richard. In San Antonio, a critic commented that Keene relied "merely upon his crooked leg and facial expression" for interpretation.[9] In La Crosse, Wisconsin, the local press was more balanced: "one could read the thoughts of Richard III in the lines and muscles of Keene's face, but at other times his facial gymnastics were similar to burlesque and distracted from the performance."[10] The strongest—and most extended—negative response came from the *New York Tribune*:

In physical aspect this performance is comic. . . . Its locomotive peculiarities suggest the Pantaloon in the pantomime. This Gloster impels himself by means of a skating motion of the legs combined with a wriggling motion of the body, so that he appears to be afflicted simultaneously with sciatica, bunions, rickets, heaves and St. Vitus' dance. His countenance meantime is, with difficult and obvious effort, kept in a state of elaborate distortion, such as commingles [sic] low cunning and lowering ferocity with a pervasive expression of impending spasms. All his movements are not only deficient of high-bred distinction, but are exceedingly awkward.[11]

Oddly enough, this strongly negative view was reprinted by Keene's manager in an advertisement in the *New York Mirror*; other reviews quoted in the same advertisement are more praising: "in mobility of feature Mr. Keene is the peer of any of his rivals." "He bears himself admirably, and his gestures are eloquent." "Mr. Keene's Richard is fairly worth seeing. In movement and facial expression he is an ideal Richard."[12] The negative response was reiterated five years later in another cultured Eastern city, Philadelphia: "it was . . . unfortunate that Mr. Keene clung so closely to tradition, and gave a performance which displayed physical vigor rather than mental discernment. In brief, he was extravagant in gait, gesture and tone, and his performance was marred by over-acting."[13]

It seems obvious that Keene's traditional approach pleased some viewers and horrified others; although evidence is scanty, enough mention is made throughout his career of his possessing a rich voice with a wide range which he employed in a manner similar to his physicalization. In 1884 one newspaper noted, "his voice has a rather large range, has sweet tones in its low register and power in its upper register."[14] While he was in Denver in 1890, the *Denver Republican* regretted "the lingering cold that destroys the force and mellowness of Mr. Keene's voice."[15] Again, those who disliked the "old school" of Shakespearean performance also disliked Keene's vocal patterns, while those who approved of the traditional approach praised him highly. In some towns, a change in reaction signalled the change in attitude which found the "old school" less appropriate as the century came to a close. In Madison, Wisconsin, for example, Keene was praised in 1885 for his "perfectly distinct enunciation . . . emphasis and modulation," but characterized in 1893 as being guilty of a "disposition to rant . . . at inopportune times."[16] By contrast, in Lexington, Kentucky, the *Leader* maintained in 1888 that "Mr. Keene never loses his portrayal so far as to resort to ranting."[17]

The sudden changes of mood and rapid shifts of physical and vocal patterns typical of the "old school" actor were, of course, singularly appropriate for *Richard III*, as was noted in La Crosse, where the newspapers indicated that Keene's style "helped show the boasting, self-praising and threatening character" of Richard.[18] The popular view of Richard is best summarized by the *Charlotte Daily Observer* whose critic said of Keene's 1880 performance there:

The character called for the expression of the deepest emotions—direful revenge, inhuman thirst for blood, deceit, indeed the worst phases of human character—and for this he is by nature especially adapted, his strong features enabling him to reveal the horrors of his deeply laid plots with a vividness which was startling. If he lacks that magnetism which thrills an audience, his individuality was so completely lost, his portrayal so consistent and intense throughout that the horrible malignity of the royal cut-throat was made a frightful realization.[19]

Even the Philadelphia correspondent for the *New York Dramatic Mirror*, writing nine years later (2 February 1889, p. 4), and disapproving of the "old school," forced himself to "admit that Mr. Keene's performance seemed to give great satisfaction to his audiences, and that audiences generally would enjoy the virility of his acting sufficiently to enable them to overlook his defects of manner."

The title character in *Louis XI*, Keene's most highly praised and frequently performed role after *Richard III*, requires similar rapid shifts of characterization. The play's tone is set early in the first scene by Commines, chronicler to Louis XI, as he muses over his history of France while providing exposition for the audience:

Ah, could Louis read this manuscript . . . he would shudder to behold the gloomy annals of his strange career. Of vice and virtue what a motley group! Here, cowardice—heroic valor, there—here, mercy—there, ensanguined butchery—humble and proud—how different by turns—courting the mass—o'erbearing to the great—miser and spendthrift, jealous—all at will.[20]

Indeed, the tyrannical monarch of the play, in his efforts to evade his impending death, runs a wide gamut of emotions, often changing radically within the course of a single speech. The play provides its central figures with strong curtains at the end of each act, and unmistakably provides a part for the star of the "old school."

It was as such a star that Keene shone on tour; while fulsome, a review from the *Seattle Press Times* is typical:

Rare, if ever, has there been seen on the stage of this city such a representation of blended wickedness, superstition and diabolical intelligence, given with such transcendent art as utterly to eclipse the man in the actor. In eccentricity of speech, manner and facial expression, Keene appears the frail old monarch, combining craftiness, deceit and hypocrisy and at rare intervals a remote suggestion of a nature not wholly abandoned. There was no defect in any feature of the performance and the king, trembling under the weight of years and remorse for accumulated crimes, was given recall after recall.[21]

Four years later in Boston, during his final tour, Keene garnered such praise to indicate that his power as a performer remained constant. One reviewer noted, "he has never played the part better. The effect was excellent, such was his care in even so minute details as the twitching of his fingers and the modulation of the voice at critical moments." Another also responded favorably: "Mr. Keene . . . gave an intelligent and forceful representation . . . bringing out in artistic antitheses [the king's] utterly false and treacherous character and his assumed devoutness. . . . Mr. Keene so conserved his earlier passages that he had plenty of reserve power for his climaxes. He made much of his trying and exacting role, and was more than satisfactory in every particular." A third newspaper critic, however, was less impressed, again demonstrating the disparate reactions Keene's performances received:

Mr. Keene performed [last night] in a way which presumably pleased him, and certainly pleased a fairly large and decidedly enthusiastic audience. The keynote of his interpretation was a restless craving for present effect, at the expense of dramatic sincerity and the harmony of the whole. Although ostensibly a tragedian, Mr. Keene's chief desire seemed to be to raise a laugh, by sudden descent from the sublime to the ridiculous. To give two instances, out of many, he gave the lines "That is not true, and you know that it isn't" in a matter-of-fact tone which made them seem like a comically incongruous bit of modern slang; and after he had travelled on his knees half-way across the stage, in a bit of passionate pleading, he rose and elaborately rubbed them, as if in pain. In all this triviality he was, of course, encouraged, and perhaps to a certain extent justified, by the temper of his audience, which was as keenly alive to the humorous side, even of what was seriously intended, as American audiences usually are. The thing was all the more regrettable from the fact that in the first act his impatience for the presence of the "holy man" was brought out consistently and with genuine power. Another admirable, but contrasted piece of consistent acting, was in the scene with the peasants in the third act, when he was frankly and irresistibly comic.[22]

The reviewer had begun his coverage with a lengthy lambasting of the play as being hopelessly old-fashioned, leading one to suspect that the style of both drama and star were at odds with the critic's expectations.

While Thomas W. Keene was indeed "popular in the provinces," as Odell remarked,[23] it is misleading to see him as little other than a mediocrity playing to audiences grateful for the respite from *Uncle Tom's Cabin* and *Hazel Kirke*, even though that judgment might seem supported by the many responses in small cities on the order of "he was an oasis in the stale, flat and unprofitable parade of mediocrity, on which the lovers of art feasted to their hearts content."[24] He drew praising reviews (although sometimes grudgingly) in the self-consciously sophisticated cities of New York, Boston, and Philadelphia even in the late 1890s, well after the traditions he represented were no longer vital and had become regarded as hopelessly old-fashioned. The existence of theatres across the continent enabled Keene to keep the classical tradition alive when it was no longer welcome in the East. Moreover, he was the first tragic actor to employ the idea, at least in embryo, of an advertising

THE
A. S. SEER
PRINT.
N.Y.

THOMAS W. KEENE
AS LOUIS XI.

3. Thomas W. Keene as Louis XI. Courtesy of the Library of Congress.

campaign to bring him to public notice; unlike many later performers whose celebrity is based on good publicity, Keene possessed the ability to satisfy audiences initially attracted by garish posters. His career, when examined in concert with other touring performers in the last two decades of the nineteenth century, suggests a far wider range of theatrical style available, and a much broader acceptance of that range, than has been previously suggested. Further, traces of traditional style survive in early silent films. If a pictorial style like that employed by Keene was widely accepted by theatre audiences, as recent scholarship has suggested,[25] such acceptance may provide one reason for the cinema's rapid spread in the first decade of the twentieth century, at the live theatre's expense. As early as the middle 1890s, some New York reviewers were becoming aware that the new, more subdued Realistic acting and dramaturgical styles were limited in their effect; Keene's Richard was described as "extreme . . . in its grotesque outlines and crude coloring, [but it has] inordinate popularity . . . among less sophisticated and more robust playgoers of the provinces. There the measured strut and rhythmic rant of the 'old school,' the noise and turmoil and sputtering violence are still in favor. And who shall decree that they are utterly wrong?"[26]

Notes

1. Biographical data on Keene has been collated from the following sources: Franklin Graham, *Histrionic Montreal* (Montreal, 1902; rpt. New York & London, 1969), pp. 261–62; *The Marie Burroughs Art Portfolio of Stage Celebrities* (Chicago, 1894), unpaginated; unidentified clipping, Players' Collection 13,401, Billy Rose Theatre Collection, Lincoln Center Research Center for the Performing Arts, New York Public Library (hereafter cited as Rose Collection); "Mirror Interview: Thomas W. Keene," *New York Dramatic Mirror*, 21 September 1895, p. 10; and "Thomas W. Keene Dead," *New York Dramatic Mirror*, 11 June 1898, p. 8.

2. Robert Grau, "Memories of Players in Other Days: Thomas W. Keene," *New York Evening World*, 1912, clipping in Player's Collection 13,401, Rose Collection.

3. *San Francisco Wasp*, 23 December 1881; as cited by J. S. McElhaney, "The Professional Theatre in San Francisco, 1880–1889," Ph.D. diss., Stanford University, 1972, p. 247.

4. *Commercial Appeal* [Memphis], 29 November 1895, p. 5; as cited by C. Powell, "The Lyceum Theatre of Memphis, Tennessee 1890–1910," M.A. thesis, University of Mississippi, 1951, pp. 122–23.

5. *Pittsburgh Gazette*, 13 September 1881; as cited by J. A. Lowrie, "A History of the Pittsburgh Stage (1861–1891)," Ph.D. diss., University of Pittsburgh, 1943, p. 159.

6. *Pittsburgh Chronicle Telegraph*, 11 March 1884; as cited by Lowrie, p. 173.

7. The performance style Keene employed has been termed the "old school," and has been well studied in recent years; there will, therefore, be no extended treatment of it here. See Attilio Favorini, "The Old School of Acting and the English Provinces," *Quarterly Journal of Speech*, 58 (1972), 204–205; the same author's " 'Richard's Himself Again!' Robert Mantell's Shakespearean Debut in New York City," *Educational Theatre Journal*, 24 (1972), 402–14; and my "Frederick B. Warde: America's Greatest Forgotten Tragedian," *Educational Theatre Journal*, 29 (1977), 333–44.

8. While Keene's complete career remains only partly compiled, enough of his touring seasons from 1880 through 1898 have been collated to permit preliminary

estimates of his annual repertoires; I have taken data from entries in the *New York Dramatic Mirror*, corrected and amplified by materials contained in the unpublished sources already cited, and elsewhere, notably the Napier Wilt Files at the University of Chicago, the Robinson Locke Collection in the Rose Collection, the L. E. Behymer Collection at the Huntington Library, and files of the Ohio Historical Society and the Ohio State University Theatre Research Institute.

9. *San Antonio Express*, 20 October 1888; as cited by C. B. Myler, "A History of the English-speaking Theatre in San Antonio Before 1900," Ph.D. diss., University of Texas, 1968, p. 277.

10. J. M. Siefkas, "A History of Theatre in LaCrosse, Wisconsin, from its Beginning to 1900," Ph.D. diss., University of Montana, 1972, p. 36, citing the *La Crosse Chronicle*, 7 April 1882, p. 3.

11. *New York Tribune*, 3 February 1884; as reprinted in advertisement, "Grand Artistic and Financial Success of the Popular Tragedian Thomas W. Keene," *New York [Dramatic] Mirror*, 9 February 1884, p. 12.

12. *Morning Journal*, *New York Times*, and *New York Sun*, all 29 January 1884, reprinted in "Grand Artistic and Financial Success."

13. "Correspondence—Philadelphia," *New York Dramatic Mirror*, 2 February 1889, p. 4.

14. *New York Times*, 29 January 1884, reprinted in "Grand Artistic and Financial Success."

15. *Denver Republican*, 13 December 1890, p. 3; as cited by E. S. Crowley, "The History of the Tabor Grand Opera House, Denver, Colorado, 1881–1891," M.A. thesis, University of Denver, 1940, p. 140.

16. *Wisconsin State Journal*, 16 April 1885 and 19 October 1893; as cited by H. C. Youngerman, "Theatrical Activities: Madison, Wisconsin, 1836–1907," Ph.D. diss., University of Wisconsin–Madison, 1940, p. 113.

17. *Leader*, 11 December 1888; as cited by J. C. Arnold, "A History of the Lexington Theatre from 1887 to 1900," Ph.D. diss., University of Kentucky, 1956, p. 51.

18. Siefkas, p. 36, citing *La Crosse Chronicle*, 7 April 1882, p. 3.

19. *Charlotte Daily Observer*, 8 December 1880; as cited by R. T. Barber, Jr., "An Historical Study of the Theatre in Charlotte, North Carolina, from 1873–1902," Ph.D. diss., Louisiana State University, 1970, p. 106.

20. W. R. Markwell, *Louis XI* (New York & London, n.d.), p. 4. As Keene's promptbook has not been located, it is impossible to know if this speech was used in his version; the speech accurately describes the king's character, however, and appears in a slightly different form in the Boucicault adaptation. Keene drew upon both Markwell and Boucicault for his own version.

21. *Seattle Press Times*, 3 January 1895; as cited by E. L. Nelson, "A History of the Road Shows in Seattle from Their Beginning to 1914," M.A. thesis, University of Washington, 1947, p. 79.

22. Three clippings, unidentified, Players' Collection 13,401, Rose Collection.

23. George C. D. Odell, *Annals of the New York Stage*, 15 vols. (New York, 1927–49), XII, 251.

24. *Nashville Daily American*, 10 October 1897; as cited by L. S. Maiden, "A Chronicle of the Theater in Nashville, Tennessee, 1876–1900," Ph.D. diss., Vanderbilt University, 1955, p. 632.

25. Donald C. Mullin, "Methods and Manners of Traditional Acting," *Educational Theatre Journal*, 27 (1975), 5–22.

26. Unidentified clipping, Locke Collection, series 2, volume 293, Rose Collection. Research for this essay was supported, in part, by a grant from the College of the Arts, The Ohio State University.

Robertson Davies   4

Mixed Grill:
Touring Fare in
Canada, 1920–1935 _____

What I offer you is not the result of patient research but an evocation of past experience in the theatre—the Canadian theatre during the last part of that period when this country relied on touring companies for its dramatic experience. When I first encountered the theatre, it was entirely an imported pleasure, and I never heard anyone say a word of regret that it was so. Canada imported pineapples and it imported plays for the same reason; such things were appreciated here but they were not of Canadian growth.

Sometimes when I talk with students I find that they cannot conceive of a Canada in which there was so little theatrical ambition and, as it appears to them, so little theatrical self-respect. It is not easy to persuade them that we felt no misgiving on this subject whatever. We thought we had quite an active theatre. I draw what I say not only from what I experienced myself, but from the experiences of my parents, who were keen theatregoers and spoke often and at length of the theatre they remembered from their youth; the store of recollection on which I am drawing thus goes back over ninety years. The self-conscious Canadianism of today was then unknown. Canada did not cease to be a colony, psychologically, until long after I was born, and in matters relating to the arts its colonialism was absolute. A national culture arises from the depths of a people, and Canadians knew where those depths were, and certainly it was not here. There were too many Canadians who were physically loyal to the new land, but who remained exiles in matters of the spirit. You might as well have asked for an indigenous form of government, or an indigenous religion, as ask for Canadian art. Theatre, music, and literature did not originate here. They came from home, wherever home might be.

As for the Canadians of long descent, among whom I am proud to number my mother's family, they were in the main aesthetic innocents. The Bible and *Pilgrim's Progress* served them for literature; music, if it figured at all in their reckonings, meant church music of no very distinguished kind. As for theatre, a common attitude is summed up in a story my mother used to tell with glee. She and some girls of her acquaintance were making up a party to go to a nearby city to see a play. One of the girls said to her mother: "Ma, can I go to Hamilton to see *Ben Hur?*" "Who's he, Annie?" asked the mother, and when she found that he was a play-actor, letting on to have had direct experience of Jesus Christ, the matter was closed with a bang. The thirst for what the theatre could give was not strong among the majority of people outside a few large towns.

One need not retreat to the 1880s to meet that attitude. My father remembered very clearly hearing, as a young man in Toronto about 1900, a fiery sermon preached by a popular local clergyman who raged against the iniquity of a woman of known blemished reputation daring to show herself on the Toronto stage. The woman was Lily Langtry, and the clergyman was the late Canon H. J. Cody, who subsequently became president of the University of Toronto, and did not greatly abate his mistrust of the theatre. I may say that, when I was a boy of fifteen, a friend of mine was forbidden to bring me to his house, because his father had discovered that I was a reader of that notorious scoundrel Bernard Shaw. That was in the 1930s and Shaw had long before received the Nobel Prize. Canada's present hydropic thirst for the delights of the theatre is a comparatively recent passion. Until 1933 touring companies served very well to satisfy the demands of those who frequented the playhouse.

When we speak of the touring theatre, we are apt to concentrate on the cities and to look eagerly for evidence that Canada was not a cultural backwater. Nor do we look in vain. We now know, for instance, that a theatregoer living in Toronto between 1830 and 1850 could have seen several—a majority—of the plays of Lord Byron, presented on the local stage. How well they were done we cannot accurately gauge, but the evidence suggests that they were not done badly. However, that was an era of resident companies in big towns. What happened to touring groups we can discover from that delightful book *A Theatrical Trip for a Wager* (London, 1861) by Captain Horton Rhys; they were greeted with suspicion, and their audiences were likely to be small and hard-bitten. We can reconstruct in imagination the entertainment offered by Rhys and his associates—Miss Catherine Lucette and Captain Bayly, the Primo Buffo of the celebrated A.B.C. Club—because he has given us their program in detail; it makes us feel sympathy for their audiences.

As a child, I lived in small towns, and I remember the touring companies that visited them. I once saw the famous Marks Troupe, though I was so small that my recollection is only of May Belle Marks, wrapped in a Union Jack and wearing a Roman helmet, singing *Rule, Britannia,* between the acts of a melodrama that has utterly escaped me. It was during the First Great

War, and patriotism was lively theatrical fare. Later, in a different small town in the Ottawa Valley, I saw most of what came to our theatre, called, inevitably, the Opera House. It showed moving pictures, but these were easily set aside when we were visited by a play.

It was, I suppose, the irreducible minimum of what the touring theatre had to offer, though I recall two visits from Blackstone, the magician and hypnotist, who was by no means an inferior performer. Greatly below that level were the minstrel shows that visited us, which I was not allowed to attend because, I was told, they were "coarse," and luckier boys who had attended assured me that this was so. However, they were not as coarse as a kind of entertainment called generically Mutt-and-Jeff Shows. These were rough-and-ready musical comedies in which the leading roles were figures from the comic strips—Mutt and Jeff, or Maggie and Jiggs—who wore masks like the faces of the familiar figures they personated. There was a theme, expressed in the title, like *Mutt and Jeff in Paris*, and the show brought a small chorus of girls who were said to be of blemished virtue, though how anybody found out I was not encouraged to inquire. A rough audience attended; it was a lumber town and our audiences were unsophisticated playgoers who had to be hit over the head with a joke—even a dirty joke—before they saw it. Again, from hearsay, I learned that the show could get really dirty if the audience seemed to like it that way. A popular comic ploy was this: a girl walks across the stage in a very short skirt, making unmistakable gestures of sexual allurement; Jeff, or Mr. Jiggs, watches her go by, saying "Oh boy-o-boy-oboy!" then spits down into the depths of his baggy pants, to cool his lust. My parents were doubtless wise not to let me go to these things, but I am glad I heard about them from some of my friends, because I am able to describe authentically what amused an audience of lumber-haulers in rural Canada in the early 1920s.

If these Aristophanic shows moved them to laughter—and I have never seen any reason to believe that the plays of Aristophanes were much above the level of *Mutt and Jeff at Delphi*—what purged them with pity and terror? I can report from personal experience that even at that late date it was the evergreen *Uncle Tom's Cabin*. I saw two Tom-shows by the time I was ten, and my recollection of them is clear. Indeed, the local school was closed so that the children could attend a matinée of this improving drama. Even to my child's eye, Little Eva seemed somewhat older than the text suggested—by a matter of twenty-five years at the least. However, Simon Legree was satisfactorily villainous, and the scene in which he flogs the noble slave was terrifying, even though the lash was plainly striking on a padded jacket. Eliza's escape over the ice floes of the Ohio River, bearing her child in her arms, was thrilling, though the scenic illusion was crude. We all applauded lustily when George Harris, the slave who is about to escape north, cried: "And when I stand on the soil of Canada, beneath the British flag, I shall never call any man 'Massa' again!" We wept at the death of Eva, who expired in considerable musical style, for a choir of slaves knelt in her bedroom singing *Nearer, My God, To Thee* in close— very close—harmony. When, in the final tableau, Uncle Tom rose from where he lay dead in the cotton field, cast his manacles from him, and advanced up a rather short staircase to be greeted by Little Eva, robed as an angel, we were purged indeed, washed whiter than snow. This was melodrama, and as such it evoked archetypes with inescapable power. I think myself lucky to have seen it when I was still innocent, before the coming of that critical spirit that robs us of so much pleasure.

There were other plays that attempted to strike the plangent melodramatic string. One was called *The Prodigal Son*; it was a Bible drama, to which even preachers went. The company included a camel, and we all agreed that it was a considerable advance in religious experience to have beheld a Bible animal of this sort. There were problem plays, too. Not Ibsen, of course, but the kind of problems our public could understand. I recall one, named *The Unwanted Child*; there were special matinées for women, who might feel some delicacy about seeing the play in the presence of men. I was not allowed to go, but I got a report on it from my mother's cook, who did. She did not want to tell me, for she was a woman of high principle who would have done nothing to smirch the pure mind of a child, but I persisted. "Please, Victoria," I begged, "what was it about?" She thought for perhaps a full minute, and then she found the answer. "Bobby," she said in a low, intense voice, "it was about a girl who Went the Limit." With that dark revelation I had to be content, for I was at an age when the splendors and miseries of The Limit were still far in the future.

I must mention another kind of travelling drama, with which I was familiar in my childhood, but which I have never seen mentioned in any record. Only part of it travelled. The director, who was also the business manager and the musical director, would arrive in town with a carload of scenery and costumes, and would let it be known that he would shortly produce a splendid musical comedy. One of these, I remember, was called *In Sunny France*. He assembled a cast of local singing amateurs, and produced his show, under the patronage of the Oddfellows or Knights of Columbus, or some such influential body. He cajoled everybody, directed everybody, provided romantic interest for everybody, and within two days of his arrival in town, knew everybody.

These musical comedies were not tightly crafted, if I may borrow an expression popular in the modern theatre. They could be enlarged to include anything anybody in town could do, which included whistling and playing the musical saw. There was always a "Prologue in Fairyland" in which virtually every female child under thirteen appeared, dancing, sometimes rather morosely, to the music dispensed by the talented director at the piano. There was always a number called "The Foxtrot of the Hours," or the "Two Step of the Flowers," or something of that kind, in which every female schoolteacher under fifty had a brief solo, as an Hour or a Flower. The costumes were gorgeous but decent.

The highlight of the evening was when the talented director himself appeared on stage and sang a song filled with references to local notabilities. These were not pungent lampoons. I recall one which ran:

> I taxi'd round to Mrs. Airth's
> To have a little frolic;
> I ate some cake the dear girl made
> And nearly died of colic.

You appreciate the appeal of this. To take a taxi in our town, except for a wedding or a funeral, was mad big city extravagance; the notion of a frolic with Mrs. Airth, who was the leading soprano in the Presbyterian choir, was suggestive if not downright salacious. However, if anyone had been feeling sorry for Mr. Airth, a local furniture dealer, they knew that he was vindicated by the joke in the final lines. In their special way, these were subtle dramas.

Where did these things originate? Where did the talented director come from? I cannot tell you, but I remember these affairs, and sometimes I think I am the only person who does. They were a form of touring theatre that stretched out a hand to amateurs. They were Broadway come to the Ottawa Valley.

Detailing these performances makes the point that there was a considerable quantity of touring theatre that was of sociological rather than artistic interest, and some of it was not far removed from the shows given by the King and the Duke in *Huckleberry Finn*. There was, however, another form of touring theatre, as I experienced it later in my boyhood in the city of Kingston, which was a first-class touring town and had a yearly theatrical season, in that there was something to be seen in its theatre for two or three nights and a matinée, every week during the autumn and winter.

At least one popular musical comedy appeared each year, sometimes more than one. They were of an innocence now unguessed at, for we have demanded of musical comedy a significance that has left it more seriously musical and hardly to be described at all as comedy. *No, No, Nanette* and *Rose Marie* were meant only to please, and they were made in a durable mold, where there were principal lovers—united to begin, parted by the caprice of fate, and united for the final curtain—secondary lovers, and comic lovers; given these and a set of comic parents, a villain or villainess, and a chorus, you could not go wrong. Another necessity was a principal dancer, invariably a woman who could, in *Rose Marie* for instance, perform the Totem Dance with a rubbery sinuosity that was agreeably erotic and gymnastic in about equal proportions. Fantasy involving these gifted women was a prominent factor in the adolescent life of the period.

My recollections of this time inevitably mingle the theatre as I saw it in Kingston, and the theatre of Toronto, because I often went there with my parents to see plays. In addition, for some years I attended a Toronto boarding school, and every Saturday afternoon was passed in one of Toronto's theatres instead of in the fresh air. I shall not differentiate needlessly, because it was all theatre of the same general sort—that is to say, a theatrical mixed grill, a remarkable sampling of everything the theatre can offer. Music-hall artists of the first rank, like Harry Lauder and George Robey, appeared, every bit as funny as legend reports. There was some very old-fashioned fare, like Bransby Williams in *Treasure Island*, which was played straight and was rather hammy, and even *George Barnwell*, which was gently guyed in a production by Nigel Playfair, in which that brilliant actor Ernest Thesiger played the ill-fated Barnwell. I saw William C. Gillette in his own play *Sherlock Holmes*, and after several plays and movies about the great detective, Gillette, dry of voice and hawk-like of profile, remains, for me, the best. Of course, the earliest illustrations of the stories were based on him. He was seventy-five when I saw him and remarkably swift on his feet.

These were productions described as "all-star" and they were starry indeed, but as we all know, the stars are immeasurably old. Such was *The School for Scandal*, with Ethel Barrymore, and the principal scandal was that she was demonstrably drunk. Such was *The Rivals*, in which James T. Powers played Bob Acres, and though not youthful, he had what used to be called the Old Comedy manner in perfection. Such was an all-star production of *The Merry Wives of Windsor* with three stars legendary even then—Otis Skinner, Mrs. Fiske, and Henrietta Crosman. Their combined ages at that time numbered 190 years, but they certainly did not look it and their speech was a revelation of clarity and witty emphasis. Skinner played Falstaff as very much a gentleman who connived at and enjoyed his own troubles, and thus never really lost dignity. I remember still his delivery of the lines: "Water swells a man; and what a thing should I have been, when I had been swelled! I should have been a mountain of mummy."

On the stage, of course, years are not so important as on the screen or (even more) on television. We now expect young characters to be young; we have seen, on television, a Juliet who was authentically fourteen. As a girl of fourteen she was credible; but as Juliet she was incredible, because she had not learned her job. These senior players knew their job to perfection. I recall Seymour Hicks, who was supreme in that now rare thing, sophisticated comedy. He played in *The Man in Dress Clothes* and in *Mr. What's-His-Name*; in one of these he was a rake, irresistible to women and devoted to women. There was a scene in which he was so down on his luck that he ate the birdseed out of the canary's cage; what made it memorable was his sincere apology to the deprived bird. He was fifty-seven at the time, and rather plump, but he was more authentically a *bon viveur* than any thin actor of twenty-seven I have ever seen. It was because he knew how to be irresistible; he had a technique for it; he did not rely on personal endowments. That is acting in one of its great modes. He possessed one physical charm in high degree; he had a delightful, witty voice. Great voices are rarities on the stage at any time.

Walter Hampden was more easily resisted. When I saw him as a soldier-saint Caponsacchi in a play made from Browning's *The Ring and the Book*, he was certainly soldier and saint, but not a heart-warming lover. Then, perhaps, neither was Caponsacchi. As Hamlet he was deeply satisfactory. I choose those words with care, because he was fifty-four and though very handsome he was demonstrably middle-aged. It was his understanding of the part, his mastery of nuance, the sense of nobility and tragic fate that he brought on the stage that made a production—he was accompanied by an admirable cast—that sent his audiences away fulfilled and sent me, as a schoolboy, treading on air, because a new heaven and a new earth had been opened to me. I have seen younger Hamlets subsequently, and some who were better; but none who were better simply because they were younger. The most subtle Shylock of this century was George Arliss; one marvelled that anybody could get the better of him. However, he wanted villainy; the finest, most believable, and most paranoid Shylock of my experience was Randle Ayrton, a great actor, whose inability to get along with anybody else robbed him of top honors; but as Shylock, Lear, and Ford in *The Merry Wives*, there was nobody to touch him for passion and tragic anguish. His later career was pretty much confined to the Memorial Theatre at Stratford-on-Avon.

From that Stratford there came some remarkable tours of Canada, playing Shakespearean repertoire in the admirable, clean, and fast productions of Bridges-Adams. A company from Stratford under the leadership of Frank Benson had come to Canada in 1913, but the company in the early 1930s brought a larger repertoire. The first visit included *Much Ado About Nothing, Richard II, Romeo and Juliet, The Merry Wives of Windsor, Julius Caesar, Twelfth Night, A Midsummer Night's Dream, Hamlet*, and *Macbeth*. The principal actors were George Hayes, Wilfrid Walter (who was especially memorable as Claudius in *Hamlet*), and Roy Byford, a naturally fat actor who was a great Falstaff; that he was fat seemed unimportant, but that he was a wit and by far the most intelligent man in the play was palpable. These tours were a revelation to young people like myself, who had seen Shakespeare only with stars; here was ensemble acting of a high order, and Shakespeare very rapidly played, with the poetry always the first consideration—a treatment which brought out the structure and drama of the plays brilliantly.

At this time, by the way, we saw a production of *Macbeth* with scenery by Gordon Craig. The scenery swamped the play, and one tires of scenery very quickly. It is of interest that it was Robert B. Mantell who first played *Hamlet* in modern dress in Toronto. I fear that economy, rather than experiment, was at the back of this, and poor Mantell in evening dress looked like an old waiter.

Another favorite visitor in repertory was the D'Oyly Carte company, playing all of Gilbert and Sullivan except the unpopular last two operettas. This was before economy destroyed the musical and production qualities of that organization. I remember in particular the superb designs for *The Mikado* by Charles Ricketts. Musical standards, established by the conductor, Isidore Godfrey, were high, and the quality of the playing in a company headed by Henry Lytton, Bertha Lewis, Darrell Fancourt, and Leo Sheffield was still under the tradition of Gilbert himself and imparted by people who had worked with Gilbert. They possessed a distinction not to be suspected from what one sees in that company now. This was fossil theatre, for it was still Victorian in the marrow of its bones; but it was the best sort of Victorian staging, and that was very good indeed. In the movement of the Chorus as a single entity— which seems so intolerable now—there was great wit, for the Chorus seemed to be a single character, multiplied by thirty.

We were ready to enjoy fossil theatre, but that was not all we enjoyed. Maurice Colborne and Barry Jones played in a repertoire drawn from the plays of Shaw; their company included a young actress, making the first of what was to be a fine reputation. She was Margaret Rawlings, brilliant as a Shavian heroine because she had in perfection the witty, dry style, the air of observing her character from without, as well as acting it from within, to which Shaw responds so well. This company did not confine itself to the most popular Shaw; its *John Bull's Other Island* was one of its greatest successes. Barry Jackson also sent a company that played what was then a modern repertoire, its newest play being *The Barretts of Wimpole Street*, with memorably beautiful designs; the part of Robert Browning was played by a young actor just coming into prominence as a leading man—Donald Wolfit. Mrs. Fiske appeared in Ibsen's *Ghosts*; Judith Anderson in Pirandello's *As You Desire Me*. We had popular London comedies, too, such as James B. Fagan's *And So To Bed*, in which Edmund Gwenn was amusing and endearing as Samuel Pepys. Nor should I forget to mention *The Chauve Souris*, which was splendid throughout, but never more splendid than when Nikita Baliev was introducing the numbers; he was named on the program as Theatre Autocrat, and that was manifestly what he was. One was left with the impression that every theatre needed such an official.

It would be tedious to go further in this direction. I hope I have made my point that the theatre we enjoyed, in our days of cultural colonialism, was very good indeed, and it doubtless gained something in mystery and delight because it came from far away, and the quarrels that ravaged it and the wrangles about finance and pride of place were not the ugly gossip of our morning papers. Our situation was, no doubt, one of child-like artistic dependence, but it was an immensely enjoyable childhood.

I have referred to fossil theatre, but I have not as yet discussed the frequent tours of Sir John Martin-Harvey, who visited Canada, all told, eight times. His was fossil theatre in that it reproduced and preserved, in many instances, productions and performances that had been originated by

Sir Henry Irving, and what Martin-Harvey undertook on his own volition was done in the Irving mode. However, I do not use the term fossil theatre derisively; this mode of acting and direction belonged to a time past, and to see it, as I once did, very close to a production of Elmer Rice's *Street Scene*, which was accounted the ultimate in adventurous modernity, was to experience some of the astonishments of travel in time. To see it, as I did also, close to O'Neill's *Mourning Becomes Electra*, produced no such shock, for O'Neill's work had its roots in nineteenth-century melodrama, and one might imagine Martin-Harvey being very fine in, for instance, *A Touch of the Poet*.

Melodrama is a constant element in theatre; it is not tragedy, because it calls heavily on pathos for some of its effects, and it often makes use of grotesque juxtapositions of villainy and jocosity which tragedy is supposed to avoid, though Shakespeare never troubled to do so. The greatest tragedy—that of Greece—treats of a world in which the gods are expected to be capricious; the greatest melodrama takes place in a world where God is not expected to be capricious, but for a time, and unaccountably, seems to be asleep, and neglecting, or perhaps simply testing, His own. The cruel justice of the Greeks is very different from the justice of melodrama, which is poetic justice. Tragedy fears the gods; melodrama looks upon God as the final righter of all wrongs, the ultimate judge. Of course, if you test melodrama by its trashy examples, you will despise it, but if you glance sideways toward some remarkable examples of poetic art—toward Goethe's *Faust*, or Byron's *Manfred*—you will see shining about them a purplish light that can only be called the light of melodrama.

Martin-Harvey appeared in what used to be called Costume Drama. It was a sort of theatre that came into being in the nineteenth century at the same time as the Costume Novel, and there was always a whiff of Sir Walter Scott about it. Romance, as evidenced in high chivalry, elaborate codes of manners and morality, and extremes of love and hatred, was always more easily accepted when it was placed at a distance in time. Furthermore, Costume Drama gave actors and actresses an opportunity to display accomplishments that found little place in plays of contemporary life; the elegant management of the dress of a bygone era, of swords, capes, walking sticks, plumed hats, combined with graceful bearing, refinement in the use of the snuffbox, the handkerchief, the fan, and all the variations of bowing, dancing, and exchanging salutations, required training, and it was expected that in an accomplished player they would become so much second nature that any suggestion of training disappeared. Was the result false in impact? Did it suggest a pageant or a puppet theatre? No indeed, because these Costume Dramas, though at a distance in matters of scene and dress, were faithful to the accepted beliefs of the nineteenth century, and the passions and the humor were of the sort acceptable to people who read Dickens, Thackeray, Trollope, and Charles Reade.

You will say, surely this seemed strange in Canada during the late 1920s and early 1930s. Yes, it seemed a little strange, but it was also pleasing, and if you will look at the moving pictures of the same era, you will see that the morality of that time was not so far removed—in the mimetic arts, at any rate—from the nineteenth century as you might suppose. It was the era of the Hayes Office in Hollywood, when scenes of sexual involvement were hedged about with elaborate rules that make very peculiar reading. Furthermore, Martin-Harvey, who was anything but a fool, did not press purely nineteenth-century conceptions to ridiculous lengths.

Consider, for instance, his version of *David Garrick*. The play was written by Tom Robertson in 1864 and by 1924 it was decidedly stuffy. Martin-Harvey used the version James Albery, who had a deft hand with dialogue, had prepared for Charles Wyndham, and had himself introduced an effective scene in the third act that was written for him by Canon Frederick Langbridge, the author of his immensely successful melodrama, *The Only Way*. So likewise his version of *The Lyons Mail* alters some of Charles Reade's lines of heavy pathos to more colloquial, though no less effective, speech, cuts comic dialogue which was in the mode of an earlier day, and alters certain emphases that throw into relief the character of Leserques.

The play is based on a true happening in which a notably good citizen, Leserques, was arrested and brought near to the guillotine because of his resemblance to the real murderer and robber of the mail-coach, whose name was Dubosc. Much of the pleasure of the play lies in seeing the same actor play both roles, and the rapidity with which he switches from one to the other—which was contrived in some instances by the skillful use of a double. Leserques, as is so unhappily common in good characters, is rather a dull dog, but Dubosc is a fascinating ruffian. Moments of terror linger in the mind of anyone who saw Martin-Harvey play the part—his high spirits as he rifled the pockets of the murdered postillion, during which he whistled the *Marseillaise* between his teeth; he got blood on his hands, which he wiped on the neck of the horse that pulled the mail-coach and then, with the good humor of a real animal lover and man hater, patted the animal jovially. One recalls the cold menace with which he treated the poor girl who was so unfortunate as to have a liking for him and, in the last scene, the goblin merriment with which he looked down from his attic at the impending execution of the unfortunate Leserques; he lay on his stomach, kicking up his heels with delight and, when the mistake was discovered and the crowd began to shout menaces at him, he threw flowerpots down on their heads. All of this, as you see, was physical action; the text was no great matter, but the blood, the jingling of the coins, and the placing of the flowerpots was of uttermost importance. It was theatre from an era when playwrights were expected to know their place, and that place was to provide a scaffold for an imaginative actor to clothe with devices that carried the heart of the drama to the spectators.

How was it done? By a technique which was never obtrusive, but which could be caught on the fly, so to speak, if you were looking for it. It was the pauses that counted. Martin-Harvey had taken careful heed of the advice Ellen Terry gave to young actors: "Act in your pauses!" Not that the pauses were too many, or portentous; often they amounted to nothing more than the careful phrasing of a line, or an instant's hesitation in the taking up of a cue. However, those pauses gave an impression of reflection, of thought, of an inner life that was not being expressed solely in speech, and they established the rhythm of the play.

As one falls under the spell of a fine romantic novelist, one fell under the spell of these plays. I have elsewhere described a personal experience that illustrates what I mean, but I repeat it because it falls pat to the occasion. When I was about eighteen or nineteen I wanted to go to the theatre one Saturday afternoon with a friend, and there was nothing to be seen but Martin-Harvey in *The Only Way*. Neither of us had seen it, but we knew all about it. We knew it was beneath us, and we despised it. Rather than stay outside in the healthy open air, however, we decided to go to jeer at the old ragbag, and pump up our egos by so doing.

The curtain rose on a Prologue, which we recognized from the novel; there was nothing to feed our scorn, but we were prepared to wait. Then the play began in earnest, in the very Dickensian chambers of Sidney Carton, where that failed barrister, painfully hung-over, drives his quill as fast as he can, preparing briefs for his master, Stryver. When the act began, Carton was asleep, sprawled over his table in a drunken stupor. It was picturesque, we were prepared to admit, and the way in which Carton dipped a towel in water and wrapped it around his aching head was both funny and pathetic. The appearance of the Little Sempstress, who is not a character in the book, but who was inserted into the play to make a role for Lady Martin-Harvey, ought to have been good for a laugh, but somehow was not; her concern for Carton, and her obvious love for him—obvious to us but not to him—was sheer hokum, of course, but we were not laughing. We would wait. The ridiculous part was sure to come. By the end of the act, when Carton said, "Well, love is good—but drink is better—and death is best of all," and fell forward over the table, insensible with liquor, we felt that something had gone seriously wrong. The play was not absurd at all. We did not know, of course, that the strong essence of Dickens, which was coming through the pauses, had seized us.

From the point of view of my friend and myself, things simply went from bad to worse, from then onward. The act in Dr. Manette's garden in Soho was admirable; there were very funny passages in it, and we had not expected anything like that. There was a love scene in it that disconcerted us, and I saw my friend furtively wiping his eye; I had something in my eye too, but I thought—I hoped—it was a speck of dust. Theatres are notoriously dusty places. The scene before the Revolutionary Tribunal followed, and that was thrilling, for it was full-out romantic management of crowds and the audience, to produce expectation, humor, suspense, and at the last a situation from which there was apparently no escape. Of course, there was; that is what melodramas and romances are about. In the next scene, we became aware—because, although we knew the book, we banished our knowledge in order to savor the play—of Carton's desperate plan to save

4. Sir John Martin-Harvey in *The Only Way*. From the Lyceum souvenir programme, courtesy of L. W. Conolly.

the life of the man who was loved by the woman whom he himself loved.

Indeed, there was a good deal of lovemaking in this scene, and boys like
my friend and myself are not the best audience for love scenes; if anything,
we favored the knock-em-down-and-drag-em-out lovemaking demonstrated
in the movies. However, we were by this time wholly in the grip of the play
and the actor. A few years ago, Sir John Gielgud, talking of Martin-Harvey,
said to me: "There is nobody on the stage today who can make love as he
did; he touched women as if they were camellias." We live in an age when
women profess not to wish to be touched as if they were camellias, but it
would be interesting to try the experiment, if the right actor could be found,
just to see how strong that determination really is. My friend and I, as we
watched, wished we had been granted the camellia-touch; we had situations
in mind in which we were sure it would have been extremely useful.

On, then, through successive scenes and the truly touching gallantry of
the condemned people in the prison of the Conciergerie. Finally came the
concluding tableau, against the background of Paris at dawn, with Carton
standing by the guillotine, and the words that have become a cliché: "It is a
far, far better thing that I do. . . . " But I do not need to remind you that
words that have never carried real meaning do not become clichés. How
many curtain calls? I do not know. My friend and I, sodden and humbled,
had the grace to admit to one another that somehow we had been mistaken.

What had we seen? A play not so much written as carpentered, using materials from a novel by Dickens, the principal theme of which is Renunci-ation. Sidney Carton was ready to die in order that the woman he loved might be happy. At the time I saw the play, I knew that was all wrong; the Freudian Revolution was far advanced, and everybody knew that a man who did a thing like that was plainly a homosexual, who did not love the girl at all, but loved her husband, because, of course, nobody ever did anything except for a selfish reason. It did not matter at all that he scarcely knew her husband; rules are rules. That day is long past, and we now recognize that the quality of insight that psychoanalysis provides has its limitations, and often leads to a crass sophistication that is as unproductive in its way as ordinary ignorance. The fault lies not with Sigmund Freud, but with his popularizers. Renunciation was a favorite theme of the nineteenth century, and doubtless they exploited it to a foolish extreme. As it appeared in *The Only Way*, the theme was not coarsely exploited, but presented with a quality of art that reached and touched hundreds of thousands of play-goers. In it Martin-Harvey was very fine, if one does not care to call him great. There have been film versions of the story since then, in which no modern actor has been able to touch him.

It was this quality of refinement in melodramatic acting that especially distinguished him. Even in the bluster of a villainous role like that of Dubosc, he never tore a passion to tatters. Instead, he suggested the unex-pected, both in the part he played and in us as we watched him. For a fine actor helps us to know ourselves better; he does not tell us, or instruct us, in emotion; he evokes emotion we had not known we possessed.

How did he do it? A splendid voice to begin with, and then a handsome presence. He was handicapped by a short stature, but the proportions of his figure were good; he had long legs, in relation to the rest of his body, so he never looked as short as he was. He had an ability to suggest the other-worldly which stood him in good stead when he played as a young man in Maeterlinck's *Pelléas and Mélisande*, with Mrs. Patrick Campbell and Forbes-Robertson. This was the quality which, in his later years, made him really great in a play of Maeterlinck's which is not often mentioned now, *The Burgomaster of Stillemonde*.

Plays that originate in patriotic fervor are not often of the highest quality, and *The Burgomaster* is not the best of Maeterlinck. However, Maeterlinck, even below his best, is not a trivial playwright, and the play had extraordi-nary strength. The scene is a town in Belgium during the First World War; the Burgomaster's son-in-law, who is a German officer, and a good one—not a conventional Hun ruffian—is ordered to direct the firing squad that is to execute his wife's father; it is a matter of discipline, as his superior explains. The Burgomaster entreats his daughter to understand that the death of an old man, under the insane circumstances of war, is not a matter that should exterminate all the love in her heart. Not an easy role to fill, but Harley Granville Barker knew it was a part for Martin-Harvey, who could not merely fill it, but expand it.

How? I have a theory. Martin-Harvey was brought up in a family steeped in Swedenborgian faith. Not many people know much about Swedenborg or his ideas, but they are deeply mystical—mystical in the sense that the believer knows that at all times he is surrounded by a cloud of invisible witnesses, and that his conduct in their eyes is fully as important as his behavior in the eyes of the world. I do not think that an impressionable child, brought up as Jack Harvey was on daily readings from the Swedish mystic's *Heaven and Hell* and the *Celestial Arcana*, will ever completely lose his sense of standing in the presence of an invisible world. Actors who can play saints, though not common, are not unknown; actors who can suggest that they move in the unseen, as well as the palpable world, are very rare, but that was the quality Martin-Harvey brought upon the stage.

That was the quality that gave uncommon eeriness to *The Corsican Brothers*, as he played it. The story is familiar. Twin sons of a noble Corsican family are bound together by a sympathy that warns them whenever one or the other is in danger; they both fall in love with the same French beauty, and they agree that one should go to Paris to woo her; he falls foul of another lover of hers who kills him; the brother in Corsica sees the death in a vision, goes to Paris, seeks out the killer, and revenges his brother.

Such a story may be rather crude. Certainly, a film that was made on this story a few years ago was as coarse as hemp. As Martin-Harvey played it, however, in Irving's version (which is not the version played by Charles Kean, but a refinement on it), it was the mystical link between the brothers that dominated the play—in the splendid first act in the Corsican mansion, in the Balzacian second act at the Paris Opera and at the rowdy party given by the Marquis de Château-Renaud, and in the third act, so magically evoked by a beautifully painted setting of the Forest of Fontainbleau during a snowstorm. Emilie de L'Esparre may have been the romantic fulcrum upon which the action turned, but when, at the end of the play, Fabien de Franchi beheld the ghost of his murdered brother Louis, we wondered if she could ever have cut much of a figure in that haunted household. Yet the uncanny effects were not heavily stressed; all the haunting and mystic sympathy were taken for granted as part of the Corsican heritage. Sometimes when I see films now in which something of this atmosphere is sought, I think of *The Corsican Brothers* and inwardly I cry, "Not like that! Do less! Do less!"

I have been describing a powerfully romantic actor. Could he do anything else? Indeed he could. I never saw him play Oedipus in Canada, but I saw it when he played it for a short season at Covent Garden to mark his retirement. It was already an old-fashioned production, because Reinhardt had devised it in 1912; the setting was spendidly ornate and the costumes magnificent, for that was before the time when anybody thought that the Greeks had possessed a barbaric streak in their history and their character. By 1936, when I saw it, we had new ideas about the old play. I went in a somewhat fearful spirit, because I knew the actor was seventy-three years old, but I wanted to see him, good or bad. It proved to be good. The voice was as ringing as ever, and because of the tragic stilts the actor wore, his small stature had vanished. It was a great evening, and next day all the London papers said so — and it was not simply the kindness that the English show toward veteran actors.

In what way was it great? It was magnificent in a somewhat Germanic fashion, and it had a large, superbly drilled crowd. It was not the Oedipus of Laurence Olivier, a splendid young barbarian chieftain in a world of mono-liths, and in the monolithic translation of Yeats. It was not the Oedipus we have seen at Stratford in Canada, which was masked, hieratic, deliberate in movement, and altogether ceremonial in spirit. The translation Martin-Harvey used was that of Gilbert Murray, lush and Swinburnean in cadence, very well matched with the elaborate setting. It is fashionable to smile at it now, but people quite as cultivated as our superbly cultivated selves thought very highly of it, in its time. Furthermore, it was the whole of Sophocles, which Yeats is not, for Murray was a great scholar, and Yeats knew no Greek and had no hesitation about lopping Sophocles when he seemed not to suit the severe restrictions of Yeats's production. Reinhardt's production was a play about a doomed king, and in Martin-Harvey we saw a king unquestionably doomed, but noble and awesome in his surrender to Fate. There was no Victorian pulling of punches about anything that happened on that stage, and the last appearance of Oedipus, his face streaming with blood, and the horror and sudden flight of that vast crowd, remains with me as one of the most startling and fearful things I have ever seen in the theatre. The slaughterhouse spirit of the Greek drama was finely served, and the poetry was splendid of its kind. Was it Freudian? Oh yes, quite sufficiently so, but it was not solely about incest; it was about the fall of a king.

No one can hope to comment fairly on the work of Martin-Harvey without taking some account of the acting of his wife, whose stage name was Nina de Silva. I have met many people who never saw her, who nevertheless speak of her as a great stage joke, a stupendously bad actress. That is unjust, for sometimes she was a very good actress; as the innkeeper's wife in *The Bells*, for instance, she was moving. However, as the heroine of *The Corsican Brothers* and in *The Only Way*, toward the end of her professional career, she was embarrassing, because the years had not been kind to her, and to put the facts bleakly she was fat and ugly. Yet she continued to play these unsuitable roles, because, I suppose, she wanted to do so, and because her husband insisted on it. There is a story that in his youth, Martin-Harvey was asked to come to New York by Klaw and Erlanger, to make his career there under their management. One of the inducements they offered was that he could have as his leading lady the finest actress in the United States. His answer was brief and characteristic: "I am married to the finest leading lady in the world." That was the end of that, for he never played in the United States afterward.

Nina de Silva appears to have been a woman of extraordinary character, and in a part that suited her, she presented a strikingly individual figure on the stage. I think it was because she was not English, but Portuguese; she came of a diplomatic family, and her manners were high-bred—sometimes rather too high-bred for the role she was playing, as, for instance, when she appeared as Vierja, the pathetically devoted factory girl in *A Cigarette Maker's Romance*. Of course, she came from an age when critics used to marvel that an actress of the distinction of Ellen Terry could assume some of the manners of a washerwoman, in *Madame Sans-Gêne*. I once saw Lady Martin-Harvey act superbly, in a comedy role in a bad play called *The King's Messenger*. She was supposed to be a harlot who had done well out of her profession; she was supposed to be fat and plain, but of boundless professional charm. She was brilliantly funny, and one wished that she had been more happily cast in more plays.

Mention of *The King's Messenger* recalls to me a custom of the touring stage that has now totally vanished—the proliferation of curtain calls. My program for *The King's Messenger*, which I saw in the early 1930s, indicates that after Act One there were three curtain calls; after Act Two, four calls, and after the third act, nine calls and a speech. We liked curtain calls, and gave them lavishly to our favorites. Nowadays the decision as to how many curtain calls there should be lies with the stage manager, who is niggardly. After two calls he wants to turn out the lights, and however enthusiastic the audience may be, it is sharply rebuked by this unseen functionary. There were sly takers of calls, like George Arliss, who pretended that he was taken unawares; there were the exhausted artists, like Donald Wolfit who, even as a young man, seemed to feel the drain of the evening's work very keenly; and there were the musical comedy players, who would have gone on bowing and smiling for an hour, if we had asked it of them. Martin-Harvey, who lived among so many shadows, including the shadow of Irving, was a master of the curtain speech in which, like Irving, he declared himself to be the public's humble, faithful, and obedient servant—bowing with his hand laid upon his heart.

Already the tide was turning. It was at about this time that I saw the Habima Players perform *The Dybbuk* at the end of which the applause of the audience mounted to hurricane proportions, but there was no call. At last, when something like a riot seemed imminent, the curtain rose to reveal some of the actors, pulling off their beards, bewildered that the public should wish to call them back in order to thank them. Another concept of the actor's art had made itself felt in the theatre.

I have seen acting during the past ten years as fine as anything I ever saw in my first twenty-five years, but it is of a different savor. It has gained much in psychological depth; it has lost nothing in refinement of technique; but it has lost the flair, the theatrical radiance of the sort of performance I have been talking about.

Is it lost forever? I greatly doubt it. Romance, like John Barleycorn, has a way of springing up again. It would be a delight to see some rebirth of the old style, shorn of the old falsities.

Douglas McDermott and Robert K. Sarlós

Founding and Touring in America's Provincial Theatre: Woodland, California, 1902–1903

The heritage of American theatre, long only a blurred background for stories about such stars as Edwin Forrest, Charlotte Cushman, the Booths, the Drews, and the Barrymores, is coming into sharper focus. Opera houses like the ones in East Haddam, Connecticut, and Wilmington, Delaware; theatres such as the Victory in Dayton, Ohio; Ford's in Washington; the Pabst in Milwaukee; the Atlas in Cheyenne, Wyoming; the Capitol in Salt Lake City; and the Orpheum in San Francisco have been restored to their former glory, while revivals of an earlier era's theatrical fare, such as *Sugar Babies* or *The Virginian*, take place in increasing numbers. An important task in this process of rediscovery is to correct the traditional American assumption that only the biggest or the oldest is significant. If that were so, Mt. Rushmore would be our finest sculpture, and the log cabin would be the prototype of our national style of domestic architecture. The results of this attitude are rather like what would happen if a physical geographer insisted that nothing less than a mile high were significant: Denver would be America's only city. The recognition seems to be growing that our cultural landscape cannot be surveyed from that altitude either.

It is finally admissible that American drama did not begin with O'Neill, nor American scenography with Robert Edmond Jones. However, those who explore the nineteenth century must continue to demonstrate that its theatre was not confined to playhouses built by the major entrepreneurs and played in by only a handful of stars. The significance of managers such as Ben DeBar, John McCauley, and Tom Maguire will never be fully appreciated until the small-time operators like John Potter are more fully revealed. Nor will the importance of touring by actors such as Joseph Jefferson, James O'Neill, Julia Marlow, and Mrs. Fiske be understood until examinations of the careers of Charles Hanford and Jessie Shirley provide a context within which to place them. The booking empires of the Syndicate and the Shuberts will be more comprehensible after an acquaintance with the adventures of

Jack Haverly, Michael Leavitt, and Alexander Pantages. It is, therefore, the overwhelming bulk of theatrical activity, that of the minor yet ubiquitous craftsmen, that needs surveying. We need to focus on the itinerant actors and managers, as well as on the playhouses they toured, and from which the syndicators eventually assembled their empire.

The Woodland Opera House was such a theatre, and housed such actors. Now to be restored after a twelve-year campaign to reclaim it from proposed transformation into a parking lot, it preserves the atmosphere of small town stopping places for itinerant entertainers and run-of-the-mill stock companies. Seen as cogs in the machine by others, these troupers may have been priests of the muses or pioneers of culture in communities that took as much pride in their own respectability and prosperity as did the urban centers of the distant Robber Barons.

The Opera House we are concerned with was not Woodland's first. The building now standing was built in 1895–96 as a civic effort to preserve the glory of one, similarly named, that stood on the same site from 1885 to 1892. It was, at least externally, more ornate than the present structure. Opulence may have been appropriate to the small town of Woodland in 1885, audience flow and civic pride having apparently outgrown all previously used theatrical facilities both as to quantity and quality of audience accommodation. Situated on the corner of Second Street and Dead Cat Alley, near the north side of Main Street, only eighteen miles from the state capital, the Woodland Opera House embodies both the glorious climax and the inglorious descent of the robust, eclectic, and mercurial American theatre that flourished on the road between 1870 and the First World War. The Opera House represents the climax of Woodland's history as well: in the theatre's heyday, from 1898 to 1907, the city was rich and proud, though it had passed its peak of growth and prosperity.

Local historians have not yet agreed whether the area of Woodland was first settled in 1853 or 1855, but the first post office was established under the name of Woodland in July 1861, and it became the seat of Yolo County in May 1862.[1] The county's population increased by more than one hundred percent during the next ten years, and by 1900 it stood at 13,618, while the city had 3,069 inhabitants.[2] Incorporation had occurred in March 1871, by which time Hesperian College (1860) was in operation, the first newspaper had begun publishing (1864), and a local bank had been chartered (1868).[3] Theatrical performances, too, were taking place with some regularity.

The first building to house theatrical performances in Woodland seems to have been Templar's Hall. That it was built by the Woodland Lodge No. 237 of the Independent Order of Good Templars, which was instituted in October 1866, is clear (Gregory, pp. 105–106). Its size, however, remains a mystery. According to the *Yolo Weekly Mail*, the Wilton Troupe performed there at least three times: in May and November 1869, and again in May 1870.[4] Their fare consisted of both the pathetic and the light-hearted, their first appearance featuring *Camille* and a shadow pantomime, their third offering *Medea* and *Andy Blake*. Details of the program presented by the Pixley Sisters in February 1870 are not known (*Yolo Weekly Mail*, 17 February 1870).

By June 1870, there was certainly another space available for putting entertainment before the Woodland public. C. P. Sprague and H. W. Atwell's *Western Shore Gazetteer* for the city contains both a description of, and an advertisement for, "Washington Hall," installed on the second floor of Adam Gerlach's Academy of Music, and "fitted with a stage and stage scenery complete" (Sprague and Atwell, p. 117). It was first occupied by a company under the management of L. F. Beatty, who supervised the application of finishing touches to the stage (*Yolo Weekly Mail*, 30 June 1870). Washington Hall was also available for rent by the night or by the week "for Theatres, Concerts, Lectures, or Balls" (Sprague and Atwell, p. 278). Some indication of its location survives, as well as copious information as to its size. The *Yolo Weekly Mail* (2 June 1870) described the entire "large brick block about to be completed" and located the hall as being "opposite Good Templar building, west of the railroad." Russell asserts that the Academy was on the north side of Main Street, between Elm and College (Russell, p. 204), and Augustus Koch's *Bird's-Eye View of Woodland, Yolo County, California*, 1871, corroborates him. Its dimensions were one hundred feet by sixty; the second floor auditorium used the entire width but only eighty feet of the length, twenty-two feet of which constituted the stage at the east end (*Yolo Weekly Mail*, 2 June 1870). The *Mail's* extravagant promise of its accommodating "about two thousand persons" could not have been fulfilled by the thirty-six hundred square feet reserved for spectators. During the 1870s, Washington Hall seems to have been the mainstay of Woodland's apparently meager theatrical life. So far, records of only thirty-two performances have been discovered.[5] By 1879, the building had changed hands and its owner pleaded through the *Yolo Democrat* (16 January 1879) for a buyer of the upper story who would commit himself to remodelling. Alterations were deemed necessary to turn the premises into "a comfortable and commodious public hall," remedy the "execrable" acoustics, and provide all visitors with a "full view of the stage" by raising the seats. A surviving program testifies that Washington Hall was still in use as late as 1882,[6] but the claim that it burned "about 1886" cannot be corroborated, except that it does not appear on the Sanborn map of Woodland published that year.[7]

Almost contemporaneous with Washington Hall, and even less frequently used for theatrical events, was Central Hall. Its completion was announced in the *Yolo Democrat* (10 June 1871):

It was lit up on Thursday evening June 8, 1871 with fourteen gas jets, which gave it an exceedingly brilliant appearance. The hall is 36 by 75 feet in the clear, and with a gallery the whole width of the entrance end. It will seat comfortably 500 persons. The seats—movable settees—have been ordered, and will be here in a day or two.

According to Russell, Central Hall was still standing in 1940 on the west side of First Street between Main and Court, but he gives the date of construction erroneously as 1858.[8] This establishment did not become a major competitor to Washington Hall for at least two reasons, which were possibly connected. First, it had apparently no stage until 1877. Second, it was alternately used for church services. However, Woodland's theatrical needs must have been expanding, for in November 1877 carpenters were reported "at work erecting a stage at the west end of the building" with a projected depth of fifteen feet (*Yolo Democrat*, 29 November 1877). Although it was expected that "with the stage completed and finished with appropriate scenery" Central Hall would become "a gem of a little theatre," the proprietor's good sense of business continued to dictate the precaution that "for dancing parties, fairs or other gatherings, the stage is so constructed that it can be taken apart, and removed, leaving the entire floor of the hall free for use." This transformation may have increased the value of Central Hall as an entertainment center. Whereas only two references to such use occurred in 1876, the seasons following the improvements provide evidence of at least four such occasions.[9]

Local newspapers do not completely reveal the history of any of the three buildings discussed so far—Templar's Hall, Washington Hall, and Central Hall—but they allow theatre historians to conclude that in Woodland, as in most other frontier settlements, the urge for culture and entertainment (overlapping but by no means identical) was present, and that the demand was supplied with some frequency if not regularity. It remains unclear what factors, other than a larger population and increased wealth, made theatre more and more popular as the years passed. Yet it cannot be denied that the amount (if not the quality) of amusement Woodland citizens demanded and could afford grew by leaps and bounds. By 1886 at least two new theatres functioned in close proximity.

Both the smaller Westend (or West End) Theatre and the more imposing Opera House show up on that year's Sanborn map of Woodland. Also known as "Prior's," and located on Main Street near the southwest corner of Elm, the Westend was noted on 5 November 1885 as "another new theatre" with an estimated capacity of sixteen hundred on seats that were removable for dancing (*Dramatic News* [Sacramento, Ca.] 5 November 1885). According to the map, it was located on the second floor, above a series of stores and offices, and behind a row of furnished rooms which fronted on the street. Dimensions are not given, but the stage is indicated at the eastern end of the hall, equipped with gas lights and a small fire hydrant. The bulk of the space is also inscribed with its alternate use: "DANCE HALL."[10] Two surviving programs from 1888 indicate its continued use, but the only further evidence is a cryptic note that it burned "some time previous" to 1892.[11]

The first of Woodland's two Opera Houses was a more ambitious affair. Although its external dimensions (104 feet by 60 feet) seem to have exceeded those of the Westend only moderately (not more than 10 feet longer and 5 feet wider), the "Gallery" opposite the stage and along the sides indicates a multilevel structure. Two surviving pictures (a photograph and an engraving) corroborate that conclusion.[12] More importantly, a document entitled "Articles of Incorporation, Woodland Opera House Association" attests to the community support rallied behind the enterprise.[13] Filed on 31 March 1884, the Articles brought into existence a corporation with a life span of fifty years and capital of $25,000 (250 shares of $100 each), for the purpose of building and maintaining an opera house. Five directors were named: John D. Stevens, J. S. White, George C. St. Louis, R. H. Beamer, and L. Dietz. *The California Architect and Building News*, the following June, identified Thomas J. Welsh as architect of a "three story brick and iron Opera House" on Second Street in Woodland, and gave what was presumably the extent of his contract as $28,000.[14]

When built, this was a richly furnished edifice with four stage boxes, a raked auditorium, and "a fairly large stage" (Russell, p. 205). It was designed to look and function in conjunction with the building on the corner of Main and Second. Not only did the two share a common wall, there was also a restaurant in the corner building, with access into the theatre's lobby. The Opera House opened on 16 February 1885, with Louise Davenport and W. E. Sheridan in *The Merchant of Venice*. Until destroyed by the great fire of 1 and 2 July 1892, it provided a varied fare of Shakespeare, melodrama, farce, musical concerts, and lectures.

During the next four years, touring companies still visited Woodland, but they were forced to play at Armory Hall. Complaints from both audiences and performers emphasized the need for a new theatre, while the Opera House remained a dangerous collection of burned walls and fallen timbers. In response to an apparent public demand, reflected by the regular urgings of the *Democrat*, the Woodland Opera House finally rose from its ashes in 1895–96. A new board of directors was formed, this time not to represent a stock company, but to guarantee an annual eight percent return for two years on an investment estimated at $160,000 put up by David N. Hershey, the astute and civic-minded businessman who had purchased the ruins and financed the new construction. Chairman of this board was R. H. Beamer, who had served on that of the first Opera House. The son of another director of the previous association, Frank Dietz, and at least two of its stockholders, Emil Krellenberg and Bert Elston, also participated. The building opened its doors for the first time on 16 June 1896 with the company of Walter Hodges in Bronson Howard's *Saratoga*.[15]

The second Opera House, less ornate but no smaller than the one it replaced, is a spacious, two-story red brick building, incorporating the east and west exterior walls of its predecessor.[16] The roof of the auditorium is about thirty-five feet above street level, while the stage house originally rose to a height of sixty feet at the northern end of the building. Almost void of decoration, the facade is imposingly serene. Nor was the interior more than moderately adorned, with unostentatious wallpaper borders.

A twenty-five-foot-deep stage, bigger than those of most contemporary California theatres, is four feet above the auditorium floor, and three traps open into the dressing room area below. The greatest improvement over the first Opera House was the provision of a stage house and counterweight system. The rigging loft originally rose fifty feet above the stage, allowing drops to fly their full height without folding. The system was operated from a double pin-rail located on a stage left catwalk. A five-foot forestage protrudes into the auditorium through the twenty-five-foot square proscenium opening. Originally, gas provided illumination both onstage and in the house. However, electricity was introduced in 1901.

The auditorium attractively combines the parterre and modified horseshoe balcony of traditional nineteenth-century American playhouses with an uninterrupted semicircular seating arrangement and large orchestra reminiscent of Italian Renaissance theatres. The unusual height from balcony to

5. Second Woodland Opera House (center background). From an undated panorama, collection of Robert L. Griffith.

ceiling (into which space a second balcony would automatically have been installed in a larger city) is responsible for the auditorium's visual and acoustical grandeur.[17] The orchestra contained eighty-eight easily removable seats, while a slightly raised box (better for being seen in than for seeing the performance) on each side of the proscenium held sixteen. Behind the orchestra, separated by a waist-high barrier, are the 224 seats of the dress circle, the most expensive area of the house. Directly above, supported by four slender, decorated cast-iron columns, is the balcony. It extends around the sides of the auditorium to the proscenium wall and accommodates three hundred spectators on three to eight rows of wooden benches. Within a total capacity of 644, very unusual for a town of Woodland's size at the time, the proportionate size of the dress circle is another indication of local wealth.

From October to May, the Opera House was hardly ever dark, averaging two to four productions a month. During the summer, the pace was considerably slower, although (as in 1898, 1902, 1904, and 1908) June and September were often quite busy. In seventeen years, over three hundred touring companies played the theatre: the annual number stayed above nineteen between 1899 and 1912, and reached its peak in 1908 with thirty. In addition, there were musical recitals, religious and political gatherings, school functions, as well as entertainment provided by local talent. While the best seat never cost more than a dollar, manager E. C. Webber must have made the Opera House commercially successful. The season of 1902–1903 was typical of his resourceful appeal to the taste of the community. It forms the subject of the remainder of this essay.

According to *Julius Cahn's Official Theatrical Guide*, Woodland and its Opera House were unchanged from 1901 to 1904. The population was given at 5,000, the capacity of the theatre as 850 (both figures are inflated), prices as ranging from twenty-five cents to a dollar. The theatre had no grooves, but had three bridges (one in back). It was served by three hotels: the Julian (across the street), the Byrnes, and the Capitol. Printing needs were indicated as "4 stands, 20 one sheets, 12 three sheets, 75 lithos." Among the staff supporting the manager, a press agent, an electrician, a prop man, a stage carpenter, an orchestra leader (with six musicians at his disposal), and two bill posters were enumerated. References were made to a transfer company, a doctor, a Southern Pacific agent, a lawyer, and a "typewriter."[18] In most cases, the names given lead nowhere, but local historians have unearthed a few interesting bits of information. Arthur C. Huston, member of a large and influential Yolo County family, doubled as press agent and attorney. After having been city editor for both the *Weekly Mail* and the *Democrat*, he achieved a prestigious career in law, and was looked upon as "Dean of Attorneys" by 1940 (Russell, p. viii). The stage carpenter, Robert Eastham, owned a cigar store (with a card room in the rear) on Main Street, adjacent to the Opera House. The orchestra leader, Eugene Marvin, was a violinist from nearby Davisville, who regularly supplied music for local dances. Among his musical companions were Edward Irwin Leake (whose family owned and still publishes the *Democrat*), Meade Everhardt, and pianist J. Harvey Hester, whose original composition "When the Silvery Moon Fell" was just about to be published by a Chicago Company (*Daily Democrat*, 31 August 1902). Of the bill posters, Frank Dietz was on the board of directors, while his partner, Glendenning, was assistant fire chief and soon to be installed as the local leader of the Grand Army of the Republic. The "typewriter" was James H. Hester, the pianist and composer. It would be interesting to know of his subsequent career in either music or politics, since, in April 1902, he was reported to have "accepted a position as stenographer for Hiram Johnson, a Sacramento attorney," who in a few years became California's governor (*Daily Democrat*, 23 April 1902).

What major issues concerned or stimulated Woodland theatregoers during the 1902–1903 season? Economic news dominated what seems to have been a year of expansion for local business. Woodland Milling Works and Woodland Canning, Condensing and Preserving were both incorporated in 1902; Yolo Winery was remodelling, Woodland Gas and Electric expanding, while the Yolo County Savings Bank prepared to move into new headquarters (now "The Bank" Restaurant); a local inventor reported brisk sales of power almond hullers, and the year-old Yolo Creamery enjoyed good business. A steamboat company considered locating near Woodland, hope lingered of an oil strike in nearby Monticello, or even in Rumsey, an electric powerplant was introduced into the city's waterworks, telephone subscribers exceeded 499, and a local flour mill was projected. There were, of course, lighter moments: dog "coursing" was an established fashionable pastime, while the new game of ping pong moved westward and claimed its first Woodland devotee; generous distribution by the Chinese population of New Year's firecrackers prompted a prohibitive ordinance. Among the more serious civic issues, the controversy about a proposed new court house was liveliest, although organized protests by temperance groups against proliferating liquor licenses also repeatedly appeared in the news. A smallpox epidemic that closed churches, as well as the Opera House, in February 1902 was only a bad memory. A shortage of mules was a temporary nuisance, a new bridge on the Sacramento River a lasting convenience. More significant was the prospect of the state fair settling in the county, since neither San Jose nor Oakland (the other applicants) had "as good a horse racing track as Woodland." The California Legislature's declared intent to establish an experimental farm and dairy electrified the Chamber of Commerce into lobbying for a bill to locate such an institution in Yolo County, in preference to Humboldt or Marin. A farmer offered a thousand dollars to purchase 160 acres if the Legislature obliged. The University Farm that began operating in Davis in 1905 crowned these efforts with success. Finally, the Opera House's owner, David Hershey, passed away on 5 February 1903.[19]

The theatrical season of 1902–1903 was one of the richest in the history of the American theatre, coming on the crest of a wave of historical development. Geographically, demographically, and theatrically, the nation had expanded steadily since the end of the Revolutionary War, and although the western frontier was officially closed in 1890, there were still vast spaces to be filled. Theatre flourished not only in the major cities, but also in the smaller towns of provincial America. In any given season around the turn of the century, there were more than twice as many productions on the road as there were in New York.[20] The provincial theatre was peaking, soon to enter a decline that would result in the virtual elimination of professional theatrical activity outside of New York by 1929.

No community (even one with several theatres) saw all the road shows this season. A large city, situated at a rail junction, like Little Rock, Arkansas (population 38,307 in 1900), would sample about a quarter of the feast.[21] A conveniently located small town like Woodland could choose from slightly less than half that much. In 1902–1903 it was visited by twenty-eight companies. Twenty-four of them stopped for only a single performance, but four stock companies stayed for two to seven performances each.[22] Statistics, however, cannot give a sense of the attractions that entertained provincial America at the turn of the century—that requires more detailed consideration.

Because Woodland was a small town in the Far West, it was not visited by the major performers that were on tour this season. There was a clear if unspoken hierarchy that ruled the road. At the top was the legendary Joseph Jefferson, who, though in his seventies, still made brief tours in his established repertoire of *Rip Van Winkle*, *The Rivals*, *Lend Me Five Shillings*, and *The Cricket on the Hearth*. Second were the romantic leading men with established New York reputations: James O'Neill in *The Count of Monte Cristo*, Otis Skinner in *Lazarre*, John Drew in *The Mummy and the Hummingbird*, E. H. Sothern in *If I Were King*, Richard Mansfield as Brutus in *Julius Caesar*, Robert Mantell on his farewell tour in a repertoire of *Monbars*, *The Dagger and the Cross*, *The Face in the Moonlight*, and *The Lady of Lyons*, William Gillette in *Sherlock Holmes*, David Warfield in *The Auctioneer*, and Henry Miller in *The Taming of Helen*. To this group can be added the season's major foreign visitors: Eleanora Duse in her repertoire of plays by D'Annunzio (*Francesca da Rimini*, *Citte Morta*, and *La Gioconda*), and John Martin-Harvey in *The Only Way*, his adaptation of *A Tale of Two Cities*. Third were the leading ladies of the New York stage: Minnie Maddern Fiske in *Mary of Magdala*, Viola Allen in *The Eternal City*, Ethel Barrymore in a double bill of *The Country Mouse* and *Carrots*, Julia Marlowe in *The Cavalier*, Amelia Bingham in Clyde Fitch's newest hit, *The Climbers*, Effie Ellsler in *When Knighthood Was in Flower*, Margaret Anglin in *The Wilderness*, and Grace George in *Pretty Peggy*. Fourth were the featured performers of the musical stage: DeWolf Hopper in *Mr. Pickwick*, Fred Stone as the Scarecrow in *The Wizard of Oz*, Francis Wilson in *The Toreador*, luscious

Anna Held in Ziegfeld's production of *The Little Duchess*, and three companies of Broadway's latest flirtation, *Florodora*. After them came the comedians: William Crane in *David Harum*, Stuart Robson in a revival of *The Comedy of Errors*, and Nat Goodwin and Maxine Elliott in *The Altar of Friendship*. Finally, there were the leading stars of the provincial stage: Frederick Warde and Louis James teamed in *The Tempest*, Lewis Morrison continued to offer *Faust*, and Walker Whiteside toured in a repertoire of *The Merchant of Venice*, *Richard III*, and *Hamlet*.[23]

If the cities and towns of the East, South, and Midwest were surfeited by at least some of these riches, what was left for Woodland? A nourishing repast of farce, musical variety, and rural melodrama, with a notable delicacy or two. At this peak of its abundance, the American theatre provided a fullness for the tables of its provincial audiences.

Woodland audiences saw one legitimate comedy, *The Man from Mexico*, on 9 February 1903.[24] A brief farce, adapted by H. A. Du Souchet from a French original, it had first appeared in New York during 1896–97 as a vehicle for the comedian Willie Collier (*New York Times*, 20 April 1897, p. 7). Most of the plays this season were musicals of one sort or another, though perhaps only one would be recognizable to a modern audience as a musical comedy. *The Liberty Belles* (11 November) was a comic operetta with book by Harry B. Smith, whose 123 librettos made him one of America's most prolific and successful writers for the musical stage.[25] The piece was only a season old, and this was one of two road companies capitalizing on its New York success. Set in a young ladies' boarding school, its most notable scene showed "the young women in their dormitory disrobing for the night."[26] It was favorably reviewed in San Francisco: "The girls are comely and go through their dances with grace and chic. The scene in the dormitory was, of course, a feature, and it certainly is novel and entertaining. It was admirably handled" (*NYDM*, 1 November 1902, p. 3).

The most common form of entertainment, however, was a kind that lay somewhere between these two extremes. Usually called a musical farce, it was loosely constructed to allow for the interpolation of specialty numbers by its performers. In effect, plot complications provided continuity for a variety show. The first of these to reach town was *Hello Bill* (4 October). It starred Harry Corson Clarke (c. 1863–1923), who had been in Woodland in *What Happened to Jones?* during 1897–98.[27] He was followed by Hennessy Leroyle in *Other People's Money* (16 October). Leroyle (born about 1870) was an Australian who had first come to America in his own play, *Squabbles* (1891), and who had been touring in this vehicle by Edward Owings Towne for nine years.[28] Woodlanders saw one of his last performances because he died in San Francisco on 28 October 1902. The master writer of the genre was Charles Hoyt, whose *A Stranger in New York* was brought to town by Jack Campbell and William Keller Mack (14 January). The sixteenth of Hoyt's eighteen plays, it had premiered in 1897–98,

and reminded reviewers too much of his earlier *A Trip to Chinatown,*
though the *Times* critic (16 February 1897, p. 7) thought "it might delight
people in Oshkosh." The play had been seen twice before in Woodland
(1897–98 and 1901–1902).

A subcategory was the ethnic musical farce. Irish brogues provided the
comic basis for the performances of Edward F. Gallagher and J. J. Barrett in
Finnegan's Ball (19 November), characterized by the Portland critic as "a
roaring horse play patch-work of jokes, songs, and rough dancing" (*NYDM*,
22 November 1902, p. 4). Murray and Mack's *A Night on Broadway* (2
February) was also Hibernian, and though this pair had been to town in
another vehicle each of the two previous seasons, the Kansas City reviewer
noted that "their new musical farce . . . differs but slightly from their former
productions. . . . Many of the old 'stunts' are employed . . . and the bass
drummer works overtime punctuating the falls" (*NYDM*, 11 April 1903, p.
3). Scandinavians were the other source of ethnic humor this season in two
plays by Gus Heege. First there had been *Yon Yonson* (31 December), which
was originally produced in 1890–91 and had been to Woodland twice
already; but more importantly there was *Ole Olson* (19 March), starring
Ben Hendricks. Hendricks (b. 1868) was the most famous Scandinavian
comic of the era, and he starred in this vehicle from 1892 to 1909.[29] Others
had played it in Woodland twice before, and would do so two more times.
As the San Francisco critic observed:

Ben Hendricks and his inseparable (seemingly) Ole Olson regaled large audiences.
. . . Considering the number of seasons Ole has been before the public . . . it is a
caution the way the entertainment draws money. Ben has surrounded himself with
interesting features in Mattie Lockette, who sings, dances, kicks, and uses her eyes in
a way that wins, and the Swedish Ladies Quartette, whose singing is always good for
a handful of encores. (*NYDM*, 11 April 1903, p. 3)

Woodland also saw its share of straight variety entertainment this season.
Most famous was *Fiddle Dee-Dee* (5 November). Written for their own use
by Weber and Fields, the best-known German dialect comics of the day, the
piece had played New York two seasons earlier.[30] Woodlanders saw a
version produced by E. A. Fischer, whose San Francisco theatre was the
western home of Weber and Fields's vehicles. The road company featured
Sam Sidman and Bob Harris as the comics. Less well known was *Pickings
from Puck* (6 December), which starred Willard Simms. An acrobatic comedian who could sing, his specialty was a sketch in which he tried to hang
wallpaper. Fred Lucier was praised for his vocal imitations, which included
a violin. The featured number of the show teamed Catherine Linyard with
Simms in a sketch, "The Opera," that had originated in *Fiddle Dee-Dee* as a
turn for DeWolf Hopper and Lillian Russell. The variety show that may
have been of the most interest to Woodlanders, however, was *One Day's*

Battle in the Wilderness by Rev. David E. Holt (16 February). Presumably, Rev. Holt preached, but he prevailed upon a local resident, Joe Taylor, who had played all over the West as a variety performer between 1850 and 1870, to provide incidental entertainment.[31]

Another form of variety was the minstrel show. Beach and Bowers (14 October) was a small group that usually played in a tent, while Gorton's (20 October) appears to have been a group of younger players, who returned in three later seasons. The most famous minstrel name was that of J. H. Haverly, who founded his Mastodon Minstrels in 1877–78.[32] By the time the organization reached Woodland (20 December), however, all that remained was the name, which Haverly's widow had sold to W. E. Nankeville. Its format was typical. The show was in two parts, each introduced by John J. Holland, the interlocutor. The first part was a series of musical numbers set against the background of ancient Venice, and featured ballads by John J. Roland, and the counter-tenor, George Morgan. The second part was a collection of specialty acts, featuring the dancing duo of Johnny and Bert Swor, the comic monologue of George Wilson, and the acrobatics of the Carl Damman Troupe. There was also Freeman and Lynn's Commercial Men's Fifty Mastodon Minstrels (16 February), an amateur group of travelling salesmen from San Francisco, who, for the third consecutive season, made a brief tour of Nevada and Northern California.

Five companies offered Woodland melodramatic rather than comic entertainment this season. Early on, there had been *The Convict's Daughter* (29 September), "a typical prison scene melodrama" (*NYDM*, 3 January 1903, p. 2), which had played Woodland the year before. It was followed by *The Iron Hand* (27 December), which may have been derived from Goethe's *Goetz von Berlichingen*, and by *Sandy Bottom* (21 January), clearly a rural melodrama. More notable was *The Honest Blacksmith* (22 November), a vehicle for Robert Fitzsimmons (1862-1917), who had been heavyweight champion between 1897 and 1899, and whose pugilistic skills were the main attraction. Boxing was illegal in most places, and stage vehicles allowed a series of ex-champions, beginning with John L. Sullivan, to evade the law to the public's delight.[33] Fitz was supported by his wife and son, playing themselves.

The most spectacular melodrama of the season was William A. Brady's lavishly mounted production of *Lover's Lane* (26 February). The most successful playwright of his day, its author, Clyde Fitch, departed from his usual practice and created a rustic play, presumably for rural consumption. When it opened two years earlier, the *New York Times* (7 February 1901, p. 9) had detailed the plot:

A group of burlesque harridans, representing the moral forces of rural society, array themselves against a liberal-minded but intensely theatrical preacher, because he countenances the presence of a divorced woman in the church choir, because he encourages pauperism by feeding the poor, because he reflects discredit on the County Asylum by harboring an obstreperous orphan it has refused to shelter.

Moreover, this minister scandalizes them . . . after he has for fifteen years refused to choose a helpmate from his flock, by openly and fervently making love to a pretty girl from a neighboring town.

Brady's production was weakly cast. The Denver critic was hostile: "If Clyde Fitch could sit through a performance of Lover's Lane by the co. that attempted it . . . he would conclude to stick to society comedy in the future and not stand such chances. It was pretty bad" (*NYDM*, 18 April 1903, p. 4).

Melodrama was also the staple of the four stock companies that visited Woodland this season. Only the Elleford Company (24–29 November) was of any significance. One of the most popular and best-known Pacific stock companies, they were making the fifth of their eight visits to Woodland. They opened with *A Lion's Heart*,[34] and followed it with *Blue Jeans*. Joseph Arthur's rural drama ran nearly the entire New York season of 1890–91, and took its place as the premiere sensation play of the decade. George Odell recorded his delight in it:

Blue Jeans, as a rural drama, had its rustic characters, even its preposterous village band, but as melodrama, it had at least one scene that gripped the audience in the suspense that atones for any lack of literary elegance. All New York thrilled in the place where the hero is strapped before the buzz-saw, helpless victim of his fiendish rival in love. Of course we knew that the girl of his heart would save him.[35]

This descendant of *Under the Gaslight* was followed on Wednesday with Augustus Thomas' equally rural *In Mizzoura*. When it opened in 1893–94, it featured Nat Goodwin as the paternally omnipotent sheriff, a role that took him from musical variety to the legitimate stage.[36] Bucolic appeal was united with patriotism on Thursday as the company presented the most successful of all Civil War melodramas, Bronson Howard's *Shenandoah*. First produced in 1888–89, it dealt with the conflict between personal affection and sectional loyalty that was the trademark of this genre inaugurated in 1886 by William Gillette in *Held by the Enemy* (Quinn, I, 57–60). The company turned to more exotic melodrama on Friday with d'Ennery and Cormon's *A Celebrated Case*. In the tradition of *Monte Cristo*, a soldier who is falsely accused, convicted, and imprisoned, escapes and vindicates himself.[37] The Saturday matinée was *Cinderella*. Some seventy dramatic versions of the story existed, all combining farce with spectacular scenic transformations.[38] The engagement concluded with *Man's Enemy*, which first appeared in New York three seasons earlier, but about which nothing else is known.

The highlights of the season were established stars in their traditional repertoire. The season saw two at the beginning and two at the end. First, there had been Robert Downing in *An Indian Romance* (8 September).

Downing (1857–1944) had debuted in the stock company of the National Theatre, Washington, D.C. (1876–80), and gone on to support Mary Anderson (1880–83) and Joseph Jefferson (1883–86). Beginning in 1886 he starred in the heroic repertoire vacated by Edwin Forrest and John McCullough. His principal vehicles were *The Gladiator*, *Spartacus*, *Virginius*, and *Othello*. He retired in 1908 to Washington where he conducted a dramatic school.[39] At the beginning of his starring career, the *New York Times* (5 September 1888, p. 4) described him:

Mr. Downing's ample physique and strong voice, which, if neither of great compass nor especial sweetness is managed skillfully enough to give impressive effect to long and involved passages of blank verse, make him a formidable figure in his chosen field. There is vigor and dash in plenty in his acting, if he is somewhat hard and mannered in pathetic moments.

Apparently, *An Indian Romance*, a new play by J. C. Nugent, did not work out well, for Downing soon reverted to *The Gladiator*.

He was followed by Charles D. Herman in *The Lion's Mouth* (28 October). Herman (b. 1847) had supported Frederick Warde since 1886, and for this season, Warde being engaged with Louis James, Herman purchased the scenery and costumes of Warde's six-play repertoire and toured in Warde's parts with Warde's company. He offered Woodland a play by Henry Guy Carleton that had premiered in 1893.[40]

The two major stars came to Woodland at the end of the season. First, there was Kate Claxton in *The Two Orphans* (31 March). After her Chicago debut in 1869, Miss Claxton (1848–1924) rose to leading parts at Augustin Daly's Fifth Avenue Theatre. Her greatest fame came at A. M. Palmer's Union Square Theatre, where she created the role of blind Louise in this play (1874–75). She became identified with the part, returning to it regularly for the rest of her career (*DAB*, II, 167–68). This adaptation of a French sensation melodrama was well received by the *Times* (27 December 1874, p. 7) at its premiere: "It is a melodrama of refinement, of deep pathos, of keen anguish, of bitter suffering, of brave contention between love and duty. . . . The piece is one of surpassing power, of strong situations, of continuous action, and of marvelously effective tableaux."

Because this was her farewell tour, "many turned out to see her who had witnessed her performance in the same play nearly twenty years ago" (*NYDM*, 23 May 1903, p. 3). While her support was not notable, the star retained her luster. The San Francisco correspondent observed, "The excellence of [her] Louise is of so broad and so high an order that it shines like a genuine gem amidst a mass of paste" (*NYDM*, 25 April 1903, p. 3).

On Miss Claxton's heels came the other major luminary to grace Woodland this season, Charles B. Hanford in *The Taming of the Shrew* (10 April). A native of Sutter Creek, in California's gold country, Hanford (1859–1926) served a long apprenticeship with the best players of the late nineteenth-century American stage. He had debuted with the company of William Stafford in 1882, spent the next two seasons with Thomas Keene, and rose in 1885–86 to Robson and Crane's *The Comedy of Errors*. For the next four seasons, he travelled with Edwin Booth, as America's greatest star was paired first with Lawrence Barrett and then with Helena Modjeska. After Booth's death, Hanford spent two years with Julia Marlowe before striking out on his own as a provincial star (1892–1910). This was the first of his eight annual visits to Woodland in Shakespearean repertoire. Mr. and Mrs. Hanford (Mariella T. Bear, whom he married in 1885 and who was billed as Marie Drofnah) offered a choice this year of *As You Like It* and *The Taming of the Shrew*. Their tours resembled Roman triumphs. To read notices is to hear echoes of hosannahs in praise of the twin theatrical deities of a strong company and the full houses they commanded.[41]

Of the miscellaneous entertainments that visited town this season, two call for some comment. In the spring there had been Professor W. B. Patty (13 March), who travelled the length of California this season demonstrating the marvelous properties of liquid oxygen: "Freezes alcohol, burns steel, boils ice." More significant for the future had been the appearance of Beatty Bros. Kinetoscope Kings of the World (23 September). Movies were sufficiently familiar to be regular attractions, but not so common as to have a separate theatre. Woodland had seen its first films in 1897, and one or two travelling shows a year was average. Audiences were offered the assassination and funeral of President McKinley, the coronation of Prince Henry, and views of the damage wrought by the Galveston cyclone.

The cultural geographer must map the territory he proposes to study before he can evaluate it. Surveying the American theatre at the turn of the century, one is immediately struck by the size of the area. It effectively covered the continental United States, involving thousands of performers and hundreds of thousands of audience members, all of whom were staking out territories and exploiting them for profit. Broadly speaking, the major avenues in the Far West were the railroad routes of the Northern Pacific, the Central Pacific, and the Atchison, Topeka, and Santa Fe, running from east to west. Tributaries, such as the Southern Pacific, and the Denver and Rio Grande, provided north–south links. Given, then, a large area in which there was considerable activity along established routes, the surveyor must choose a vantage point. He can choose that of the traveller, following a particular one along a given route, describing and analyzing the process of getting from one place to another. Philip C. Lewis chose this approach in *Trouping*, as he followed the path of Dustin Farnum in *The Virginian* during the season of 1905–1906.[42] We have chosen the opposite vantage point— that of the settlement through which the travellers passed.

We do not suggest that one approach is better than the other, only that they address different concerns and produce different results. Emphasis on the travelling theatrical combination tells of the lives and working conditions of its members. It defines the road from the standpoint of the performers. Each settlement is important only insofar as it helps or hinders them in making a living by means of their craft. Emphasis on the settlements tells of the lives of the audience. Who the travellers were and what they purveyed provides some insight into an aspect of small-town life that otherwise remains closed. We can determine the political and economic heartbeat of Woodland at the turn of the century, but we cannot know what it was like to live there. Theatrical visitors allow us to take the pulse of the cultural life of the town. We glimpse something of the emotional and imaginative life of its people.

From our survey of the Woodland Opera House season of 1902–1903, a few generalizations can be drawn about theatrical life in small-town America at the turn of the century. First, the performers were clearly seen as more important than their vehicles. In the hierarchy that ruled the road, a small town would, at best, see only the lower strata: established provincial stars, such as Ben Hendricks, Downing, Herman, and Hanford, or a fading star from New York, such as Kate Claxton. Second, most of the vehicles were between five and fifteen years old. Of the three major exceptions, two (*The Liberty Belles* and *Fiddle Dee-Dee*) were relatively recent New York successes, the latter in a West Coast production. Only once in the season observed was the town used for the tryout of a new piece, *An Indian Romance*. Third, there was a high rate of repetition in both performers and vehicles. Much of the season had been seen before in one way or another, and a good part of it would be seen again. Clearly, familiarity was more potent than novelty in small-town theatre. Fourth, the genres of musical comedy, variety, and melodrama dominated among the familiar vehicles. Fifth, there was no discernible pattern in the playing schedule as to the days of the week on which performances were given, or the number or type of attractions presented in a given period. Apparently, a small town took everything it could get, when it could get it. A considerable amount was available. From September through April, the town saw fifty-two performances on forty-eight days, out of a total of 242 days available; or, on the average, one performance every five days. Averages, however, can be deceiving, since thirty-six performances (69 percent) were staged between the first of September and Christmas.

We might conclude, then, that the typical Woodland audience in 1902–1903 desired at least a weekly break from whatever was routine. It wanted to be diverted by song, dance, humor, and thrills. While it recognized the potent cultural brand names of New York (Clyde Fitch, Charles Hoyt, Harry B. Smith, Weber and Fields, William A. Brady, Kate Claxton), it relied on personal experience. It had seen Murray and Mack before, knew them to be funny, and so would see them again. It trusted in the Irish and the Swedes as a source of humor. It was confident of musical farce, melodrama, and minstrelsy, and it favored those performers, like Downing, Herman, and

Hanford, who catered to it and who seemed to have its best interests at heart.

Standing on the corner of Main and Second streets in Woodland, we have watched the parade passing down the American theatre's vanishing road. We have attempted to tell the story of those travellers who turned down Second Street, to play the Opera House, and we have derived a sense of the soul of small-town America in its theatrical taste: pragmatic about taking advantage of what met its needs, but with a strongly conservative preference for the familiar and the comfortable.

APPENDIX:
Attractions Appearing at the Woodland Opera House during 1902–1903

Day	Date	Attraction
M.	9/8/02	Robert Downing in *An Indian Romance* by J. C. Nugent
M.	9/15/02	Allen Stock Co. in *Rosedale* by Lester Wallack
Tu.	9/16/02	Allen Stock Co. in *Davey Crockett* by Frank Murdoch
W.	9/17/02	Allen Stock Co. in *The Power and the Wealth*
Th.	9/18/02	Allen Stock Co. in *A Fair Rebel* by Harry P. Mawson
F.	9/19/02	Allen Stock Co. in *A Player's Night Off*
Sa. (m)	9/20/02	Allen Stock Co. in *The Real Lord Lenox*
Sa. (e)	9/20/02	Allen Stock Co. in *The Good Little School Boy*
Tu.	9/23/02	Beatty Bros. Kinetoscope Kings of the World
M.	9/29/02	*The Convict's Daughter* with W. R. Ogden
Th.	10/2/02	Hugo Mansfeldt, piano recital
Sa.	10/4/02	Harry Corson Clarke in *Hello, Bill* by W. M. Goodhue
Tu.	10/14/02	Beach and Bower's Minstrels with Bobby Beach, Otis Bowers
Th.	10/16/02	Hennessy Leroyle in *Other People's Money* by E. O. Towne
M.	10/20/02	Gorton's Famous All White Minstrels
Sa.	10/25/02	Charles D. Herman in *The Lion's Mouth* by H. G. Carleton
M.	10/27/02	Carl Berch Co. in *A Better Atonement*
Tu.	10/28/02	Carl Berch Co. in *Hazel Kirke* by Steele Mackaye
W.	10/29/02	Carl Berch Co. in *A Cross of Gold*
Th.	10/30/02	Carl Berch Co. in *A Black Flag*
F.	10/31/02	Carl Berch Co. in *Dr. Jekyll and Mr. Hyde*
Sa. (m)	11/1/02	Carl Berch Co. in *My Uncle from New York*
Sa. (e)	11/1/02	Carl Berch Co. in *Oliver Twist*
M.	11/3/02	*Fiddle Dee-Dee* by Weber and Fields
Tu.	11/11/02	Frank Hennessy's Co. in *The Liberty Belles* by H. B. Smith
W.	11/19/02	Gallagher and Barrett in *Finnigan's Ball*
Sa.	11/22/02	Robert Fitzsimmons in *The Honest Blacksmith*
M.	11/24/02	The Elleford Co. in *A Lion's Heart*
Tu.	11/25/02	The Elleford Co. in *Blue Jeans* by Joseph Arthur
W.	11/26/02	The Elleford Co. in *In Mizzoura* by Augustus Thomas
Th.	11/27/02	The Elleford Co. in *Shenandoah* by Bronson Howard

Day	Date	Attraction
F.	11/28/02	The Elleford Co. in *A Celebrated Case* by d'Ennery and Cormon
Sa. (m)	11/29/02	The Elleford Co. in *Cinderella*
Sa. (e)	11/29/02	The Elleford Co. in *Man's Enemy*
Sa.	12/6/02	Willard Simms in *Pickings from Puck*
Sa.	12/20/02	Haverly's Mastodon Minstrels
Sa.	12/27/02	*The Iron Hand* by Charles Townsend
W.	12/31/02	*Yon Yonson* by Gus Heege
W.	1/14/03	Campbell and Mack in *A Stranger in New York* by Charles Hoyt
W.	1/21/03	*Sandy Bottom* with Mr. and Mrs. R. E. French
M.	2/2/03	Murray and Mack in *A Night on Broadway*
F.	2/6/03	Rev. David E. Holt, *One Day's Battle in the Wilderness*, assisted by Joe Taylor
M.	2/9/03	Leslie Morosco and Lula Shaw in *The Man from Mexico* by H. A. DuSouchet
M.	2/16/03	Freeman and Lynn's Commercial Men's 50 Mastodon Minstrels
Th.	2/26/03	W. A. Brady's production of *Lover's Lane* by Clyde Fitch
F.	3/13/03	Liquid Air Experiments by Prof. W. B. Patty
Th.	3/19/03	Ben Hendricks in *Ole Olson* by Gus Heege
Tu.	3/31/03	Kate Claxton in *The Two Orphans* by d'Ennery and Cormon
F.	4/10/03	Charles B. Hanford and Marie Drofnah in *The Taming of the Shrew* by William Shakespeare
W.	4/22/03	Readick Stock Co. in *The Vendetta* by D. K. Higgins
Th.	4/23/03	Readick Stock Co. in *The Unknown* by John A. Stevens
W.	6/17/03	Kapta String Quartette, presented by the senior class of Woodland High School

Notes

1. Tom Gregory, *History of Yolo County, California* (Los Angeles, 1913), p. 94, gives 1853. C. P. Sprague and H. W. Atwell, *The Western Shore Gazetteer and Commercial Directory for the State of California: Yolo County* (San Francisco, 1870), p. 114, cites 1855. William O. Russell, ed., *History of Yolo County* (Woodland, Ca., 1940), p. 196, says "between 1853 and 1855." The date for the establishment of the post office comes from Walter N. Frickstad, *A Century of California Post Offices, 1848–1954* (Oakland, Ca., 1955), p. 222. All sources agree on the date of Woodland becoming the county seat.

2. U.S. Census reports provide the following figures for Yolo County's population: 1860: 4,716; 1870: 9,899; 1880: 11,772; 1890: 12,684; 1900: 13,618; 1910: 13,926; 1920: 17,105. The town of Woodland appears as part of Cache Creek township in the 1880 census, with 2,257 inhabitants. The 1890 census notes that the township of Cache Creek had split into Cacheville and Woodland. At this time the township's population was pegged at 4,523, the city's at

3,069. During the following decade, both figures declined, rising again by 1910 to 4,584 and 3,178, respectively.

3. Gregory, pp. 98–103, and Russell, pp. 196–198, are in agreement.

4. *Yolo Weekly Mail*, 29 April 1869; 25 November 1869; 28 April 1870; 5 May 1870; 12 May 1870; and 19 May 1870.

5. In an unpublished paper (Sacramento State College, January, 1969), Charles A. Grover listed that many events recorded in the *Mail* and the *Yolo Democrat* between 28 July 1870 and 10 December 1879.

6. Will Weider, "Woodland Opera Houses, Early Entertainment," *The Daily Democrat* [Woodland, Ca.], 5 August 1968.

7. The burning is referred to by Russell, p. 204. For the Sanborn map see note #10 below.

8. Russell (p. 204) actually says "on the west side of Main Street between Main and Court Streets," an obvious misprint. The correction is based on Grover's paper, and Augustus Koch's 1871 map, which shows Central Hall on the corner of Dead Cat Alley.

9. *Yolo Democrat*, 21 January 1876 and 30 March 1876 records events before alteration that are clearly nontheatrical. Performances recorded in the *Democrat* on 18 December 1879, 4 and 6 March 1880, 15 April 1880, and 24 June 1880 seem more nearly theatrical.

10. Sanborn Map Publishing Co., Woodland, 1886, sheet #6.

11. Programs referred to by Weider, n.p. The fire is recounted in the *Daily Democrat*, 31 December 1895.

12. The photograph shows Woodland's Fire Department lined up in front of the Opera House on 4 July 1888 (Russell, opposite p. 202). The engraving is in the *Pacific Coast Commercial Record, Yolo County Edition*, 1 February 1889.

13. A xerographic copy of this document is in the Performing Arts Collection, Shields Library, University of California, Davis.

14. *California Architect and Building News*, 5 (June 1884), p. 114.

15. All dates of performances in both Opera Houses, unless otherwise indicated, are taken from the *Daily Democrat*.

16. This and the next four paragraphs are based on our article, "The Woodland 'Hershey' Opera House: The End of an Era in California Theatre," *California Historical Society Quarterly*, 48 (December 1969), 298–300.

17. This is the opinion of Iain Mackintosh, a British architect and theatre consultant, experienced in restoring nineteenth-century theatres.

18. Identical entries for Woodland can be found in Cahn for 1901 (p. 251) and 1903 (p. 253).

19. Information in this paragraph (and much in the previous one) is derived from a day-to-day perusal of the *Democrat*. Members of the Yolo County Historical Society, especially Mary Aulman and Eleanor Emison, have been tireless helpers in this task.

20. Larry T. Menefee, "A New Hypothesis for Dating the Decline of the 'Road,'" *Educational Theatre Journal*, 30 (1978), 345-47.

21. Road show figures are from Menefee, while population figures are from Edwin D. Goldfield, ed., *Statistical Abstracts of the United States* (Washington, D.C., 1960), p. 19.

22. For a complete listing of the season's attractions, see chapter appendix.

23. This survey of the season's major touring attractions is based on the *New York Dramatic Mirror*, 2 August 1902 to 30 June 1903, hereafter referred to as *NYDM*.

24. All dates for appearances in Woodland are based on the *Daily Democrat*, 1 September 1902 to 31 August 1903. All other information about the attractions, unless otherwise noted, is from the pages of *NYDM*.

25. Stanley Green, *Encyclopedia of the Musical Theatre* (New York, 1976), pp. 388–90.

26. *The Theatre*, 1 (September 1901), pp. 6–7.

27. Clarke's obituary appeared in the *New York Clipper*, 7 March 1923, p. 3.

28. Leroyle's obituary appeared in *NYDM*, 1 November 1902, p. 21. The play was first reviewed in the *New York Times*, 20 August 1895, p. 5.

29. Dixie Hines and Harry Prescott Hanaford, eds., *Who's Who in Music and Drama* (New York, 1914), p. 162.

30. Felix Isman, *Weber and Fields: Their Tribulations, Triumphs, and Their Associates* (New York, 1924), p. 264.

31. For his earlier career, see J. H. Taylor, *Joe Taylor, Barnstormer* (New York, 1913).

32. Robert C. Toll, *Blacking Up: The Minstrel Show in Nineteenth-Century America* (New York, 1974), pp. 146–47.

33. *DAB*, III, 443–444; William A. Brady, *Showman* (New York, 1937), pp. 82–83; Eugene C. Elliott, *A History of Variety-Vaudeville in Seattle from the Beginning to 1914* (Seattle, Wa., 1944), p. 16.

34. A play of this title by Arthur Shirley and Benjamin Landeck played in London in the summer of 1892: Allardyce Nicoll, *A History of English Drama 1660–1900*, 6 vols. (Cambridge, 1923–1952), V, p. 564.

35. George C. D. Odell, *Annals of the New York Stage*, 15 vols. (New York, 1927–1949), XIV, 557–59.

36. Arthur Hobson Quinn, *A History of the American Drama from the Civil War to the Present Day*, 2 vols. (New York, 1936), I, 245–46.

37. John Bouve Clapp and Edwin Francis Edgett, *Plays of the Present* (New York, 1902, 1969), pp. 59–62.

38. Nicoll, VI, 80–81.

39. John Bouve Clapp and Edwin Francis Edgett, *Players of the Present* (New York, 1901, 1969), pp. 91–92.

40. Frederick B. Warde, *Fifty Years of Make-Believe* (Los Angeles, 1923), pp. 240–264.

41. *Who's Who in America*, 1926–1927 (Chicago, 1926), p. 878; Hines and Hanaford, p. 152.

42.

Ambrose Small:
A Ghost in
Spite of Himself _____

Beyond the official mystery of Ambrose Small's disappearance in Toronto in 1919, following the sale of his theatrical assets to Trans-Canada Theatres Ltd. for $1,750,000, is the ghost of the man himself. Elusive in death as in life, he haunts the theatre he built, notes the profit and the loss and, no doubt, casts a spectral frown on the subsidies that are a way of life in our time. Only students of the theatre have the leisure to ponder the equations of profit with artistic prostitution or of high art with a perpetual state of imminent bankruptcy. Small concentrated, rather successfully, on the logistics of a circuit through which flowed a continuous stream of professional companies. Like many of his American counterparts, he apprenticed in the box office and lived his life behind the scenes, booked his shows in New York or Chicago or at home in Ontario, and made a fortune.

Ambrose Small's contemporaries in the late nineteenth and early twentieth century either damned him for exploitation or praised his enterprise and organizational skills. Hindsight allows us to see that both views were correct. Just as Klaw and Erlanger were not *simply* syndicated villains, so Minnie Maddern Fiske, who opposed them with all the ardor of a St. Joan on tour of the provinces, was an astute businesswoman who listened to the voices of her bankers quite as respectfully as she did to her Muse. Similarly, we will never know whether James O'Neill might have created the definitive Lear or Othello which generations of actors would strive to surpass. Nevertheless, the fortune he made with *The Count of Monte Cristo* did not mar the excellence of his performance, though his son would have us believe that he was destroyed, dollar by dollar, thousands of times. *A Long Day's Journey Into Night* is, of course, a great play but one of the reasons it has special resonance for North Americans is that we recognize in it our compulsion to diminish the mythic idols we have ourselves created, as if some balance must be struck by counterweighting exaggerated goodness with exaggerated badness.

This is not so simple, I think, as saying that the nineteenth century was a heroic age and the twentieth century an anti-heroic one. In Canada, Louis Riel is one figure now ripe for a re-viewing. Hanged for treason in 1885 and translated to the stage a year later by Arthur Forrest in Clay Greene's *North-West Rebellion*, Riel has become the "good guy" in our time, a symbol of all oppressed minorities, a Metis martyr canonized, not by the dramatists of Quebec but, ironically, by the English, whose expiation of ancestral guilt has gathered momentum with every new generation of writers. Logically, the next play about Riel will be an exercise in demythification—Louis Riel as beautiful loser. One hardly dares to think what the future holds for another legend, the Jesuit, Father Brébeuf, whose heart and mind E. J. Pratt captured in a long, dramatic verse narrative which is, at the same time, a superb apologia (*Brébeuf and His Brethren*, Toronto, 1940). Do not be surprised to read in tomorrow's paper that someone has produced a play in Quebec, the thesis of which is that Brébeuf, far from being a Christian martyr, was a frustrated miscreant who satisfied his own masochistic needs by destroying all that was sacred and natural in the religion of the Hurons, and whose death at the stake was the prescribed torture for anyone who dallied with an Indian maiden. Dramatic literature is, more frequently than not, antithetical to the authorized version of history. Theatre Passe Muraille's *1837* and James Reaney's Donnelly trilogy are recent plays which remind us that truth is seldom simple. So it is with the Small story. Like other skeletons in our national stage closet, he needs to be rattled out to see what made him dance.

However obliquely, I am trying to preserve Ambrose Small from the simplistic fate which history often assigns those who have been praised, or damned, not wisely but too well. The easy (too easy) way is to describe him as a stereotype, "rags to riches" or usher to theatrical magnate. That would be appropriate only within the context of Victorian melodrama. The romantic mode implicit in the term Founding Father (poor but honest *pater* whose vision promotes the common weal) won't do either, for he was neither poor nor honest and the weal he promoted was his own. Hector Charlesworth, a contemporary of Small's, tells a story of the New York producer who was so exasperated with Small that he took a train to Toronto and a taxi to the theatre, marched into the manager's office and said:

Mr. Ambrose J. Small, I have never seen you before, but you will know who I am when I tell you I am John C. Fisher of the New York Casino. And let me tell you, Mr. Ambrose J. Small, that I have come all the way from New York to give myself the pleasure of saying to you that you are a damned liar and a damned thief.[1]

Charlesworth's book is full of little tributes of this kind, and since he was a professional journalist and, presumably, familiar with the laws of libel, his anecdotes have a certain validity.

That "damned thief" is the same Ambrose Small whose gambling instincts were as sure in the theatre as they were at the racetrack and who thereby gave people in the small towns and cities of Ontario the chance to see more professional companies every year for thirty years than were seen by their children or their children's children.

Between his first job as an usher in the early 1880s and his disappearance in 1919, Small changed the history of theatre in Ontario. He leased, managed, built, and bought theatres and filled them with Shakespeare and minstrels, new musicals and such old standbys as *Uncle Tom's Cabin*, *Richelieu*, *The Lady of Lyons*, and *Ingomar*. Small made a fortune, but the real winners were the two generations of actors and audiences trained and entertained in his theatres by a panoply of stars. Not until Tom Patterson realized his dream of a festival in Stratford was Ontario part of the international theatre scene again.[2]

The building of theatres in Ontario began in earnest in the 1870s, and the first theatre in many towns and cities was often a 1,300-seat house. Canadians missed the whole period of Georgian theatre with its patrician patronage, eclectic dramas, and tiny, jewel-like theatres—unless one counts Lady Dufferin's private theatre in Rideau Hall and, even there, the fare was distinctly Victorian. What audiences saw was whatever had proven itself on the road or in New York. A few people must have seen Denman Thompson in a Toronto variety house working up the sketches which became *The Old Homestead*, but on the whole the shows seen here were road-tested. Small's patrons saw few premieres, but neither did they see the disasters of Broadway or London.

Ambrose Small's business was theatre as Molson's was ale. The comparison is not entirely capricious. Molson built the first good theatre in Montreal in 1825; Small grew up working in his father's pub next door to the Grand Opera House in Toronto and subsequently married into malt. His wife's money accelerated his progress from theatre owner to one-man syndicate. An association with C. J. Whitney of Detroit, who had been connected with the management of the Holman Opera House and the first Grand Opera House in London as well as theatres in Toronto and Hamilton, gave Small access to Whitney's circuit in Michigan, Ohio, and New York states. Together, they built a new theatre in London in 1900. Small subsequently bought the Toronto Grand Opera House, and Grand Opera Houses in Hamilton, Kingston, Peterborough, and St. Thomas.

Between 1890 and Whitney's death in 1903, Small learned to orchestrate the routes of hundreds of companies for whom eastern Canada was a natural extension of several American circuits (e.g., C. R. Gardiner's, H. S. Taylor's, H. R. Jacobs', and F. F. Proctor's). The most important of these in Ontario was Whitney's, with twenty-two theatres in eighteen cities.[3] Another dozen theatres, more or less at various times, were under Small's control through his booking agency. The Whitney-Small circuit, therefore, could tour a show through more than thirty-two theatres, half of which were in Ontario. The route in this province was the Grand Trunk Railway line, except for northern towns which were serviced by the Canadian Pacific.

Ambrose Small successfully combined the functions of owner or lessee and booking agent in the 1890s precisely at the time when it was most profitable to do so, after the heyday of resident stock companies and before the cost of salaries, production, and travel killed the road. By 1890, virtually all permanent stock companies had disappeared, with the exception of Palmer's, Daly's, Frohman's, and Madison Square in New York. The combination system, which followed, used New York as a launching pad. "Direct from New York" was good newspaper copy, but the profits accrued not in New York but on tour of the American states and the provinces of Canada. Broadway was simply the most convenient place to put a show together because the actors, designers, technicians, and suppliers were there. New York productions were designed to travel to the audiences; after World War I, the pattern was reversed and, today, the bulk of tickets in New York are sold to tourists who travel to the shows.

The number of touring combination companies peaked in 1900. Bernheim estimates there were 339 productions on the road that year.[4] By 1914, there were only 124, and in 1919, when Ambrose Small sold his theatrical assets, there were only forty-nine. A year later (1920), only thirty-four touring companies were available and the new owners of Small's theatres had to resort to various means to pay the taxes. In Hamilton, Ontario, Arthur Holman was imported from Milwaukee to organize a season of summer stock, one example of the revival of resident stock in the early twentieth century. The Toronto Grand Opera House was closed and then demolished. Other theatres were converted to accommodate moving pictures with vaudeville.

As I suggested earlier, Ambrose Small was not a "Founding Father" in any artistic sense but an entrepreneur who imported, exported, and transported good, current theatre for forty weeks a year. Each season began, typically, the last week in August and ran into June. In early September, during Fair or Exhibition Week, the entertainment was light, something like (in 1901, for example) William Brady's production of *Way Down East* followed by Hanlon's *New Superba* and Roland Reed's *Humbug*.[5] By mid-October, more serious fare was in order and almost every year brought well-known actors or shows to Ontario. In 1897, for example, between 11 and 19 October, the Grand Opera House in London presented William Farnum in *When London Sleeps*, *The Geisha*, Paul Cazeneuve in *The Three Guardsmen*, and the comic opera *Wang*, the theatrical ancestor of *The King and I*. In 1903, William Faversham starred in *Imprudence* on 13 October; he was followed by Lily Langtry in *Mrs. Deering's Divorce*, Julius Cahn's production of *David Harum* and, on 20 October, by William Greet's "Original London [England] Production" of Wilson Barrett's *The Sign of the Cross*. By 1913, Edison's Talking Pictures played the Grand from 3 to 8 October, but we can take some consolation from the fact that they were preceded in September by May Robson, Lawrence Brough, and Mrs. Fiske, and followed by Cyril Maude and the Stratford-upon-Avon Players who, in this first American tour, presented *The Taming of the Shrew, Henry IV, Twelfth Night,* and *Hamlet.* The Christmas season was reflected in family plays, concerts, minstrel shows, and melodrama; Easter was occasionally marked by a passion play or Hall Caine's *The Christian* or *Uncle Tom's Cabin,* though this pattern is by no means consistent. Each season ended, as they still do, with *amusettes. Giroflé-Girofla,* or Anna Held in *A Gay Deceiver* and *The Cat and the Cherub* (1898) or *Living Canada* and *Russo-Jap War Pictures* projected, in 1904, by "The Finest Picture Machine on the American continent" are typical examples.

Each season held its own highlights. Audiences in Ontario saw Sarah Bernhardt, James O'Neill, Ellen Terry and Henry Irving, Mrs. Drew, Sr., Tyrone Power, several Barrymores and Drews, Henrietta Crosman, and Otis Skinner. Among the stars and lesser lights were to be found Canadians like Julia Arthur, Margaret Anglin, Mme. Albani, Marie Dressler, Henry Miller, George Primrose, "Canada" Lee, Richard B. Harrison, McKee Rankin, and Ida Van Cortland.

Such were the riches Ambrose Small provided. He may, perhaps, be best described as an Inadvertent Patron, in the spirit of Leslie Fiedler's title for the 1978 Massey Lectures.[6] Although Small's achievements may have been higher than his goals, he was responsible for the continuity of the Canadian theatrical tradition; without him, the record of the last seventy-five years would have been quite different. The vitality of the shows he brought is reflected in the amount and quality of dramatic news and criticism in the daily and weekly press. We have yet to collate many of these columns of theatrical criticism and to rediscover the diaries and journals in which the highlights of each season must have been recorded. Meanwhile, it is a challenge to assay the golden puffs to be found in newspapers and programs and to identify the nuggets and the dross. Whatever became, one wonders, of The Royal Midgets who, in 1891, toured *Gulliver's Travels?* What of Daniel Ryan, who starred in *Wife for Wife, The Fatal Wedding, The Lost Paradise,* and *20 Years After?* We do know that Mathews and Bulger became one of the outstanding blackface vaudeville teams after the turn of the century when they toured a three-act, "rag time opera" called *By the Sad Sea Waves* through Ontario. This old gem, the program tells us, was set in the Finishville Habit Cure Institute. It sounds edifying and dull which certainly was not the case with Florenz Ziegfeld's production of *The Turtle,* a French farce which the predominantly male audience found offensive. "No London audience would sit through it a second time," commented the local critic.

Familiar names reward the searcher. Lionel Barrymore toured Ontario in his grandmother Drew's 1893 production of *The Rivals.* Hattie Anderson, who later married C. P. Walker of Winnipeg, "trouped" in the province in 1888 and starred in *Three of a Kind* in 1890. A stage version of Ralph Connor's *The Sky Pilot* arrived in 1902, the year that John C. Fisher stormed into Toronto to blast Ambrose Small about the way his production of *Floradora* had been handled. Sam Lucas, famous as the first black actor to play Uncle Tom, toured in a rewritten version of Cole and Johnson's *A Trip to Coontown*. Effie Ellsler starred in *When Knighthood Was in Flower* and Henrietta Crosman in *The Sword of the King. The Wizard of Oz*, starring Anna Laughlin and with Edwin Stone, Grace Kimball, and Arthur Hill was billed during the Christmas season of 1902.

There are other nuggets in those dusty old files. James O'Neill brought *Monte Cristo* in 1891, 1896, and 1902. He also appeared in Ontario in *Fontenelle* (written by the Fiskes) in 1893, in *Virginius* and *The Dead Heart* in 1897, and in support of Viola Allen in *The White Sister* during his last visit in 1910. Thomas Keene, I believe, brought more productions of Shakespeare to Canada than anyone else in the nineteenth century. He toured almost annually from 1882 until his death in 1898. It is said he played the Colley Cibber version of *Richard III* 2,525 times.[7] Mlle. Rhea was another hardy trouper. Beginning with *Camille* in 1882, she toured Ontario twice a year, most frequently in Bernhardt roles. Her last appearance, so far as I can tell, was in 1896 in *Josephine, Empress of the French.* Bernhardt, whose roles in North America were repeated by many lesser lights, was in London twice, in 1896 and 1910. Montreal audiences saw her first in 1880, and her *Camille* on that occasion was not only copied but parodied, in Ontario as elsewhere. One early example is a burlesque opera called *Sarah Burnt Heart* which was part of a minstrel program in 1883.

After 1900, we must add William Faversham (four tours), and Forbes-Robertson in 1905 and again five years later in *The Passing of the Third Floor Back*. Mrs. Patrick Campbell starred in *The Notorious Mrs. Ebbsmith* in 1907, and Canadian-born Marie Dressler returned briefly in 1913 with Dressler's Players before she went off to fame and fortune in Hollywood.

The years between 1900 and 1912 represented a period of consolidation for Small. In 1896 he was business manager of the Toronto Opera House for Jacobs and Sparrow. Two other Toronto theatres, the Grand Opera House and the Princess Theatre, belonged to the Whitney chain. About 1899, Small leased the Royal Opera House in Guelph. In 1900 the theatre in London burned and Small, in partnership with Whitney, built a new Grand Opera House. About the same time, Whitney leased the Opera House in Hamilton. Then in 1901 Small leased the Russell Theatre in Ottawa for the 1901–1902 season. When it was destroyed by fire in 1901 and replaced the following year, Small and Whitney became joint lessees. Small acquired the St. Thomas Opera House in 1903.

In 1902 Ambrose married Theresa Kormann, the daughter of a wealthy brewer (and his stepmother's sister). They planned to invest in theatre properties; when the Toronto Opera House burned in 1903, they decided to expand and diversify their holdings. The impetus to so do was fortified when Small's partner, C. J. Whitney, died that same year.

The probate of Whitney's will revealed their mutual holdings. The estate claimed two-thirds of 90 percent of the profits from the Princess Theatre, one-third of the net profits from the Grand Opera House (Toronto), the Toronto Opera House, and the Russell Theatre in Ottawa. In addition, the estate claimed one-half of the net profits of Grand Opera Houses in Hamilton, London, and Kingston and of the Canadian one-night stands controlled by Whitney and Small.[8]

In 1904, Small bought the Hamilton theatre for $25,000 and in 1905 the Kingston theatre. In 1906 he became the owner of the Grand Opera House in Toronto. Later, he acquired the Grand Opera House in Peterborough.

By this time, he was well established and had considerable experience. M. B. Leavitt, who had been playing in Canada for at least thirty years, praised Small for developing theatres in Canada "so successfully that time is now [1911] eagerly sought by all leading producers and owners of prominent productions."[9] At the back of Leavitt's book, one finds an advertisement for The A. J. Small Circuit, the "most carefully booked territory in the world."

By 1919 Small realized that road companies were an endangered species, almost, in fact, extinct. The wars of the syndicates, rising production costs, the introduction of "family Vaudeville," the novelty of radio and moving pictures, and the revival of less expensive, resident stock signalled the end of an era.[10]

Small sold his theatrical assets for $1,750,000 to Trans-Canada Theatres Limited, deposited a check for one million dollars (the down payment) in his bank on 2 December 1919, and disappeared. His "vanishing act" has never been satisfactorily explained and the police did not close the case until 1960. There were various theories: he had "gone larking" with a woman not his wife, or he found success traumatic and was lost and suffering from amnesia, or he had been murdered. Because Theresa Small was convinced that he was either at the racetracks or with the aforementioned female, the police were not notified for several weeks. When the story hit the press, it made international headlines. Conan Doyle offered to come to Toronto, but his help was refused. Houdini was sure he had seen Ambrose in a gambling casino in Mexico. A $50,000 reward was posted but was never paid.

Foul play seems the most likely explanation. Several times in the correspondence over the sale, mention is made of Small's desire to close the deal by 1 December, and this in spite of the fact that he was receiving interest at 6 percent on the down payment of one million dollars from 1 September, when the first agreement was drawn. Still, no hard evidence of blackmail was found. Neither has anyone discovered what Small planned to do with his time and money after the sale. Speculation provided journalists with many columns of print for several years, as police continued their investigations and Small's sisters fought his widow over the estate.

I have two theories to offer. One is the story of an old stagehand at the Grand Opera House in London, Ontario. He claimed that Theresa was having an affair with a Londoner and that, on the night after Small's disappearance, the two lovers incinerated Ambrose in the furnace of a heating plant close to the London theatre. There were, apparently, particularly noxious fumes from that plant on the evening of 3 December 1919, when the stagehand was working a show.

The other theory is based on correspondence of Robert J. Haire of New York, a retired attorney. The correspondence is found in the papers of E. W. M. Flock, the London lawyer who acted for Small when he sold his assets to Trans-Canada Theatres Ltd.[11]

Haire sent a copy of the following letter to Flock, with a covering note in which he said he did not know the author, but that the Chicago police might be able to identify him. The letter reads (errors and all):

New York Jan. 4th., 1920.

Col. R.J. Haire;

It will not be necessary for me to introduce myself furthan to say, that when I knew you, you knew me to be a friend of Big Bill H.

If you will read first page and first colum of the New York World, of to-day, you will see the disapearance of A.J. Small.

I have known of this case for three weeks, but did not know the name until I saw it in to-days paper. I do not know just where Mr. Small is, but I do know the "Gang" that is holding him, and they are doing so for a reward, and waiting for him to sufficiently recover his health, (For he was badly injured and is not yet able to write) as they intend to make him do, as soon as he recovers his mind.

You must have known something of the Chicago "Gang" which was controled by the respectable Gates. He died about the time Big Bill was pinched in Chicago.

Here is what I want you to do, and be quick about it. Jump the train and go to Toronto, and make such arrangements as will in no wise involve me, and I will furnish, through you the necessary information to run the "Gang" down and locate Small. I must not be known in the matter, it would cost me my life, or something else equally as bad.

I know Big Bill trusted you with delicate matters, and what was good enough for him will do me.

Until I receive your assurance, that you will protect me & keep me in the background, I shall not further make myself known.

I am not looking for money in this matter, but for satisfaction, and I have no doubt that you can get paid for your time and expenses. You can reach me by putting an Ad in the New York Herald. Address to_____and sign_____, and I will then correspond with you, and if necessary meet you here or in Montreal, with the understanding, that I am not to meet, or give information to any other party than yourself. Make this plain in your Personal.

Come what may, or the result be what it may, I must never be known in this matter, and if, you cannot so pledge yourself, then go no further.

Put your Personal in the Herald not later than next Saturday.

For the present I will sign myself,

Yours truly,
B. B. Friend.

Flock forwarded this intelligence to a Toronto legal firm which was acting for Mrs. Small, as he did subsequent offers of assistance. He continued to receive "clues" for several years because he was named in the press as Small's lawyer. Small's disappearance provoked many curious responses. One letter was dated 10 January 1920, within a week of the first news release.

Dear Sir:

Having read of the disappearance of A. J. Small of your City, in the Billboard Magazine I would like a description of him, including his teeth, as to dental work & etc.

Please find stamps for reply also notify if any reward is offered for knowledge of his whereabouts.

> Yours truly,
> G. P. Rugg,
> Pablo Beach Fla.

Another letter was written by a Thomas A. Body, Master Psychist of St. Alban's, Ontario, on 14 April 1922, while the search for Small continued. It contains two pages addressed to Mrs. Small in which Body says, "the end of this matter does not look very cheering as both planets ruling . . . are aspecting evil planets in 3 directions. . . . " The Master Psychist enclosed an astrological chart to prove his point and assured Flock that satisfied clients included a prosecuting attorney, a dentist, and Mlle. Gladys, a medium with "Professor Herman's Magician Show." Mlle. Gladys, apparently, spoke in public about Mr. Body's "wonderful psychic powers."

The most important documents in the Flock papers, however, are the Agreement of Sale, made between Ambrose Small and Henry W. Beauclerk (representing Trans-Canada Theatres Ltd.) and the legal descriptions of some of the properties.

The Agreement of Sale, which went through several revisions, provides for the payment of one million dollars "in good and lawful money of Canada," plus interest on that amount at 6 percent per annum from 1 September 1919 (to closing) and $750,000 to be paid in twenty equal, consecutive, annual payments ($37,500 per annum), without interest. Security for this amount was given in the form of shares of capital stock rather than in the form of a mortgage which Small had suggested. They gave Small no voice in the management of the new company since they were nonvoting shares. They were to be redeemed on the first of September each year as each annual payment was made by the purchasers.

Trans-Canada Theatres Ltd. was a consortium of Montreal businessmen, including financiers like the Hon. W. J. Shaughnessy with whom Small and Flock negotiated. The only theatrical person involved in the new company was Robert Driscoll, manager of Her Majesty's Theatre in Montreal. They bought from Small the Grand Opera Houses in Toronto, Hamilton, London, St. Thomas, Kingston, and Peterborough, and "all booking contracts for all other theatres now existing" (in Small's control). Rental from offices and concessions would accrue to the new company; Small retained, rent-free, his office in the Grand Opera House in Toronto. Schedule "A" of the 1 September agreement reveals that Small had one-year contracts with theatres in Pembroke and Brockville, three-year contracts in ten more towns (North Bay, Sudbury,

6. *Polly of the Circus*, a painting by Anna Baker, with Ambrose Small in levitation above the proscenium. *Polly of the Circus* toured London, Ontario, in 1912. From the collection of Mary Brown.

Orillia, Barrie, Trenton, Galt, Stratford, Midland, Lindsay, and Sarnia), two five-year contracts in St. Catharines and Renfrew, and a contract of unspecified duration in Brantford. Nine of these fifteen booking contracts expired in 1920, while the remaining six ran to 1922.[12]

Letterhead for Trans-Canada Theatres Ltd., dated 1920, also lists Her Majesty's Theatre in Montreal, the Walker Theatre in Winnipeg, the Grand in Calgary, the Empire in Edmonton, "and other high class theatres in one, two, three night and week stands from the Atlantic to the Pacific" which would enable the company to offer "25 to 35 weeks of consecutive and profitable booking." The letterhead notes plans for new theatres in Regina, Edmonton, and Vancouver. Newspapers of the period refer to another theatre in Victoria and one in London, England, but these are not on the company's stationery. Patrick O'Neill, in a paper on the British Canadian Theatrical Organization, quotes from the London *Times* of 29 July 1920 to show that Trans-Canada Theatres Ltd. had by that date a circuit of eighty theatres in Canada. He also documents the reasons for its demise in 1922, but that is another story.[13]

However one measures achievement, Ambrose Small ranks high on the scale. That he earned $1,750,000 *in the theatre* and *before 1920* is one measure of his success. The number of Canadians and Americans who learned to act in the road companies that played his theatres is another. A further measure is the delight of audiences whose memories were richer for having seen James O'Neill in *Monte Cristo* or Julia Arthur in *A Lady of Quality* or Julia Marlowe, Modjeska, Cushman, Nethersole, and Janauschek, or extravaganzas like *Ben Hur* or William Faversham in *All Hail Herod* ("with Julie Opp and a cast of 200!").

Success did not spoil Ambrose Small. It killed him. What *really* happened to Small is that he became *A Ghost in Spite of Himself*, to borrow the title of an old play. His restless spirit is with us still, in Anna Baker's paintings[14] and in the stories of his mysterious disappearance which appear annually in newspapers and magazines. A legend in his own time, he caught the popular imagination and has held it, post mortem, for sixty years. That restless spirit, that Inadvertent Patron, can still be seen occasionally, on a dark night, in theatres across the land, casting an ectoplasmic glow somewhere in the vicinity of the box office.

Notes·

1. Hector Charlesworth, *More Candid Chronicles* (Toronto, 1928), p. 285.
2. See Ross Stuart's essay in this volume, pp. 173–91.
3. In 1893, the Whitney circuit included Henck's Theatre in Cincinnati, Burt's Theatre in Toledo, the Lyceum and the Cleveland Theatre in Cleveland, the Grand and Powers Theatre in Grand Rapids, the Star Theatre in Buffalo, four theatres (New Detroit Opera House, Lyceum Theatre, Whitney Opera House, Empire Theatre) in

Detroit, and theatres in Saginaw, Bay City, and Jackson. Canadian theatres on the circuit were the Grand Opera House and Princess Theatre in Toronto, the Grand Opera Houses in London and Hamilton, as well as theatres in Woodstock and St. Thomas.

4. Alfred Bernheim, *The Business of the Theatre* (New York, 1932), p. 75.

5. Performance dates are for London, Ontario, unless otherwise noted. I have compiled a calendar of performances for London, from which I derive information used in this paper. These dates and performances are typical for the circuit, though not every show played every theatre on the Small chain. The two London theatres involved were the first Grand Opera House, built in 1880–81 as part of the Masonic Temple, and the second Grand Opera House, built by Small and Whitney when the Temple was destroyed by fire in 1900. For many years the home of the London Little Theatre, the second Grand is now called Theatre London and is, once again, a professional theatre.

6. Leslie Fielder, *The Inadvertent Epic from Uncle Tom's Cabin to Roots* (Toronto, 1979).

7. See Alan Woods' essay in this volume, pp. 31–40.

8. Clippings and other information supplied by the Burton Collection, Detroit Public Library.

9. M. B. Leavitt, *Fifty Years in Theatrical Management* (New York, 1912), p. 567.

10. See Bernheim, chapter 6.

11. A collection of papers concerning Ambrose Small that belonged to his lawyer, E. W. M. Flock, was donated to the Regional Collection of the D. B. Weldon Library at the University of Western Ontario in 1979.

12. Schedule "A" sets forth the following agreements: 1. Pembroke; J. H. Bruck to A. J. Small, 1 August 1919 to 1 August 1920; 2. Brockville; J. McLennan to A. J. Small, 1 November 1919 to 1 November 1920; 3. St. Catharines; Colonial Amusement Co. to A. J. Small, 1 August 1915 to 1 August 1920; 4. North Bay; John Blanchet to A. J. Small, 1 September 1917 to 1 September 1920; 5. Brantford; James T. Whittaker to A. J. Small, 5 September 1919 to 5 September 1920; 6. Galt; Galt Opera House Company to A. J. Small, 1 August 1919 to 1 August 1922; 7. Stratford; W. I. Kemp to A. J. Small, 1 August 1919 to 1 August 1922; 8. Linday; W. H. Roenigk to A. J. Small, 1 August 1919 to 1 August 1922; 9. Sudbury; J. R. Bissett to A. J. Small, 1 August 1919 to 1 August 1922; 10. Sarnia; John F. Myers to A. J. Small, 1 December 1919 to 1 December 1922; 11. Trenton; R. H. Weller to A. J. Small, 1 August 1917 to 1 August 1920; 12. Barrie; John Powell to A. J. Small, 1 August 1917 to 1 August 1920; 13. Orillia; T. W. Robbins to A. J. Small, 1 August 1917 to 1 August 1920; 14. Midland; Arthur Bugg to A. J. Small, 1 August 1917 to 1 August 1920; 15. Renfrew; Ottawa Valley Amusement Company to A. J. Small, 1 August 1917 to 1 August 1922.

13. "Not a Golden Age: British Theatre in Canada, 1912–1929;" paper given at the conference of the Association for Canadian Theatre History in Fredericton, New Brunswick, May, 1977.

14. Anna Baker was born in London, Ontario and now lives in Barton, Vermont. In 1973 she exhibited a series of 26 paintings she called Ambrose Small productions. The ghost of Ambrose Small appears in levitation above the proscenium arch in several of these rich, theatrical fantasies.

Jean-Cléo Godin

Foreign Touring Companies and the Founding of Theatres in Quebec, 1880–1900 and 1930–1950

Jean Béraud was, for many years, an attentive witness and a well-appreciated critic of the Montreal stage. For an understanding of the long process of the creation of an authentically francophone theatrical life in Quebec, Béraud's *350 ans de théâtre au Canada français* (1958) and other writings of his remain, despite a few errors that are gradually being corrected by patient research, a necessary starting point.

In the 2 November 1940 issue of Montreal's *La Presse*, Béraud comments on the arrival of the French actor Victor Francen, who had first visited Montreal, with Paul Marcel and Claude Ritter's company, in 1908. Béraud takes the opportunity to speculate on the significance of tours to Quebec by distinguished foreign performers. The (incomplete) list he gives covers more than half a century; there are thirty-one names on it, including those of Sarah Bernhardt—she came five times, between 1880 and 1910—Réjane, Firmin Gémier, Sacha Guitry, Yvonne Printemps, and Gabrielle Dorziat. The balance sheet is impressive and, spanning such a long period, the series seems to constitute a well-established tradition, of which the most prestigious period coincides with the first "golden age" of theatre life in Montreal, around the turn of the century; and we must note that the first attempts at establishing professional companies in Montreal can be dated to those very years. Recollecting them, somewhat nostalgically, Béraud writes: "Quand je me replonge dans ces fastes du théâtre à Montréal, je m'étonne chaque fois que l'art dramatique ne se soit jamais implanté et n'ait jamais fleuri chez nous autrement que de façon spasmodique."[1] As a matter of fact, things had regressed since Victor Francen's first tour, owing to the birth of cinema, the development of radio, and the great economic crash of 1929. Despite all that, Béraud has good reason to wonder why, in 1940, one should still be talking of theatre in terms of beginnings: "Chaque fois qu'un artiste d'envergure paraît, on reparle de renaissance du théâtre. C'est bien la preuve que le théâtre n'a jamais pris racine."[2]

The words chosen by Béraud to describe the failure of numerous efforts to establish theatre in Montreal are significant, for they imply that professional theatre must come from the outside (mostly from France) to be transplanted and take root in Canadian soil. Béraud neglects, perhaps, the importance of amateur theatre, not only in Montreal, but also throughout the province. One might have expected some development of professional theatre out of amateur activity, but this did not occur. Nor did the frequent presence of touring companies manifestly engender professional theatre. We are, therefore, faced with the fundamental question of why the establishment of solid and permanent professional theatre in Quebec was so slow. The question of the relationship between the founding of permanent local institutions and the touring of foreign companies is a secondary question, but one which might lead us more quickly, perhaps, to a correct answer to the main question. Two periods lend themselves well to such an investigation: the first one, which I have already described as the "golden age," extends from 1880 to 1910; the second one is considered by Béraud as the beginning of a new era, and extends approximately from 1935 to 1950.

The first French company to come to Montreal and Quebec City was that of Scévola Victor in 1827. John Hare relates the visit to the opening of the first Montreal Theatre Royal in 1825, and to the appearance in Montreal in the summer of 1826 of Edmund Kean.[3] The latter, Hare conjectures, could have met French actors in New York and suggested that they pay a visit to the former "Nouvelle-France." We can at least note that the touring itinerary is always the same from then on: whether they were American or French, foreign companies generally came from New York, and Montreal seemed nothing more than an extra stop after an American tour. It was almost a century before European artists crossed the Atlantic to come especially to Montreal. They had to wait until the city became large enough to make such a visit profitable. Scévola Victor made a profit only by disappearing with the company's funds, leaving his actors distressed and unprovided for in Quebec City. However, it might be to this unfortunate incident that we owe the first beneficial effect of a foreign company, since many local amateur actors immediately joined a few members of the stranded Victor Company and staged a play the following season.[4] Two years later, for the first time, two amateur troupes played simultaneously in Montreal, such a sudden effervescence perhaps being due to the continuing presence in the city of a few members of Victor's company. Similar examples are not numerous at the time, but we can legitimately suppose that local theatre life was on occasion enriched by the more or less permanent, more or less accidental addition of foreign elements. We should note also that theatres were successively built in Montreal from 1825 to 1890,[5] thus stimulating local activity and increasing the number of foreign visiting artists. These theatres belonged to the English bourgeoisie and were primarily concerned, quite naturally, with English drama. We know, however, that the French-speaking public was not neglected. In 1852, for instance, the third Montreal Theatre Royal, only a week after its opening, greeted a French company from New Orleans, which attracted a large French-Canadian audience with two vaudeville shows, *Deux paires de bretelles* and *En manches de chemise* (Hare, p. 81): hardly great drama, but clear evidence of the existence of a significant popular French-speaking audience.

In the half-century following the opening of Montreal's first Theatre Royal, theatrical activity in the province of Quebec increased rapidly, attracting a wider and more popular public, and a greater number of foreign artists. The evolution was such that, touring in Quebec in 1871, the French company of Alfred Maugard thought it worthwhile to settle in Quebec City. The time was not yet ripe, but both the positive and negative aspects of this enterprise are revealing. The company experienced rapid success at first, mainly because Maugard had established good relations with the local bourgeoisie. Most important, he obtained the support of local politician and future premier of Quebec, Félix-Gabriel Marchand. Marchand was eager to show the French director his own play, a vaudeville piece called *Erreur n'est pas compte*. Maugard then prepared "une grande representation extra-ordinaire . . . [sous] le patronage de l'honorable orateur et MM. les députés de l'assemblée législative," featuring two Canadian plays: one adapted from Marmette's novel *l'Intendant Bigot*, and Marchand's play (Hare, pp. 81–82). This unusual accord between the worlds of theatre and politics was particularly fortunate, uniting as it did the experience and expertise of foreign actors and the creative effort of local authors. However, the singularity of such an accord probably caused the setback that followed, for Maugard's success attracted the attention of the clergy and moral censors. On 7 November 1873, Monseigneur Taschereau condemned Maugard's company and ordered Catholics not to attend his plays (Hare, p. 82). The unfortunate Maugard was forced to find an alternative means of livelihood. He became a restaurateur, not turning back to the theatre until 1878, this time in Montreal.

Maugard's misfortune would be relatively unimportant, if it were not so typical. It recalls, of course, the famous *Tartuffe* affair which, in 1694, set Frontenac against Monseigneur de Saint-Vallier[6] and, as a consequence, confined all theatrical activities to colleges and convents, up until the 1760 conquest. The Maugard and *Tartuffe* condemnations both took place in Quebec City, but it would be wrong to suppose that the Montreal clergy were less vigilant. Between 1789 and 1874, there were three major clerical attacks on the theatre in Montreal.[7] In 1789, the Notre Dame parish priest condemned the Théâtre de Société, and in 1859, Monseigneur Bourget sent his flock a pastoral letter condemning theatre in general. It was not by chance that this letter coincided with an active season at the Theatre Royal, a season which brought the Sanford Opera Company in June, the French Theatre and the Parodi Italian Opera in July, and the Cooper English Opera in November (Camerlain, p. 54). Evidence in contemporary newspapers indicates that the bishop particularly had in mind the French and the Italian companies, since they were likely to draw large numbers of francophone (and therefore Catholic) Montrealers. In 1872, Bourget's target was unequivocally the touring companies: "J'apprends qu'il nous arrive des Etats-Unis deux troupes de comédiens, que l'on m'assure être très immorales."[8] The Maugard Company is again cited, but also the Wallack Company and the French Company from New York and New Orleans. Now, while it is usually difficult to evaluate the precise consequences of episcopal condemnations, this episode would seem to support a reasonable hypothesis. Maugard, as we have seen, suffered additional rebuffs from Bourget and soon retired (albeit temporarily) from the stage; Wallack, on the other hand, was professionally unaffected by the strictures of the bishop. Ecclesiastic censorship, it seems, affected primarily French-speaking companies, touring and resident, in Quebec. The hypothesis is further supported by a circular issued by Bourget in 1874, this time against the Dominion Theatre. The Dominion, whose first manager, Fortin, was a French-Canadian, attempted to draw a popular French audience with a repertoire of vaudeville, light comedy, and circus. The Dominion opened on 4 August 1873. It was quite successful for some months, but soon experienced financial difficulties that forced many changes in the management but not in policy. The bishop stepped in on 28 February 1874, and on 18 April, the Dominion closed and was replaced by the Opera House. Since, at that time, the box-office receipts were good (Camerlain, p. 113), it seems reasonable to assume that Bourget was directly responsible for the Dominion's closure.

Evidently, the francophone theatre was by now under general clerical and secular suspicion. Lorraine Camerlain suggests (p. 117) that "Les multiples interventions de Mgr. Bourget et de ses successeurs entretiennent dans l'esprit des Canadiens-français une forte connotation 'immoralité-théâtre francais'."[9] Such a bias would explain Bourget's quick and aggressive comment upon the arrival of the French actress Marie-Aimée in October 1874: the bishop saw in her "ce que le théâtre français produit de plus sale et de plus révoltant pour la pudeur."[10] A paradoxical effect of this linking of French theatre and immorality was that French-Canadians gradually came to neglect French theatre—only to attend more English plays, or translations of foreign plays. At least, that seems to be the general meaning of a commentary found in *la Minerve* on 8 April 1874, in which the author complains that too few "Canadiens" (i.e. French-Canadians) went to see the Génot Company from Paris, a company of very high standards and to be preferred, says the author, to the "burlesque" and other "comique américains" to which the francophone public gave its support.

We can only speculate on the theatrical tastes of French-Canadians in nineteenth-century Quebec, but we can say with some certainty that church initiated censorship curbed the spontaneous and natural development of francophone theatrical life. The censorship seriously restricted the founding of local companies in the second half of the nineteenth century, though it was not able to completely halt the momentum.

The first visit of Sarah Bernhardt to Quebec, in 1880, marks the beginning of an era of great visiting stars, and, as Jean-Marc Larrue has pointed out, Montreal quickly became "[un] centre de théâtre important" for American and European artists.[11] The stars came in ever-increasing numbers and, as public enthusiasm increased, episcopal censorship became harsher, more widespread and concerted, precisely because "le théâtre se fait [aux yeux des éveques] de plus en plus menaçant parce que de plus en plus présent dans la société."[12] In 1886, for instance, the bishops united at their seventh provincial council to warn their congregations against touring companies and amateur theatre. Nonetheless, the former kept growing in number, and amateur groups continued to multiply in Montreal and throughout the province.

Toward the end of the century, we finally see the first attempts, under the influence of touring companies and with the help of some foreign directors and actors, at establishing permanent professional companies in Quebec. "Le Conservatoire," described by John Hare ("Panorama," p. 92) as "le premier théâtre francais permanent à Montréal," was founded in 1887 and fostered the career of Blanche de la Sablonnière, "la Sarah canadienne." Professionalism developed as new theatres opened: the Nouveau Théâtre Empire in 1893, the Monument National in 1894, the Théâtre des Variétés in 1898, the Théâtre National in 1900. New companies were founded, among them the Compagnie franco-canadienne, so called because it joined together French and Canadian actors (many French-Canadian actors began their careers with this company). According to John Hare, "de 1898 à 1914, Montréal vit la fondation d'une vingtaine de troupes professionnelles."[13] Few of these, it is true, lasted more than two seasons, but such a sudden proliferation clearly shows that Montreal and Quebec were now ready for a fully professional and permanent theatre life.

To what degree did foreign touring companies contribute to this new situation? Given the current state of research in this area, conclusions can only be tentative, but just as visits of the "divine Sarah" built up hopes for a Canadian Sarah—hopes at least partially satisfied by Blanche de la Sablonnière and Juliette Béliveau, "la petite Sarah"—so it seems natural that frequent visits of French and American companies should favor the development of local activity and create sound competition. We know that some foreign actors came to Quebec and contributed to the founding of local theatres: Maugard, Antoine Bailly (later known as Godeau), and Eugène Lassalle, founder of the Conservatoire Lassalle. (A complete list of actors, directors, or producers who came on a tour and stayed in Quebec remains to be compiled.)

During this "golden age" of Quebec theatre, many Canadian stars were born, the most famous being Palmieri, Juliette Béliveau, Fred Barry and, later on, Ovila Légaré and Albert Duquesne. Opportunities for these and other actors were bright but not without restrictions. I have already mentioned the Compagnie franco-canadienne in which foreign and local actors played together. In 1901, the Comédie-Française du Nouveau Monde was created, a company "dont on confiait le sort à des artistes français pour les premiers rôles et canadiens pour les seconds emplois."[14] That well expresses the relationship between the two groups: theatrical life was now intense in Montreal, but it was well understood that leading parts must be held by foreigners, who also frequently assumed managerial and artistic control of theatres as well. The best-known actor-director of this period is the Frenchman Godeau, who landed in Montreal in 1897 and was destined to be associated with various companies for a good half-century. (His daughter, Marthe Thierry, was Albert Duquesne's wife and became one of the greatest actresses of the twentieth century.) Béraud quips, perceptively enough (*350 ans*, p. 89), "le théâtre montréalais avait attendu Godeau," before giving itself permanent theatres and a true theatrical tradition.

From 1900 to 1914, theatre life in Montreal progressed in a sort of fervent disorder; companies multiplied but they were shortlived. The war put an end to the great impetus, but it had started to slow down as early as 1904, when the Théâtre National tried to grab a share of the new fascination exercised by moving pictures by introducing short films between the third and the fourth acts of the main piece. Béraud aptly comments (*350 ans*, p. 102): "C'était introduire le loup dans le bergerie." In 1906 Ernest Ouimet inaugurated his famous "ouimetoscope", and theatres began to convert into movie houses. The young "golden age" was over; the age of "troubled adolescence," as Béraud puts it, was beginning. The good days were over even for touring companies; because of rising costs, Montreal could now afford no better than third-rate performers (Hare, "Le Théâtre," p. 244).

World War I sent many Quebecois actors to the battlefield; it drastically affected social life; and it brought the rapid growth of theatre to an abrupt halt. The big play was staged somewhere else, in the "vieux pays."

After the war, theatrical revival was not easy. The movie industry had progressed, and broadcasting, born in Montreal in 1918,[15] offered a new type of entertainment, while at the same time tempting actors with better incomes than the theatre could provide. This double competition, says John Hare, led to a decline in the quality of theatrical performances. "Ce fut la belle époque des revues et sketches humoristiques."[16] However, even this variety of show business experienced difficulties with the onset of the 1929 economic crash.

We can date the beginnings of a revival to 1930, with the founding of Montreal's Théâtre Stella. As in the earlier period, foreign companies provided a means of acceleration. However, the relationship between local companies and foreign artists had changed considerably since the turn of the century. The initiative was taken by the Barry-Duquesne company whose members were all Montreal-born. During its first season, the Stella hired "des vedettes de France pour venir jouer à côté des interprètes canadiens dans l'espoir de créer un intérêt plus grand encore,"[17] but local actors were determined to share the leading parts. Interestingly, too, one of the first "Parisian" guests invited to the Stella was Antoinette Giroux, a Quebec actress who had won a scholarship to study in Paris in 1923.

The Stella actors worked industriously and imaginatively to attract audiences, educate their taste, and create theatregoing habits. They endured a gruelling tempo and schedule and accepted a heavy financial sacrifice. Not surprisingly, there were clashes between the French stars who demanded and received high wages and the regular company members who had to share what was left. Yet the public was not overly impressed by anything bearing the Paris stamp. The French stars such as Liliane Gérane did not always please (Cunningham, p. 73), and were not so successful as had been hoped in luring Montrealers back to theatre. After six years of heroic efforts, many actors from the Barry-Duquesne company opted for radio work, and the Stella became a movie house.

Between 1935 and 1945, other attempts at theatrical revival were made. Many failed, but the attempts persisted, and now new companies were looking less to outside help. Touring companies still came to Montreal, some to His Majesty's—at least two American companies played there in 1939, as did Gaby Morlay with a play by Henry Bernstein—others to the Saint-Denis or the Monument National. If we are to believe Jean Béraud, some people still thought touring companies a necessary part of theatrical revival. On 7 September 1940 Béraud wrote: "La direction [du His Majesty's] tente cette saison l'expérience de spectacles donnés par des troupes américaines à des prix d'admission vraiment modérés à l'extrême. Elle espère que le grand public reprendra le goût d'aller entendre chaque semaine une pièce interprétée par de bonnes troupes ayant à leur tête une grande vedette qu'il a pu apprécier déjà sur la scène ou à l'écran."[18] His Majesty's continued to specialize in foreign touring companies, but frequent closures in the early 1940s indicate that the policy was not as successful as it assuredly once would have been.

The Second World War caused the expatriation to the United States or Latin America of many French companies and stars. French-speaking Quebec seemed to be a natural land of adoption, but such a possibility, which would have been accepted with enthusiasm around 1900, was, forty years later greeted rather coldly, even as a threat. Thus, "la rumeur voulant que Louis Jouvet, réfugié en Amérique du Sud, vienne s'installer à Montréal, avec les vingt-quatre membres de sa troupe"[19] was harshly opposed by the young Union des Artistes, which was willing to welcome the great artist only on condition that he came alone so that members of his company could not jeopardize opportunities for the young and talented Quebecois actors trying to make a career in Montreal. One can find an echo of this incident in

Gratien Gélinas' annual stage review of 1942. Celebrating in his own fashion Montreal's tricentenary, Gélinas depicts "une troupe d'acteurs français à l'accent déjà fort évolué fondant la ville un an avant M. de Maisonneuve et promettant aux 'bons sauvages' tous les bienfaits de la civilisation."[20] By the middle of the twentieth century, Quebecois actors no longer considered themselves to be "bons sauvages" in need of instruction from foreigners. On the contrary, by the early 1940s, Montreal could boast of many excellent local actors, and, theatrically speaking, the city stood on the threshold of a new era. To be sure, the theatrical life of Quebec remained open to French influences, mainly because Quebecois actors and directors studied in Paris and then returned to found their own companies. However, the appearance of a few French actors—François Rozet, Françoise and Jean Faucher, for instance—now represented only a minor factor in Quebec's theatrical evolution.

In his analysis of the 1930 decade, the highlight of which was the failure of the Stella, together with the creation in 1937 of the Compagnons de Saint-Laurent, Béraud rightly speaks of a "crise bienfaisante," and he explains that it is "durant ces années périlleuses qu'auront vu le jour des initiatives individuelles ou collectives qui doteront le Canada français d'un art du théâtre encore hésitant, mais . . . détaché enfin des imitations serviles. Le salut ne viendra pas de l'étranger, il faut se déterminer à agir soi-même."[21]

Those who took action and whose endeavors were particularly effective were Emile Legault and his Compagnons, in 1937, Gratien Gélinas in 1938, and, later, Pierre Dagenais' Equipe in 1943. From the Compagnons came many of today's prominent actors, including the two founders of the Théâtre du Nouveau Monde, Jean Gascon and Jean-Louis Roux. Furthermore, one must not neglect the impact of Gratien Gélinas' annual reviews, which greatly heightened the quality of a genre considered minor, a genre of which the popular French-speaking public was very fond, and with which it was deeply identified. During these crucial ten years for the development of theatre in Quebec, no one attracted a larger public than Gélinas. As for Dagenais' Equipe, it lived no more than five years during which it experienced both triumphal artistic success and heavy financial loss. To this day, Dagenais speaks with bitterness about his endeavor and judges it a failure.[22] His company, however, was the first one in Montreal to stage Sartre (in 1946, before London and New York), Cocteau, and Salacrou; the first one, also, to try and develop truly international standards of production.

Dagenais' efforts may have been premature, since the audience he aimed at was not sufficiently large to make his work financially feasible. However, his decade, the 1940s, must be seen as years of gestation, years during which a full range of theatrical genres was explored, from burlesque to sophisticated dramas, from classical works to avant-garde plays. In the midst of such a rich but somewhat unstable and eclectic period, l'Equipe was an essential experiment. Unfortunately, it disappeared just as theatrical life in

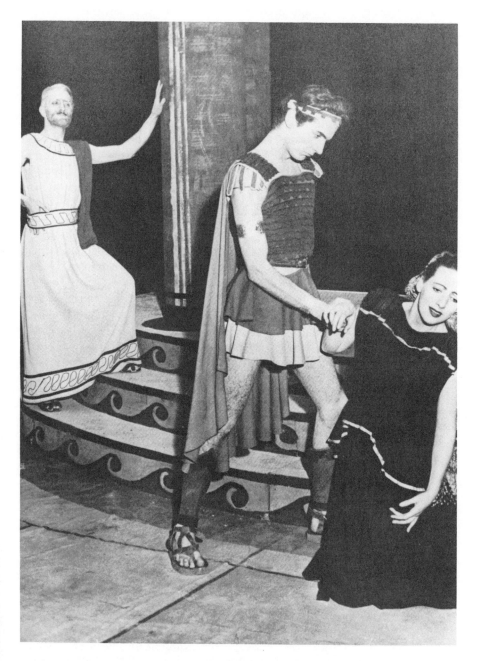

7. Scene from Racine's *Andromaque*, played by Les Compagnons de Saint-Laurent in 1947. By permission of Le Père Emile Legault, of Les Compagnons.

Quebec was about to soar. *Tit-Coq*, generally accepted as the first work of the contemporary period, appeared in 1948; the same year saw the founding of the Rideau-Vert on the premises of the former Stella, where it is still successful. In 1952, one hundred and twenty-five years after the first visit of a foreign company to Canada, the Théâtre du Nouveau Monde was founded; it first played at the Gésù (a church basement belonging to the Jesuits) and then in various halls, before settling in its own building in 1972.

In the past twenty years, these two Montreal companies—the Rideau-Vert and the Théâtre du Nouveau Monde—have made several European tours; more recently, younger groups and companies have followed, playing in Paris, Brussels, and other European cities works by Quebec playwrights such as Michel Tremblay, Antonine Maillet, Michel Garneau, Roland Lepage, Jacques Duchesne, Jean Barbeau, and Robert Gurik. Quebec playwrights have become well-known in English-Canada and the United States. The time when Montreal was "waiting for Godeau" and fetched him from Paris is well past; now Quebec theatre radiates through North America, Europe, and even North Africa. Ironically, and it is a just turn of events, in this cultural milieu where ecclesiastical censorship so often tried to curb the progress of theatre, Père Legault and other members of the clergy[23] were among those who, with patience and some passion, educated theatregoers and trained many actors in the 1930s and 1940s. It is to these actors that we mainly owe the great impetus of the 1950s. Hélène Beauchamp-Rank writes: "Le théâtre qui s'est fait à Montréal depuis 1950 a suivi plusieurs modes lancées par des créateurs, des animateurs qui croyaient en un style de jeu, de présentation, en un répertoire. Au-delà de l'attirance à ces modes, il faut noter l'esprit d'aventure de ces gens, leur goût du risque, de la recherche de renouvellements. Ils ont souvent donné à Montréal l'élan nécéssaire, une vitalité essentielle."[24]

The last thirty years have been a success, despite setbacks and crises. Francophone theatrical life in Quebec now seems well-structured, institutions are lasting and, more important still, playwrights have for a good many years built up a valuable repertoire. If he were still with us, Jean Béraud would happily record that theatre has taken firm root in Quebec.

Notes

This paper was originally written in French. The translation is by Jean-Cléo Godin and L. W. Conolly. The help of Professor Ramon Hathorn, University of Guelph, is gratefully acknowledged.
   1. Jean Béraud, "Est-il encore temps?" *La Presse* (Montreal), 2 November 1940, p. 7. ["Whenever I immerse myself again in these Montreal theatre annals, I am astonished every time that drama never took root and flowered among us, except spasmodically."]

2. Ibid. ["Every time an artist of any renown appears, once again we speak of a theatrical renaissance. That is proof indeed that the theatre has never really taken root."]

3. John E. Hare, "Panorama des spectacles au Québec: de la Conquête au XXe siècle," *Archives des lettres canadiennes*, 5 (1976), 67.

4. Two actors of the Victor company and four amateurs from Montreal played *Le comédien sans argent ou le retour d'Alvic en Canada* and *Le sourd ou l'auberge plein* on 17 December 1827. (Hare, p. 67.)

5. The first Theatre Royal opened in 1825 and closed in 1845. The second Theatre Royal opened in 1847, closed in 1851, and burned in 1852. The third Theatre Royal had a longer career, from 1852 to 1913. See Hare, "Panorama," pp. 80–81, and Raymond F. Montpetit, "La construction des théâtres à Montréal au dix-neuvième siècle; critique de l'historiographie," *Aspects du théâtre québecois* (Actes du congrès de l'ACFAS 1977; Trois Rivières, 1978), pp. 41–55. According to Montpetit, a fourth theatre, the Royal Olympic, existed between 1845 and 1847.

6. The bishop banned a performance of Molière's comedy planned by the province's governor. See Jean Béraud, *350 ans de théâtre au Canada français* (Montreal, 1958), p. 13.

7. See Lorraine Camerlain, "Trois interventions du clergé dans l'histoire du théâtre à Montréal: 1789–90, 1859 et 1872–74." M.A. thesis, University of Montreal, 1979.

8. "Lettre adressée par Monseigneur l'Evêque de Montréal à tous les curés de la ville et de la banlieue," cited by Camerlain, p. 87. ["I understand that two companies of actors are coming from the United States, which I am assured are very immoral."]

9. ["The numerous interventions of Bishop Bourget and his successors denote in the minds of French-Canadians the strong connotation of immorality and French theatre being synonymous."]

10. Circular of 18 October 1874, cited by Camerlain, p. 115. [". . . the filthiest and most shameful product of the French theatre."]

11. Jean-Marc Larrue, "Le théâtre à Montréal de 1890 à 1900," M.A. thesis, McGill University, 1979.

12. Camerlain, p. 125. ["in the eyes of the bishops the theatre is becoming more and more dangerous because of its ever-increasing presence in our society."]

13. John Hare, "Le théâtre professionel à Montréal de 1898 à 1937," *Archives des lettres canadiennes*, 5 (1976), 244. ["from 1898 to 1914, Montreal saw the founding of some twenty professional companies."]

14. Béraud, *350 ans*, p. 98. ["whose future was entrusted to French actors in lead roles and to French-Canadians for the lesser parts."]

15. Gilles Proulx, "La radio canadienne a 60 ans," *La Presse* (Montreal), 28 November 1978, p. A-4. According to Pierre Pagé, it is only from 1931 that one can legitimately speak of a "littérature radiophonique," but "quelques oeuvres brèves de littérature ont été jouées—sketches ou dramatiques par épisodes" before 1930. P. Pagé, *Répertoire des oeuvres de la littérature radiophonique québecoise, 1930–1970* (Montreal, 1975), p. 23.

16. Hare, "Le théâtre," p. 246. ["This was the high point of reviews and comic sketches."] See also Jean-Cléo Godin, "Les gaietés montréalaises: sketches, revues," *Etudes françaises*, 15 (April 1979), 143–57.

17. Joyce Cunningham, "L'ancien théâtre Stella (1930–1936)," *Jeu*, 6 (Summer/Fall, 1977), 67. ["some stars from France to come and play alongside French-Canadian performers in the hope of creating still wider interest."]

18. Jean Béraud, "Au Majesty's—chez Fridolin," *La Presse* (Montreal), 7 September 1940, p. 37. ["The Management (of His Majesty's) is experimenting this season with shows given by American companies at extremely reasonable prices. It hopes

that the public will develop again a taste for going every week to see performances by good companies headed by a great star whom it has already admired on stage or on screen."]

19. Béraud, *350 ans*, pp. 247–48. ["the rumour suggesting that Louis Jouvet, a refugee in South America, may come to set himself up in Montreal with the twenty-four members of his company . . . "]

20. Béraud, *350 ans*, p. 248. ["a company of French actors with strongly developed local accents founding the city a year before M. de Maisonneuve and promising to the 'noble savages' all the benefits of civilization."]

21. Béraud, *350 ans*, p. 226. ["during these perilous years that saw the dawn of individual or collective initiatives which would endow French Canada with a theatrical art still tentative, but . . . finally freed from servile imitation. Salvation will not come from abroad; we must decide to act by ourselves."]

22. See an interview with Lise Hétu, "L'équipe de Pierre Dagenais;" typescript deposited in the Centre de documentation des études québecoises, University of Montreal.

23. Particularly the Jesuit priest Georges-Henri d'Auteuil who, at the Collège Sainte-Marie in Montreal, was the first teacher of Jean Gascon, Jean-Louis Roux, and other prominent actors. He died in 1978.

24. H. Beauchamp-Rank, "La vie théâtrale à Montréal de 1950 à 1970: théâtre, troupes, saisons, répertoires," *Archives des lettres canadiennes*, 5 (1976), 267. ["Theatre produced in Montreal since 1950 has followed several fashions initiated by creative talents who believed in a style of acting, of production and of repertoire. In addition to the attraction of these fashions, one must take note of the adventurous spirit of these people, their taste for risk, and searching for new forms. They have often given to Montreal the necessary push and an essential vitality."]

Andrew Parkin   8

The New Frontier:
Toward an
Indigenous Theatre
in British Columbia _____

The beginnings are many. They exist now in British Columbia in the form of new companies which spring up, produce a few plays, and then disband. They exist also in history: the previous efforts to provide entertainment for the growing and changing theatre audiences in the far West over the last one hundred and thirty years. During this period, the emergence of regional drama has been slow and, until recently, disappointing. Not so the theatre history of the region. This has been rich and interesting. To investigate the founding of indigenous professional theatre in British Columbia is to discover a wealth of amateur and professional activity and the building of many theatres. This activity can be charted alongside the economic and social factors that stimulated and depressed it: the Cariboo gold rush, the transcontinental railroad, the Yukon boom, the post-1918 Little Theatre boom, the Depression, and then post-war growth, with the effort to build a Canadian culture having its own identity.

There is no comprehensive survey of British Columbia theatre in book form. There are a number of articles in newspapers and journals, and some unpublished dissertations, such as studies of an individual theatre or an amateur group.[1] Mr. Chad Evans, a heritage researcher for the British Columbia government, has almost completed a book on frontier theatre in the province up to 1900.[2] It is my purpose here to give some idea of the materials available to the researcher of the theatre history of British Columbia, to sketch some of the early theatre activity, and then to discuss in a little more detail the ways in which Canadian professional theatre emerged in British Columbia.

The available sources for a study of the founding of theatre in the province are varied and many. The Public Archives of Canada in Ottawa cannot be relied upon alone, since there is material in British Columbia archives that has not yet been properly catalogued and microfilmed. The Provincial Archives of British Columbia[3] contain manuscript collections such as the Bullock-Webster papers, and records of the British Columbia Drama Association, as well as those concerning the Dominion Drama Festival. The departmental papers of the British Columbia government contain reports and publications on drama and theatre in education. The correspondence files and newspaper files—clippings and microfiche—are essential. Besides the two major Vancouver papers, the *Sun* and the *Province*, the researcher has such sources as the *Daily Colonist*, the *New Westminster Times*, the *Victoria Gazette*, the *British Columbia Chronicle*, the *Vancouver Times*, and the *Nanaimo Gazette*. As well as national theatre journals, one should not forget specifically West Coast publications, such as *Theatre B.C.* There are also the unpublished diaries of early settlers. There is a fair amount of photographic evidence in the provincial archives. The Vancouver City Archives also contain some early photographs and about eight feet of shelves devoted to the Vancouver Little Theatre Association. Some of the records of the Vancouver Playhouse can also be investigated there. Furthermore, the Chilliwack Military Museum holds the records of the Royal Engineers, with their papers for the military theatre in New Westminster. *The Emigrant Soldier's Gazette*, bound, printed, and distributed to survivors of the *Thames City* voyage, is useful too. If the theatre of Europe grew out of church theatricals, that of Canada grew out of garrison theatricals.

The university libraries in British Columbia are, of course, very useful, but researchers should be especially alerted to the Rushton papers in Special Collections at the University of British Columbia library. These contain records of the Vancouver Little Theatre Association and the theatre-in-schools group known most recently as Holiday Playhouse, before it ceased to exist.

The theatre historian should not overlook the value of aural history. Some recollections of life in British Columbia are stored on tape in the provincial archives, but the most valuable example for the student of theatre history is the tape in the University of British Columbia library of Dorothy Somerset and Sidney Risk, interviewed by Laurinda Daniells. Here, the aspects of Vancouver's theatre history leading to the growth of indigenous professional theatre are recalled in much detail (and with some inaccuracies) by two people who helped to make it happen. In the Provincial Archives Orchard Collection, the reminiscences of early settlers in British Columbia amount to about 2,000 hours, and contain accounts of touring theatre, Chinese theatre, amateur activity, and theatre in the Kootenays. There is also a collection of CBC radio plays in the provincial archives, including radio plays written in British Columbia. So far, approximately 1,000 hours have been catalogued out of a total of 12,000 hours.[4]

Indigenous British Columbia theatre, as it exists now, is an offshoot of British and American theatre, so far as they are distinguishable; it owes little or nothing to Chinese or Indian theatre. This is not to say that there has been no theatrical activity of any sort among the Chinese and Indian populations, but it would be a different topic, and one only marginally relevant to this discussion. Professional theatre in British Columbia arose from the amateur activities of settlers, forming a tradition from the naval and military performances to the activities of the British Columbia Drama Association, the Vancouver Little Theatre Association, the regional stimulation of the Dominion Drama Festival, and the growth of university and school drama as well as the little community theatres. It also arose from the stimulation of American and British touring companies, the stock companies of gold rush days and later, together with a local determination to provide an alternative (legitimate) theatre to the fare offered by the vaudeville circuits.

The first recorded theatrical event for the settlers occurred technically on British soil, for it was aboard Her Majesty's ship *Trincomalee*, anchored in Esquimalt harbor on 18 October 1853.[5] At about this time, there were fewer than five hundred British settlers living in the Fort Victoria area.[6] The diary of Martha Cheney reveals that members of the audience went aboard at about six in the evening; Robert Melrose confided to his diary that the performance was "splendid theatre."[7] These "on-boards" were welcome entertainment. A handwritten program for one of them is in the provincial archives. It tells us that the "Theatre Royal" aboard HMS *President* presented a farce in one act, *The Irish Lion*. The comic song, "Jack Rags" was rendered by one C. Brian, and the "sentimental" song "Give Me a Lot by Side of a Mill" was sung by C. Saunders. Another farce, *The Captain of the Watch*, was played with *The Irish Lion*, and there was dancing after the plays. The cast, of necessity in this on-going naval tradition of gun-boat theatre, was all male. According to an account in the *Colonist* of 26 February 1863, the on-board offered by HMS *Devastation* was set up by clearing the quarterdeck and arranging rows of seats on it facing the stern. A canopy decorated with flags was rigged up to shelter the audience. Beyond the wheel and compass were situated the proscenium and drop curtain. A fire-basket warmed the audience. In the interval, apples, oranges, cakes, and ginger beer could be had from the temporary saloon placed on the starboard upper deck.

The nautical habit of floating theatre spread to the contingent of Royal Engineers who sailed to the newly created colony of British Columbia aboard the *Thames City*. They came, they mapped, they acted. Having staged farces, laced with songs and dances, during the long voyage to the townsite of New Westminster, they soon set up "the first genuine dramatic society in far Western Canada" (Evans, "Frontier Theatre," p. 7). At their own expense, the sappers built a club room which could be used as a theatre. It was nicknamed the Theatre Royal. Although a dance was held in this camp theatre in December 1859, references to theatricals do not start until the following winter. Apparently, casts were made up mainly from NCOs and other ranks, the younger men playing female roles. The townsfolk, about 250 of them at the time (Akrigg, p. 200), left these comedy evenings in high spirits.[8] During their last season, 1862–63, they raised as much as $311 for a six-hour benefit show for the Lancashire coal miners. In January 1862, they combined with some of the people in the tiny community of Yale on the lower Fraser River to put on J. M. Morton's farce, *Sent to the Tower* (*British Columbian*, 2 January 1862). Among the comic songs between the acts, there was one called "The Cariboo." Evidently, the engineers were beginning to respond to their strange new environment. However, they had to give their last performance on 20 October 1863 and soon disbanded, for many returned home to England.

Meanwhile, in the more important and more populous Victoria, the Hudson's Bay Company had been quick to respond to the challenge of gun-boat theatre. On 23 December 1853, the company put on a "Theatrical Play and Ball, held at F[ort] Victoria" (Melrose diary). Three years later, a handwritten playbill (PABC) proudly announced an ambitious production in what had evidently become a regular series: "Annual Amateur Theatricals Vancouver's Island Wednesday Jany 14th 1857 *The Rivals* (By Richard Brinsley Sheridan)." An all-male cast apparently played with hilarious effect, the fun being intensified by the recognition of familiar people in incongruous garb.

In 1858, the gold rush resulted in Victoria's being suddenly full of Californians. It rapidly became an extension of San Francisco. The new population and resultant trade boom meant that money could be made by providing professional entertainment. To keep miners from retreating down the coast in the winters, theatres were built and professional actors arrived in the hope of making a good living. By the end of 1858, there were over 3,000 permanent residents in Victoria. By October 1859, the officers of HMS *Ganges* had fixed up a little theatre in part of Reid's storehouse, playing in cramped conditions to over 400 people, all of them doubtless conscious of the salmon in the storehouse. Not surprisingly, there was a general sense that Victoria merited something better. The following February saw Mr. Cusheon of the Union Hotel opening a hall which he dubbed his Naval and Military Theatre. It opened with men from HMS *Satellite* performing *The Inchcape Bell* and *Blackbeard* on 16 February 1860. Meanwhile, James Wilcox of the Royal Hotel had men from HMS *Ganges* performing in his hall. Amateur performances were now firmly enough established in the minds of local residents for thirty people to subscribe a total of $150 to form the Amateur Dramatic Association of Victoria (ADAV) on 29 October 1862. His Excellency the Governor, James Douglas, was patron. The next eighty years were to see an amazing growth of significant amateur theatre in the province. The first ADAV performance was on Boxing Day 1862, in aid of the Royal Hospital. Their second production was marred by an accident which merited comment in the press: "We regret to state that a scene of much disorder and uproar was occasioned at the

Theatre last evening in consequence of the indiscretion of a man in the dress circle throwing an apple at the gentlemen on the stage in the last play" (*Colonist*, 31 January 1863). As a result, one young lady fainted and was carried outside.

The ADAV players were assisted by professional actresses and by the use of the resident professionals' theatre. The first professional legitimate theatre group to perform in the province was the George Chapman Pioneer Dramatic Company. Chapman and his company disembarked from the steamer *Constitution* in March 1859. On 5 March they opened in the Assembly Rooms with performances of *The Young Widow*, a comedy, and *The Limerick Boy*, a farce. It was a two-week engagement, the beginning of a long chain of visits by stock companies, variety acts, vaudeville, and touring stars. The tourers, and the stock companies, which might stay for as long as money could be made, were necessary for the founding of indigenous theatre for two main reasons: they precipitated the building of local theatres, which could then be used, and even, at some later time, be taken over by local actors. Second, the audiences exposed to a variety of theatrical experiences would grow in numbers and eventually be able to support a Canadian professional theatre, to some extent itself inspired by the touring stars.

When the Chapmans returned to Victoria, they managed to transform a newly built music hall into the first legitimate stock theatre in the province, the Colonial on Government Street. It opened on 4 February 1860 with Kotzebue's *The Stranger*. This theatre was modest. It seated 365, had three separate entrances, a parquette holding 125, with side entrance for ladies, and a pit and gallery. Respectable citizens could book for the parquette at one dollar; itinerant miners booked for the pit at fifty cents, while "Indians and such ilk" were denizens of the gallery, also at fifty cents per seat.

The arrival of John S. Potter's Company in Victoria in 1860 soon led to the building of another frontier theatre. After a run of three months at the Colonial in late 1860, they went to New Westminster for three weeks, where J. T. Scott, owner of the Pioneer Saloon, added "an extended wooden shack" to his premises, fitted it out, and called it the Pioneer Theatre. F. E. Herring remembered that:

a company of actors, landing from no one knew where at Port Moody . . . walked in over the Indian trail, carrying on their heads and backs the paraphernalia and dresses of their craft. Here they played for three or four months, every night in the week except Sunday, to "No Standing-room left," a dollar seat being the price of admission to any part of the house. "Come early and take your choice" was the rule, although a few seats were always reserved in front, in case any gentleman was so fortunate as to accompany a lady there. . . .
The leading woman was not in her first youth, and one night when she was playing "The Lady of Lyons," in the most pathetic part, when all was silence, "Liverpool Jack" made inquiries as to her pretty hair, which changed the tragedy to farce, and

brought down the house. Scarcely a night passed but something occurred which was not on the programme.[9]

Such were the conditions under which foreign professional actors worked in British Columbia. Theatres were quickly built, converted to music halls and vice versa, demolished, rebuilt, sold, resold, and refurbished. It was with the coming of the railroad, however, that the big commercial circuits could establish themselves, bringing Eastern business capital and methods and the more permanent and often opulent theatre buildings to Vancouver, the new terminal of the West.

The first theatre to open in Vancouver was Blair's Hall, where on 17 May 1886 the Smith Comedy Company performed. Less than three weeks later, the Columbia Hall opened with an acrobatic song-and-dance team known as Webster and Stehle, playing to an audience of about 400. Only eight days later, Vancouver was destroyed in large part by fire. The mayor telegraphed to Prime Minister John A. Macdonald requesting government aid. He received $5,000. Rebuilding was rapid. There was time to create a variety hall in the Globe Hotel and one called Agret's Hall at Abbott and Water streets. Moreover, F. W. Hart transplanted his Port Moody roller skating rink to Carrall Street in Vancouver, where he added a small stage and seating to create Hart's Opera House. By May 1888, the population of Vancouver had topped 8,500. It was definitely time for a better theatre. Crichmay and Robson obliged by building the Imperial Opera House in April 1889 at Abbott and Pender. This $10,000 theatre was 120 feet by 50 feet, had a waiting room for the ladies, and one for the gentlemen, two ticket offices, and a bar. It could accommodate 600 people. The 30-by-49-foot stage had a proscenium 15 feet high and 23 feet wide. The Imperial had six dressing rooms, sunken footlights worked from the wings, and a one-foot rake to the stage. The acoustics were exceptionally good.

The Vancouver Opera House, built by the Canadian Pacific Railway, opened on 9 February 1891. It seated about 1,200 people. By 1911 Vancouver, really booming, had a population of 120,000 and, according to Sidney Risk, contained nine legitimate theatres.[10] The largest was the Columbia, but the Avenue Theatre at Main and Georgia was full of character, decorated in white, pale green, and gold. It was near the water, so that dressing rooms would sometimes be flooded, and rats wallowed and scrambled beneath the stage. It was torn down for lack of business during the Depression.

The Pantages circuit built two theatres in Vancouver, and one in Victoria, which eventually became the McPherson Theatre. For Sidney Risk, the second Pantages in Vancouver was "one of the most beautiful theatres" he had ever seen. It had marble and gilt and was upholstered beautifully in red plush. It was used, of course, for vaudeville, but later became a cinema called the Imperial, before it was torn down after the end of the Second

8. Interior of the Vancouver Opera House. Courtesy of the Provincial Archives, Victoria, British Columbia.

World War. The pattern was that the theatre circuits grew before the First World War, and in the 1920s there was a boom in professional and amateur theatre alike in Vancouver. Various stock companies played at the Empress. There was burlesque and vaudeville at the Columbia and the Royal. Distinguished touring companies such as the Stratford-upon-Avon Company, the Abbey Theatre, and the Birmingham Repertory Company played at the Vancouver Opera House. It was used for the annual reviews brought to Vancouver in the 1920s by the Dumbells, a successful, all-Canadian professional company.

Sidney Risk is a convenient example. His career as a British Columbia actor is instructive. He was given his first job in the professional theatre by Charles Royal who had formed the Royal Players. Risk appeared under the stage name of Dickson McNaughton in *The Better 'Ole*, while he was a student. He went on to direct the Player's Club at the University of British Columbia, get more experience in England, work again in Canada and, in 1946, he formed the Everyman Theatre Company, whose policy was to hire young Canadian actors. The company had no theatre of its own and very little money. It existed by touring in a Ford truck and bus from Vancouver to Winnipeg. They toured in winter and were caught in blizzards, sometimes finding themselves on trains without heat or food. Dr. Shrum gave them the use of an office and rehearsal room; they continued to tour, and then found a small studio theatre they could use on Main St. Their ambitious repertoire included Ibsen's *Ghosts*, Chekhov's *Uncle Vanya*, and Eliot's *Murder in the Cathedral*. They were soon "pushed out" of the studio, and moved into the State Theatre. It had 900 seats and was far too big for them. The company was brought to a full stop when they were taken to court for their production of *Tobacco Road* in 1952, but Everyman had kept up its battle for survival for six years as a professional Canadian company. Risk's company proved that in the years after the Second World War, a truly Canadian professional theatre company could work, even if it did not flourish, in the West.

The setting up of the civic theatres, Victoria's McPherson, with its Bastion Theatre Company organized by Peter Mannering on the Manitoba Theatre Centre model, and the Vancouver Playhouse, was soon to be approved. These two major theatres have ensured a varied yet continuing professional pool of actors in the West. Both have also pursued a policy of theatre for children, so vital for the building of future audiences and the nurturing of actors and playwrights. They also provide valuable opposition for other actors to react against and emulate, and surpass.

The leap from the circuit theatres and stock companies knocked out by the Depression, the Second World War, rising prices, and cinema, to the recent growth of professional companies indigenous to British Columbia is not an absurd leap across a gaping chasm. There are bridges, such as the tradition of amateur acting in the province and the movement of individual actors in and out of British Columbia, bringing ideas, knowledge, and experience. We can hardly overestimate the stimulus and excitement provided by the Dominion Drama Festival on all the amateur groups throughout Canada, let alone those in British Columbia—but that story is too well-known for us to rehearse it here. Moreover, the Dominion Drama Festival was a means to stimulate the arts of the theatre, rather than theatre itself. My emphasis, therefore, will be on the two kinds of amateur drama, educational and adult. Without the efforts to stimulate drama in schools and the education of the local adult population to become theatregoers, it is unlikely that the province could support more than one or two very mediocre theatre companies. At this point, one has to remember that there have been some crucial people and organizations in British Columbia's theatrical development that will have escaped mention in a brief account such as this. Their efforts form part and parcel of the entire amateur scene which I characterize now in the work of Major Llewellyn Bullock-Webster and of the Vancouver Little Theatre Association.

Bullock-Webster was a man of extraordinary vigor and a certain bizarre panache. He was born in June 1879 in Wales and educated at Ampleforth

College and later Cheltenham College, in an attempt to prepare for Sandhurst. He did not get into Sandhurst, but obtained the Associate of the Royal College of Music in 1900. He acted in London and seems, after a while, to have been reduced to an equestrian act. During this period, he had two injuries, and could not continue to act. After coming to Canada, he started the Prince Rupert Little Theatre in 1910. After the First World War, he worked tirelessly in Victoria at a variety of theatrical projects. In 1921, he set up the British Columbia Dramatic School with Victoria and Vancouver offices to give private or group lessons in elocution, dramatic work, and public speaking. The school undertook to read and comment upon plays and sketches submitted at $10 each. It gave a number of plays per year featuring senior students. A brochure dated September 1927 is illustrated with a photograph of four girls in a sort of tableau vivant of eurythmic poses. The brochure asserts that "one of the principal undertakings of the school is a series of DRAMALOGUES . . . (The name was originated by Mrs. T. S. Gore, for the school and is the property of the school.) These are Dramas in which speech takes the place of action. The parts are taken by society people."[11]

There could be few better descriptions of what Peter Brook calls "the deadly theatre." Yet Major Bullock-Webster sent some of the students (from among more than 700 who attended between 1921–33) to win scholarships at the Royal Academy of Dramatic Art and to join professional companies. He also found time to write improbable plays with impossible titles, such as *The Curse of Chirra-Pooje*, under intolerable pseudonyms, such as Chareh Sultan El Osman. As if this were not enough, he insisted upon the Alfresco mode of production: "the alfresco play requires two stages, one large and one smaller. The audience sit in a position from which they can see both."[12]

On 21 September 1931 in the Victoria premises of the British Columbia Dramatic School, Bullock-Webster held the first meeting of the British Columbia Drama Festival. By 1932–33, it had attracted twenty-nine groups. In spring 1933, there were thirty-five groups affiliated and sixteen more joined by the summer of 1933. By 1935, it had membership of the British Drama League. In the president's report of October 1938, Bullock-Webster complimented his fellow committee members: "This Association has done what I believe has never been done before on the North American continent, namely, sell admission to between thirty and forty plays for a price of one dollar, which works out at about two and a half cents per play. This has been possible only because the officers and so many of you yourselves have year after year given generously of your time and talents."[13] As if all this were not sufficient, Dr. George M. Weir as Minister of Education for the province appointed Bullock-Webster Drama Director of the Department of Education. He now travelled widely throughout the province, setting up drama groups. He divided British Columbia into fifteen drama districts, each with its own association and drama festival. By September 1939, there

were in British Columbia 177 adult groups (Little Theatres or drama organizations) with 86 high school clubs developing. During the war, the logical
thing was to concentrate on the schools. By 1945, approximately 325
school drama clubs were active. Deeply hurt by the failure of the Dominion
Drama Festival to appoint him as British Columbia Director from the
beginning, he resigned from the British Columbia Drama Festival and in
1935 started a rival organization called The Canadian Drama Award.
Despite his quarrels with other drama associations and despite his taste
which was already outdated in the 1920s and 1930s, he definitely worked
hard and enthusiastically for the development of Canadian theatre.

Meanwhile, over in Vancouver, the Vancouver Little Theatre Association
(VLTA) was formed in 1920 and put on its first season of plays in 1921. Its
first president was R. L. Reid, its first vice-president, E. V. Young, and its
directors H. H. Beeman, H. B. Coleman, and Frederic Wood. A surviving
membership drive poster sets the tone:

Keep Theatre *Alive*

Join

The Vancouver Little Theatre Association
Studio and Green Room 2237 Main Street

ACTING. DIRECTING. MAKE–UP.
READINGS. STUDIO NIGHTS. SOCIAL ACTIVITIES
HAVE FUN!
MEET NEW FRIENDS
PLUS
6 TICKETS FOR FIVE MAJOR PRODUCTIONS
MEMBERSHIP $5[xx] [14]

West Coast flapper energy was, in fact, well disciplined.

There are seven charts recording the VLTA personnel and their produc-
tions over the fourteen seasons 1921–35. The one-acters we might expect by
Harold Brighouse, W. W. Jacobs, and Lord Dunsany are also accompanied
by Maeterlinck's *The Intruder*, Arnold Bennett's *The Stepmother*, J. M.
Synge's *The Shadow of the Glen* and, surprisingly, W. B. Yeats's *The Land of
Heart's Desire*. In fact, the VLTA's program in its regular series was extremely enterprising and varied. Pirandello's *Sicilian Lines* was produced in
March 1923, J. M. Barrie's *Dear Brutus* in May 1923, and Karel Čapek's
R.U.R. in the 1924–25 season. In 1925, too, Shaw's *The Devil's Disciple*
and *How He Lied to Her Husband* were produced. From then on, the VLTA
regularly did full-length plays. Shaw, Ibsen, Noel Coward, Somerset Maugham,
Galsworthy, Sheridan, Henry Arthur Jones, and Chekhov were all produced, together with many other worthwhile playwrights. Special produc-

tions, repeat performances, Christmas plays, and pantomimes were all part of the VLTA's activities.

On 15 February 1929, there was an All Canadian Night with the production of three Canadian plays: L. McFarlane's *The Root House*, C. H. Dowling's *Three Nights with Cupid*, and I. E. MacKay's *The Second Lie*. In November 1932, VLTA did a production of W. B. Yeats's *The Only Jealousy of Emer*, following it up in January 1935 with a production of the same writer's *Deirdre*. This repertoire will indicate the range of interest in the VLTA productions. It is also a proof of their good taste and understanding of the need to give audiences the work of some of the best dramatists in their contemporary repertoire. Their choices are alert, up-to-date, and judicious.

It is clear also that the VLTA gave Vancouver a stable training ground for actors, technicians, and directors for an extended period of time. In combination with the Player's Club at the University of British Columbia, the Summer Extension program, and other work of Dorothy Somerset in the Theatre Department at the university, the VLTA has trained several generations of successful people in theatre.

There remains a postscript to this account of British Columbia theatre. A Canadian theatre must serve the best in the world repertoire and the best work of new playwrights; it must serve Canada's own best plays and the best of her new plays. British Columbia has one organization which has been taking the latter task very seriously. In 1965, Sheila Neville and Doug Bankson wrote to the Dominion Drama Festival, outlining a scheme for aid-to-playwrights centers to be set up across Canada. The idea was that playwrights should be able to have a play read and criticism given, free of charge to the playwright. The scheme was turned down. Neville and Bankson, therefore, started in 1969–70 The New Play Centre in British Columbia on an $800 grant from the Koerner Foundation. In 1971, Pamela Hawthorne was recruited. She has run the center most energetically ever since, existing from year to year on funding from a variety of agencies such as the British Columbia Cultural Fund, the Canada Council, the Vancouver Foundation, and the Koerner Foundation. In 1978, one hundred and twenty-five to a hundred and fifty scripts were received. Scripts are read by two professional directors and advice given. About twenty-five to thirty-five scripts are selected for workshop treatment, during which the playwright will attend and work for perhaps thirty to forty hours of rehearsal with a director and actors. Many revisions may be made as a result of this experience. Of these plays, about four to six are selected for stage production in a little theatre. Playwrights such as Tom Cone and Sheldon Rosen have emerged from The New Play Centre.

The various movements, organizations, and the many people who have contributed to their development and interaction have created a situation in British Columbia in which fine theatres have been built and equipped to replace older ones so ruthlessly destroyed. Actors and directors are being trained, and enough companies exist for good actors to get work. In the last three years, there has been about a 30-percent increase in Vancouver theatre audiences. Looking back from this contemporary situation rich in local theatrical ventures, the theatre historian can acknowledge the vitality of theatre in British Columbia over the last sixty years. Enthusiasm and willingness to work hard and risk much are qualities that link the amateurs and professionals of the region in theatrical endeavors which have achieved, in a surprisingly short time, a very real transformation. In short, we have charted the transition from theatre dominated by United States circuits and foreign stars to one capable of maintaining an indigenous crop of actors and technicians employed in the production of international classics and new plays from Canadian and foreign writers.

Notes

1. See, for example, Michael Booth, "The Beginnings of Theatre in British Columbia," *Queen's Quarterly*, 68 (Spring 1961), 159–68, and the same author's "Gold Rush Theatre: the Theatre Royal, Barkerville, British Columbia," *Pacific Northwest Quarterly*, 51 (July 1960), 97–102; C. A. Long, "Community Theatre Groups," M.A. thesis, University of British Columbia, 1974; Irene T. Barber, "A History of the Bastion Theatre, 1963–1975," M.A. thesis, University of Victoria, 1975. In addition, I am indebted to Mr. Jim Cliffe, currently engaged in research on British Columbia theatre at Western Washington State University, for his help in discussions of the Bullock-Webster papers in the Provincial Archives of British Columbia (hereafter PABC).

2. Most of what I say about frontier theatre in the nineteenth century derives from Chad Evans' unpublished typescript, "Frontier Theatre: A History of Theatrical Entertainment in the Canadian Far West during the Nineteenth Century." I am deeply indebted to Mr. Evans for his conversation, the loan of his typescript, and some photographs of early British Columbia theatres.

3. I must gratefully record my thanks to Mr. B. A. Young and his colleagues at the Provincial Archives.

4. Information from Dr. J. Cauther of the Aural History Archive.

5. Bullock-Webster refers to the first performance as taking place in a tent, but I have no corroborating evidence of that.

6. See G. P. V. Akrigg and Helen B. Akrigg, *British Columbia Chronicle: Gold and Colonists* (Vancouver, 1977).

7. Quoted by Evans, "Frontier Theatre," p. 3. See Martha Ella Cheney, "Diary, 1853–1856," and Robert Melrose, "Diary, August 1852–July 1857," PABC.

8. See the review in the *New Westminster Times*, 2 February 1861.

9. F. E. Herring, *In the Pathless West* (London, 1904), pp. 66–67.

10. Information in this and the following paragraph is from a taped interview (25 February 1979) with Dorothy Somerset and Sidney Risk (introduction by Laurinda Daniells) held in Special Collections, University of British Columbia Library.

11. Bullock-Webster Collection, PABC.

12. Program in the Bullock-Webster Collection, PABC.

13. Minute Book, BCDF, Bullock-Webster Collection, PABC.

14. Poster in the Margaret Rushton Collection, Special Collections, University of British Columbia Library.

Richard Moody 9

Theatre U.S.A., 1909–1919:
The Formative Decade _____

No decade in the history of the theatre in the United States has been so crowded with theatrical activity as the ten-year span from 1909 to 1919. No decade left such a mark on the theatre that was to follow, the theatre we know today.

There was Winthrop Ames at the New Theatre, Maurice Browne at Chicago's Little Theatre, George Pierce Baker with his famous 47 Workshop, Professor Thomas Dickinson and his Wisconsin Dramatic Society, Mrs. Lyman Gale and her Boston Toy Theatre, the introduction of the New Stagecraft with the Reinhardt production of *Sumurun*, the exhibition of New Stagecraft designs, Sheldon Cheney, missionary for the new movement, in his books and his *Theatre Arts Magazine*, the Drama League, the Neighborhood Playhouse, the Washington Square Players, the Province-towners, the Little Country Theatre in North Dakota, the Carolina Playmakers, and Little Theatres in practically every city in the country.

It was a crowded decade. Too crowded for the present space. Some of the prophets and playmakers will be silenced too quickly.

The dedication of the New Theatre on Central Park West at Sixty-Second Street on 6 November 1909 was an auspicious event in the social and theatrical life of New York. J. Pierpont Morgan sat in the center of the platform group flanked by such notables as Nicholas Murray Butler, Woodrow Wilson, George Pierce Baker, William Lyon Phelps, W. D. Howells, Thomas A. Edison, William Winter, William Archer, and Richard Gilder, father of Rosamond Gilder.

Following a series of dedicatory addresses, an ode by Percy MacKaye, a recitation of Hamlet's advice to the players by Forbes-Robertson, and a lusty rendering of "America," the celebrities retreated to the house, and the curtain went up on a final dress rehearsal of *Antony and Cleopatra*, starring Sothern and Marlowe. The dedicatory prelude turned out better than the main event. The production was not ready.

The idea for the New Theatre had originated with Henrich Conried, director of the Metropolitan Opera, and in 1905 he had persuaded a number of his wealthy patrons to undertake the project. Ground was broken in December 1906, and in September 1907, *Theatre Magazine* carried an article entitled "Who Will Direct the New Theatre?" Among those suggested were Henrich Conried, Richard Mansfield, Daniel Frohman, David Belasco, and Harley Granville-Barker. Barker was regarded as the prime candidate.

He had already been marked in London as a member of the new wave, and he and William Archer were about to issue their *Schemes and Estimates for a National Theatre* (1908). After a tour of the construction, Barker declared that the theatre would only be suitable for spectacles. He was not interested.

Someone among the founders had heard of a young man in Boston, Winthrop Ames, who had studied with Baker at Harvard, had operated the Castle Square Theatre, had just returned from a trip to Europe visiting the theatrical centers, and was about to build his own art theatre in Boston. He was literate and appeared to have good taste. Furthermore, he was wealthy and their social equal. In July 1909, Ames was named managing director with a contract to run until 30 April 1911.

Like Granville-Barker, Ames was not completely sold on the plans for the New Theatre. He wrote to the Executive Committee: "I personally feel convinced that if these dimensions are not otherwise altered now, they will be later at a greater expense; or that otherwise the theatre will become the home of opera or spectacle."[1]

Ames's objections were ignored. The founders went full-steam ahead in spite of Ames and the objections they heard from other quarters. They were proud of their magnificent Italian Renaissance structure. It would accommodate the general public, some 2,500 of them, and provide boxes and anterooms for them and their friends.

Probably the best summary account of the inauguration of the New Theatre is that provided by Walter Prichard Eaton, a college friend of Ames:

Over the orchestra pit there yawns a mighty void, wherein the voices of the actors wander tentative and dim. From the balcony not only is it a strain to hear, but the stage is so far off that it seems to be viewed through the wrong end of an opera-glass. . . . As a result of the double blunder in the original scheme, the plan to mix drama and opera in the same house and the plan to make of it a social diversion for the wealthy founders, the theatre has started on its career under a well-nigh insurmountable handicap. Gloom rested on the New Theatre, and it was not visibly dispelled on November 11, when the second drama production was made, of the light fantastic comedy by Edward Knoblach, called *The Cottage in the Air.*[2]

Of the eleven productions that constituted the first season of twenty-four weeks, only Galsworthy's *Strife* and Edward Sheldon's *The Nigger* came close to satisfying those who expected something new from the New.

During the summer, Ames and the founders took stock of the first year's experience and decided on some alterations. The upper balcony was closed off. The boxes were reduced from twenty-three to eighteen.

Still, lack of a firm policy was apparent throughout the second season. The only notable productions were those of two American plays: Josephine Preston Peabody's *The Piper* (she was a Baker student) and Mary Austin's *The Arrow Maker*. In February, the founders announced that they intended to lease the theatre to someone else and that they would build a more suitable theatre. This undertaking never materialized. Ames apparently resigned when he completed his contract at the end of April 1911, though he did take *The Piper* on tour.

Two years was a short life for such a major enterprise, but it did have "an uplifting influence," as one observer remarked. The lessons were clear, if expensive. An art theatre could not be bought with dollars. The new movement demanded a theatre that was smaller, not larger, than the usual commercial theatres.

Ames was quick to profit from the lesson. On 21 September 1911, he wrote to Baker: "Please come on early in the winter and see my 'little' theatre a-building. It's going to be a little Pullman car of a place — and most attractive I hope" (MacArthur, p. 196). It seated 299, was built on a small plot of land on the south side of West 44th Street just west of Broadway. It still stands, next to Sardi's. It was constructed in four months and opened on 11 March 1912, with Galsworthy's *The Pigeon*. During the five years that Ames operated the theatre, he produced thirteen plays, and although outside the province of the present story, it must be noted that Ames also built and operated the Booth Theatre. Another Ames undertaking does belong here. It was Ames who brought the Reinhardt production of *Sumurun* to the Casino Theatre on 16 January 1912.

The demise of the New Theatre signalled a remarkable burgeoning of theatrical activity of a new kind in other parts of the country. The Wisconsin Dramatic Society began in December 1911. Boston's Toy Theatre, the Little Country Theatre in Fargo, and the Chicago Little Theatre all began early in 1912. They had Percy MacKaye's *The Civic Theatre* (1912) to guide and support their cause and the visit of the Irish Players to inspire them. (They also had Huntly Carter's *The New Spirit in Drama and Art* to acquaint them with the latest European innovations.)

The Wisconsin Dramatic Society was organized by Professor Thomas H. Dickinson in Madison and had a branch in Milwaukee directed by Mrs. Laura Sherry. Mrs. Lyman Gale set up her Boston Toy Theatre in an old stable on Beacon Hill. She called it Toy because "toys that people make themselves, toys made of string, and wood, and anything that comes to hand, mean more to children, and are far more valuable both in educating and amusing them than the finest ready-made toys the shops afford."[3]

Alfred Arvold's Little Country Theatre operated in a chapel in the administration building of the North Dakota Agricultural College at Fargo.

There were early alternative theatres in Chicago. The Hull-House Players were organized in 1901, and when Maurice Browne arrived in Chicago in 1911, he was much impressed by their rendering of Galsworthy's *Justice*. There was a New Theatre in Chicago in 1906 directed by Victor Mapes. Like its New York counterpart, it became known as a coterie theatre and endured for a single season. Donald Robertson's Chicago Drama Players made a stronger impact in 1912.

Chicago was alive with artistic activity. These were the years of Carl Sandburg, Edgar Lee Masters, Vachel Lindsay, Maxwell Bodenheim, Ben Hecht, Alfred Kreymborg, Sherwood Anderson, George Cram Cook, and Floyd Dell. Chicago was ready for Maurice Browne and his Chicago Little Theatre.

Browne was born in England, graduated from Cambridge, and is now most often remembered for his production of *Journey's End*, although Bernard Shaw once said, "None of these things matter a tuppenny damn. The work this man did years ago on a fourth-floor back in Chicago—this is what matters."[4]

Browne met Ellen Van Volkenburg in Florence in 1910, fell in love with her, and followed her back to Chicago where she proposed to continue her career as an actress and specialist in solo performances. Browne had read Craig and had seen the Irish Players even before they turned up in Chicago soon after his arrival, and he and his wife-to-be had already begun talking about founding an experimental theatre that would deal in art rather than in commerce.

They saw all of the Irish Players productions in Chicago and talked regularly with Lady Gregory. She advised them to trust their dream and proceed: "By all means start your own theatre; but make it in your own image. Don't engage professional players; they have been spoiled for your purpose. Engage and train, as we of the Abbey have done, amateurs; shopgirls, school-teachers, cut-throat thieves, rather than professionals. . . . Strike out, my children. And God bless you."[5] They followed her advice.

Browne found quarters for his theatre on the fourth floor of the Fine Arts Building on Michigan Boulevard. The auditorium seated ninety-three. The stage was even more confining. It measured "fourteen feet across, twenty feet to the back wall and eight feet to the solid ceiling above. Stage-left, four-fifths of the way downstage a structural pillar three feet square stood like Stonehenge; except for this and a tiny toilet [they had to establish ground rules for the use of this facility] there was almost clear wing space of nearly two feet" (Browne, *Too Late*, p. 123).

With an inadequate supply of male performers—at the beginning there was only Browne—they had begun rehearsing *The Trojan Women*. When it was not ready, they turned to Wilfrid Wilson Gibson's *Womenkind* and

Yeats's *On Baile's Strand* for their opening in February 1912. *The Trojan Women* did not reach the stage until January 1913, but with this production they hit their stride and with later revivals it was to become their most noteworthy production.

In spite of Browne's frugality, they were perpetually on the verge of collapse. Anonymous donors kept them afloat. Even Bernard Shaw, contrary to his usual custom, lent a hand. When they produced *The Philanderer*, Shaw wrote, "My attention has been called to the fact that you are paying me a royalty of 6% on a house seating less than $100. This is unnecessary extravagance. I am perfectly prepared to take 5%" (Browne, *Too Late*, pp. 155–56).

In May 1917, *Theatre Arts* announced that the Chicago Little Theatre had just received an endowment for three years. Unfortunately, the subscribers did not honor their pledges, and on 7 December 1917, Mr. and Mrs. Browne announced the closing of their Chicago Little Theatre.

In five seasons, Browne had produced forty-four plays, among them *Medea*, *Hedda Gabler*, Andreyev's *The Pretty Sabine Women*, Rupert Brooke's *Lithuania*, *Candida*, *Mrs. Warren's Profession*, and Synge's *Deirdre of the Sorrows*, which they produced jointly with the Washington Square Players when they visited Chicago in February 1917. Under the auspices of the Women's Peace Party, they toured the country with *The Trojan Women*. They did forty-two performances in thirty-one cities in fifteen weeks to a total audience of 33,000.

Browne made his mark not only by what he did in the theatre, but in what he wrote about what he did and was trying to do. On 3 September 1913, in a letter to the editor of *The Drama*, published under the heading "The Temple of a Living Art, Being a Plea for an American Art Theatre," he said that he had found America "imbued with such an extraordinary sense of the dramatic, that he knew that there must be an unsatisfied demand for a new supply of drama."

In two other essays, "The New Rhythmic Drama" and "Lonely Places," he wrote in more detail about the drama, about the actor, about the New Stagecraft. "Art is founded on the recognition of reality," he wrote, "and for mankind the supreme reality is human destiny. Whence? Whither? Why?" To these questions "the tragic artists have made the same reply, unfalteringly. The whence and the whither were unknown, they said: they might be unknowable; or on the other hand they might be discovered in the fullness of time. But the why has its own response: the game for the game's sake."[6]

In directing and design, he followed Craig. He regarded *The Art of the Theatre* as his bible. Like Craig he tried to "create a place which harmonized with the thoughts of the poet." "The simple things," he wrote, "are the only ones that permanently satisfy the human soul, and the greatest master is he who uses one line where others use two."[7] In the battle for a new kind of theatre "three main issues were directly joined: stage-decoration, acting, and the play. The first battle has been won and won on the stage of the Chicago Little Theatre, by my wife and Raymond Johnson, even before Sam Hume's exhibit or Granville-Barker's 'discovery' of Robert Edmond Jones, and long before the rhinoceros-hided magnates knew that six such midges as we were biting them."[8]

Whether one credits Mrs. Dainty Pelham, Maurice Browne, Percy MacKaye, or someone else as the generator of the Little Theatre movement, the impact of the pioneers on our theatrical landscape was immediately apparent and can still be seen. Although an accurate tabulation of the Little Theatres that came into being before 1919 is probably impossible, I have encountered at least thirty in one way or another.

As Kenneth Macgowan and others have noted, these and the other art theatres had much in common with their European progenitors. They aimed to provide their audiences with plays and productions the like of which were unavailable in the commercial theatre and to provide their participants with an opportunity to fulfill their creative aspirations and to learn the arts and crafts of the theatre. Most of them limited themselves initially to one-act plays, and for good reason. This was the principal repertoire of the Irish Players. One-acts were rarely offered by the commercial theatre, and they could be more easily rehearsed, required less demanding stage facilities, and a program of short plays could employ the talents of more members of the group.

These groups were distinguished from their European counterparts in sponsoring auxiliary educational enterprises: lectures and reading programs, encouraging courses in the theatre arts in the colleges, keeping up with *The Drama*, with *Theatre Arts Magazine*, reading MacKaye's latest books and Constance D'Arcy Mackay's *The Little Theatre in the United States* (1917), Thomas H. Dickinson's *The Case of American Drama* (1915) and his *The Insurgent Theatre* (1917), and, of course, joining The Drama League.

The Chicago suburb of Evanston was home base for The Drama League, as it was for the Women's Christian Temperance Union. Evanston apparently provided an invigorating environment for ladies who wished to do good. The Drama League was founded in 1909, held their first convention at the First Congregational Church in Evanston in 1910, with 162 delegates in attendance, elected Mrs. A. Starr Best as temporary chairman, and held a constitutional convention at the Art Institute on 25 April 1910.

Sixty-three clubs were represented at this convention. A year later the League had 12,000 members in twenty-five states. By the early 1920s, they boasted of 23,000 members, 100,000 affiliated members, and 114 centers throughout the country. Their high moral stand worried some producers and critics, but there is little evidence that this fear was justified, though their moral tone and call for uplift may well have influenced the stipulations for the Pulitzer Prize when it was instituted in 1917. The prize was to be awarded to "the original American play performed in New York which shall represent the education value and power of the stage in raising the standard of good morals, good taste, and good manners."

The Drama League did wield tremendous power and most of it for the good of the theatre. In 1911, the League initiated *The Drama*, a quarterly "to cultivate a deeper understanding and appreciation for American drama and theatre," with a board of editors that included George Pierce Baker, Thomas H. Dickinson, Brander Matthews, and Stark Young. They also issued regular bulletins of advice regarding current productions through the country—some 250 bulletins between 1910 and 1916. Professor Baker, later succeeded by Brander Matthews, was in charge of devising a series of courses for the study of drama. Every year they held a convention, moving from Chicago to Philadelphia, to St. Louis, to Pittsburgh, to Detroit where their 1915 meeting sponsored Hume's exhibition of the New Stagecraft. They published twenty volumes in their Drama League Play Series, the last and final volume in 1916 devoted to the Washington Square Plays. In 1917 the national headquarters was moved to Washington. During the 1920s they expanded their educational programs with a series of summer institutes in Chicago, and in 1931, held their final convention at the Hotel McAlpin in New York.

George Pierce Baker was not only active in the national organization, he had been elected president of the Boston center on 13 March 1911, one of the strongest centers in the network. In 1912, they had 2,500 members. Baker, of course, had already begun his work at Harvard and Radcliffe. His English 47, "Technique of Drama," first tried out at Radcliffe in 1903, was later augmented with an English 47A, open to students who had shown unusual ability in the first course, and in February 1913, with the 47 Workshop where the plays could be produced.

Baker was born in Providence, had gone to Harvard, and it may have been when he heard Henry Irving speak in the Sanders Theatre that he found his calling. Right here in this audience of Harvard students, Irving had said, "there may be some who will enter the profession which I represent."[9]

Baker's playwriting course received a tremendous boost after the Broadway successes of two of his students: Edward Sheldon with *Salvation Nell* (1908) and Edward Knoblock with *Kismet* (1911). In 1912, so many students submitted acceptable one-act plays that he was obliged to increase his enrollment. He told a reporter, "Really this work of mine has been pushed ahead rather faster than I ever expected or perhaps desired. . . . I naturally shrink from being expected to turn out working playwrights every year, as has chanced to happen of late. That is too much to ask, you know. To instill in a single student, however able, a sense of the great difference between a string of episodes and a really cumulative plot, is a large order for one year, and much larger when multiplied by eighteen."[10]

In 1912, Baker acquired a large room, 30 feet by 150 feet, in Massachusetts Hall, a building that had served as a barracks for Revolutionary soldiers. Here everyone from director to stagehands cooperated in getting the "47" plays to the stage, always mindful of the wishes of the playwright.

Baker recognized, as he once said, that "no one, no system, can create a dramatist. No one can help him as much as himself. But the difficult road may be shortened for him, and above all he may be helped to help himself. That is all the 47 Workshop tries to do."[11] After a trial run, the plays were moved to the auditorium in the Agassiz House on the Radcliffe campus where they were given the stage for two rehearsals and two performances before an audience whose price of admission was a written criticism of the play. (Baker continued this practice at Yale.)

Baker acknowledged his debt to the Irish Players. "My workshop, like the many other experimental theatres throughout the country," he wrote, "would probably never have been founded had not the Abbey Theatre, under the brilliant guidance of W. B. Yeats and Lady Gregory, shown how much may be done from the smallest beginnings, if courage and wisdom assist."[12]

Probably no college professor in any discipline has had such a profound effect on the future activities in his field as Baker had, first at Harvard and later at Yale. Here are a few of the most conspicuous students, not including those already alluded to: Phillip Barry, Sidney Howard, Eugene O'Neill, Heywood Broun, VanWyck Brooks, Kenneth Macgowan, George Abbott, Donald Oenslager, Lee Simonson, Theresa Helburn, Thomas Wolfe, George Freedley, and Elia Kazan.

The best short piece about Baker is that of John Mason Brown, another student, called "The Four Georges." Brown wrote: "He never abused dramatic literature by treating it as if it had no connection with the stage. He kept it smudged with grease-paint and managed to give the impression that the desk behind which he was lecturing was surrounded by footlights."[13]

I would like to share one of my own stories about Mr. Baker. When I was playing in summer stock in Whitefield, New Hampshire, after my first year at Yale, Mr. Baker came to see us every week, and we regularly took one of our productions to his garden theatre at Silver Lake for the benefit of the local hospital. When I once played there as Percinet in *The Romancers*, Baker came up to me after the performance with some kind words about my performance and then said that he had once played the part himself, opposite Josephine Hull. "She made the professional stage. I didn't."

Further discussion will follow shortly of two Baker students, Sam Hume and Robert Edmond Jones. In the fall of 1913, one of the workshop productions was a pantomime called *The Romance of the Rose* by Samuel J. Hume with stage settings by Hume. When Percy MacKaye's *The Scarecrow* had its first production in Cambridge on 8 December 1909, Robert Benchley appeared as Captain Bugby, Gluyas Williams painted the posters, Kenneth Macgowan was stage manager, and Robert Edmond Jones played the violin in the orchestra.

College theatre productions and courses in the theatre arts proliferated remarkably during the decade. Among the leaders were Thomas Dickinson at Wisconsin who had taught earlier at Baylor where he had introduced a course in the "staging of plays" in 1902. The same year Brander Matthews was appointed Professor of Dramatic Literature at Columbia. Alexander Drummond, with James Winans, organized the Cornell Dramatic Club in 1909 and in 1912 became its director. Frederick Koch, another Baker student, worked first at North Dakota in 1905, then at North Carolina in 1918, and Thomas Wood Stevens established the first Drama Department at Carnegie Tech in 1914. This was a new concept in American education.

Perhaps no innovation appeared so new and revolutionary as the New Stagecraft, the shift from scene painting to scene designing, the dawning awareness of the visual artist's power to speak for the play.

New York was introduced to the New Stagecraft at the Casino Theatre on 16 January 1912. Ames had seen the production of *Sumurun* at the Deutsches Theater in Berlin and again in London and had persuaded Reinhardt to bring the entire German company to New York for a four-week engagement. *Sumurun* was a wordless play in nine scenes based on the Arabian Nights. The total effect, according to one viewer, was of an atmosphere impregnated with incense, and the action was so swift and convincing that one often forgot that the actors were silent. Some critics were shocked by the expanses of bare flesh and the torrid lovemaking. The *New York American* reporter (17 January 1912) thought some of the Oriental wooing came "as near justifying the ringing down of the asbestos curtain as anything which has ever been disclosed." The simple and colorful settings, however, received most attention. "They are unique," one critic wrote, "and in them the splendor and squalor of Eastern life are cleverly portrayed. They have, like the music, repellent charm, alluring and antagonizing at the same moment. . . . There is one moment when, the curtain drawn, you sit breathless with surprise. Against a deep-blue, cloudless sky is silhouetted a skyline of mosques and minarets as if a clever pair of scissors, of gigantic size had cut the picture from velvet paper and artistically placed its work."[14] It is "impressionism applied to the stage. . . . It sweeps by like a landscape— scarcely touching more than one's eyes and ears and taste for wild romance. Here is a play which is real 'play,' which sends one back into Broadway with the delightful sensation of having been away from New York."[15]

The new concepts in staging had, of course, been heard of earlier: in Walter Prichard Eaton's "The Question of Scenery" in *The American Magazine* in July 1911. Between 1903 and 1912, there were six articles about Craig in American periodicals. *On the Art of Theatre* was published in January 1912, *Towards a New Theatre* in April 1913. There had been American designs in the new manner: John Alexander's settings for Maude Adams' *Chantecler* in January 1911; Joseph Urban's *Pelleas and Melisande* at the Boston Opera House, opening six days before *Sumurun*; Livingston

Platt's experiments with overhead lighting and plastic scenes at the Toy Theatre. In 1914, Hiram Kelly Moderwell's (another Baker student) *Theatre of Today* included thirty-two illustrations of settings by Appia, Craig, Platt, Jones, and others.

After *Sumurun*, there were two other landmarks in the rise of the New Stagecraft: Samuel Hume's exhibition of the New Stagecraft and Robert E. Jones's designs for *The Man Who Married a Dumb Wife*.

Hume had just completed a Master's degree in art at Harvard and had a large studio near Harvard Square. Here he exhibited sketches and photographic prints of settings by Craig, Bakst, several of Reinhardt's designers, Joseph Urban, and Robert E. Jones from 5 to 14 October 1914. Macgowan reported that there were some three or four hundred items plus twenty-three models, ten of them constructed by Hume, and a model stage demonstrating the use of a sliding stage and the lighting effects that could be achieved against a skydome. The demonstration lasted almost two hours and "everybody sighed when it was over."[16]

Chance played a role in moving Hume's exhibition to New York on 9 November 1914 and chance led to Jones's first major design assignment. Emilie Hapgood, the president of the New York Stage Society, had intended to bring over an exhibition of the latest European stage designs but World War I made that impossible. She saw Hume's show in Boston, persuaded him to send it to New York, with Jones to supervise the installation at 714 Fifth Avenue. Emilie Hapgood was so impressed by Jones that she commissioned him to design and stage Anatole France's *The Man Who Married a Dumb Wife* to be produced by the Stage Society. When Granville-Barker came to see the exhibition, he met Jones and sat in on a rehearsal of *Dumb Wife*. He was about to open *Androcles and the Lion*, was in need of a curtain-raiser to fill out the program, and Jones's production seemed the logical choice.

Although contemporary reviewers gave the Jones costumes and setting only passing attention—one did note that the design was in the manner of *Sumurun*—photographs of the design have probably now been reproduced more frequently than those of any other stage setting. With its neatly modulated rectangles of black, white, and gray, so simple and so clean, it has become the "classic" example of the New Stagecraft.

With *Dumb Wife*, Jones established himself as Broadway's first professional scene designer, as the leading exponent of the new movement; and four months later he told a reporter: "The modern producer seeks for a synthesis of color, sound, and movement, and the artist helps him by supplying the decoration which binds the whole. . . . The desire for unity in the theatre is the kernel of the new theatre movement."[17]

Jones had begun his artistic career at an early age. In October 1904, he wrote to the *St. Nicholas Magazine*: "Dear St. Nicholas: My Badge came last night and I am more than delighted with it. I shall always keep it, and shall

9. Robert Edmond Jones's original design for *The Man Who Married a Dumb Wife.* From *Theatre Magazine,* May, 1915.

always look with pleasure to the time 'when my first picture was printed.' I mean to work hard this summer all by myself, and shall send in more drawings, even better, I hope, than the one which was printed. Thanking you again for the beautiful badge, I remain, Most gratefully yours, Robert E. Jones."[18]

After graduating from Harvard in 1910 with a major in fine arts, he stayed on for a year as a graduate instructor in art—the year W. B. Yeats lectured at Harvard on the work of Gordon Craig—and began designing costumes and stage settings. He then went to New York where he renewed his acquaintance with Harvard classmates, particularly John Reed. Reed thought that Jones should go to Craig's school in Florence, and with contributions from classmates and from Mabel Dodge organized the "Robert Edmond Jones Transportation and Development Company."

In partial payment for Reed's efforts in his behalf, Jones contributed his services as designer for Reed's labor pageant at Madison Square in the spring of 1913 in support of the silk-weavers in Paterson, New Jersey who were striking for an eight-hour day. This was Jones's first design in New York.

Jones reached Florence in July 1913, and when Craig refused to see him, for some reason or other, he joined a Dodge excursion to Paris and then to

Berlin where he called on Reinhardt. Reinhardt was more generous than Craig, liked him and agreed to let him work at the Deutsches Theater as an apprentice. Had not the war intervened Jones would probably have continued his study with Reinhardt.

The first season back in New York, 1914–15, Jones began the hectic pace he was to continue throughout most of his life. In addition to the Hume exhibition and *Dumb Wife*, he designed the first productions for the Washington Square Players and the Provincetown Players, Arthur Hopkins' *The Devil's Garden*, Percy MacKaye's masque, *Caliban by the Yellow Sands*, in the spring of 1916, and also that spring, the costumes and settings for Nijinsky's *Til Eulenspiegel*.

Some of his most notable work was done for Arthur Hopkins, the only commercial producer who was charmed by the New Stagecraft. Sheldon Cheney thought that the Hopkins-Jones *The Devil's Garden* was the best example of the new movement to reach the stage: "That simple room fairly breathed bureaucracy, the bureaucracy that was about to grip the clerk. . . . It showed the possibilities of the new art."[19]

Jones often spoke and wrote about his work. "A good scene," he said, "should be not a picture but an image. . . . It is a presence, a mood, a symphonic accompaniment to the drama, a great warm wind fanning the drama to flame. It echoes, it enhances, it animates. It is an expectancy, a foreboding, a tension. It says nothing but it gives everything."[20] Jones had a strong influence on later advances in scenic art through the publication of *Continental Stagecraft* (with Macgowan) and through the work of his apprentices, Donald Oenslager, Mordecai Gorelik, and Jo Mielziner.

Three of Jones's contemporaries were exponents of the New Stagecraft: Joseph Urban, Norman Bel Geddes, and Sam Hume, but only Hume will be discussed here.

Samuel Hume had the only direct link with Gordon Craig. He had gone to Florence from Berkeley in October 1909, and apparently struck the master when he was in a good mood (in contrast to Jones's later experience). Craig accepted him as an assistant and took him into his household. Hume swept the stage, cut out costumes, mixed paints, moved scenery, manipulated lights, and pasted together stage models, the only activity that engaged his artistic talents.

In spite of the limited opportunities Craig offered him, he regarded himself as the master's disciple and missionary when he returned to the States in the summer of 1912 to join Baker's 47 Workshop. Here he experimented with his version of Craig's screens and assembled his New Stagecraft exhibit. In the spring of 1915, Hume took the exhibition to Detroit for the Drama League convention, and here his work came to the attention of George Booth who was about to dedicate a Greek theatre at his Cranbrook estate. Hume was hired as director and designer of the masque, and this led to his appointment as designer of the new theatre for the Arts and Crafts Society and then to being its director for the opening season of 1916–17. The theatre seated 350, had an ample stage, a dome cyclorama, and lights that could achieve the plasticity envisioned by Appia.

Hume was an all-around theatre man. He managed, directed, designed, lighted, acted many of the principle roles, and chose plays that could use the flexible unit setting that he had demonstrated in his model—such plays as *Interior, The Glittering Gate, Abraham and Isaac*, and a short version of Marlowe's *Doctor Faustus* by Samuel Eliot, Jr. (The first of Sam Eliot's *Little Theatre Classics* had just been published. Four volumes were issued between 1917 and 1922.)

After the 1917–18 season, Hume left Detroit and accepted a post as Assistant Professor of Dramatic Literature at Berkeley and director of the Hearst Greek Theatre.

The Detroit theatre became more widely known than any of the other art theatres because Hume had the good fortune to find quarters in the Arts and Crafts building for Sheldon Cheney, who was about to launch his new quarterly, *Theatre Arts Magazine*. The first issue appeared in November 1916, and in 1917, Cheney's *The Art Theatre* carried sixteen photographs of Hume productions.

In 1913, Cheney had gone to Harvard to study with Baker and, although he was not accepted, he became acquainted with some of Baker's students and began writing a series of articles on the new movement for *The Theatre* and for *The Forum*. These came to the attention of Alfred Knopf and became the nucleus for his first book, *The New Movement in Theatre*, published in 1914, the same year as Moderwell's *The Theatre of Today*.

Early in 1916, Cheney met Hume on a street corner in Berkeley. They had been at the Berkeley High School together. Cheney told him about his plans for a magazine, and Hume proposed that he sound out his sponsors in Detroit about the project. They approved and provided space for Cheney.

Theatre Arts Magazine, later to be called *Theatre Arts Monthly*, was launched in Detroit in November 1916 and immediately became a house organ for the Art Theatres and for the New Stagecraft. In the foreword to the first issue, Cheney outlined his goal. The magazine was to be devoted to a new generation of artist-workers who had grown up outside the business theatre. It was to be "designed for the artist who approaches the theatre in the spirit of the arts and crafts movement, and for the theatre-goer who is awake artistically and intellectually."[21] To assist him, he had enlisted the help of a distinguished group of contributing editors: Winthrop Ames, Maurice Browne, W. P. Eaton, Clayton Hamilton, Sam Hume, Kenneth Macgowan, Percy MacKaye, Hiram K. Moderwell, and Thomas Wood Stevens.

Regularly, the magazine carried news of the Little Theatres throughout the country and repeatedly Cheney and others attempted to describe the essence of the new movement: "The synthetic ideal has to do with the attainment of that elusive quality which makes for rounded-out, spiritually unified productions. . . . To find a synthesis of all the forces of the theatre, [that] is the most typical earmark of the insurgent movement."[22]

Occasionally, Cheney opened his pages to the opposition. When Belasco told a newspaper reporter that the new art was just so much nonsense, Cheney reprinted his views. Belasco had said, "This so-called new art of the theatre is but a flash in the pan of inexperience. It is the cubism of the theatre, the wail of the incompetent and degenerate."[23]

In the August 1917 issue, Cheney printed a photograph of the Volksbühne am Bülowplats in Berlin, a theatre that had been designed by Oskar Kaufmann and opened in 1914. Cheney's caption under the picture read:

Those Germans

Now that everybody is busy showing up the barbarism of the Germans, we wish to expose their cruelty as seen in the playhouse. For many years the Germans have been building theatres so much finer than those of England and France and America that a comparison is extremely humiliating. . . . This picture shows how the German architects spoiled the playgoer by making him comfortable. . . . Any American manager could show them how to squeeze in two more rows of seats. . . .

(Remember that the United States had now entered the war!)

When I met Cheney in San Francisco in November 1978, and this ninety-two-year-old man, speaking in a whisper, told me that he had lived in San Francisco at the time of the earthquake, it was difficult to see him as the young rebel who had started *Theatre Arts* and who had written this caption.

In the next issue, December 1917, Cheney announced that their offices had been moved to 220 West 42nd Street in New York where his friend Alfred Knopf had given them quarters. He also announced that the move to New York had been precipitated by his remarks on "Those Germans." The board of the Society of Arts and Crafts had deprived them of their rooms.

When Cheney moved the magazine to New York, a number of theatres that subscribed to the new movement were flourishing in the city: The Neighborhood Playhouse, the Bramhall Playhouse, The Portmanteau, The Greenwich Village Theatre, and, of course, the Washington Square Players and the Provincetown Theatre.

The Neighborhood Playhouse, like the Hull-House group, was a community center enterprise, at the Henry Street Settlement House, organized by Alice and Irene Lewisohn, Radcliffe graduates and Baker students. On 12 February 1915, they opened with *Jephthah's Daughter*, a ritual festival based on biblical sources.

The miniature Bramhall Playhouse, a remodelled Armenian church at Twenty-Seventh and Lexington, was opened on 1 April 1915 by the actor

Butler Davenport to serve as a showcase for his talents as actor and playwright.

Stuart Walker's Portmanteau Theatre, "the theatre that comes to you," was a portable, collapsible theatre that could be set up in three hours in any hall or park. It had its first performance in early 1915 at the Christador Settlement House.

The Greenwich Village Theatre was organized by Frank Conroy and some other defectors from the Washington Square. They opened in November 1917, in a small theatre at Seventh Avenue and Christopher Street.

The Washington Square and the Provincetown ventures were both generated in Greenwich Village, drew their companies from among the painters, sculptors, journalists, novelists, poets, anarchists, and assorted bohemians who inhabited that section of New York, and initiated their excursions into theatrical production within a half-year of each other. They each began at a distance from the Village, both were to continue after the war—the Provincetown under a different management and the Washington Square reincarnated as the Theatre Guild—and each was to leave an indelible mark in their time and later, the Provincetown with the discovery of O'Neill and the Washington Square with a host of designers, directors, and actors who were to continue in the theatre.

The idea for the Washington Square Players originated with Lawrence Langner, a young patent attorney, and Ida Rauh, a former actress who was then married to Max Eastman, the editor of *The Masses*. They talked up the idea among their friends, Robert Edmond Jones, Sam Eliot, Edward Goodman, Phillip Moeller, and others, and in the fall of 1914 staged their first production, Dunsany's *The Glittering Gate* with settings by Jones, in the back room of the Washington Square Bookshop before an audience of forty. This effort sealed their resolve to move ahead. They incorporated, rented the 299-seat Bandbox Theatre at 205 East Fifty-Seventh Street near Third Avenue, and issued a manifesto which read in part:

The Washington Square Players believe that a higher standard can be reached only as the outcome of experiment and initiative. . . . We believe that hard work and perseverance, coupled with ability and the absence of purely commercial considerations, may result in the birth and healthy growth of an artistic theatre in this country.[24]

On their first program at the Bandbox on 19 February 1915, they offered three one-acts: *Licensed* by Basil Laurence (Lawrence Langner), *Eugenically Speaking* by Edward Goodman, and Maeterlinck's *Interior*. The scenes were devised by Robert Edmond Jones, reportedly at a cost of thirty-five dollars. They played only on Friday and Saturday nights, and during that first spring they offered four different bills of one-acts, including John Reed's *Moondown*, Phillip Moeller's *Two Blind Beggars and One Less Blind*, Chekhov's *The Bear*, and Andreyev's *Love of One's Neighbor*. Broadway theatregoers began to notice them even in this first season. Here was a theatre that offered a great variety of unusual plays, some even a bit shocking, plays that would never be seen on Broadway. The actors were earnest, and the scenery, though often simple, even barren, seemed always to capture the atmosphere appropriate to the play.

Their second season, beginning on 4 October 1915, was more ambitious. They gave seven performances per week, increased their admission price to $1.00, and put all workers on a $25.00 a week salary. For most of the season, they stuck to one-acts: Alice Gerstenberg's *Overtones* which antici-pated O'Neill's *Strange Interlude* in the use of stream-of-consciousness asides; *Bushido*, in which Katharine Cornell appeared in a small part; and to close the season they attempted two long plays, Maeterlinck's *Aglavaine and Selysette* and Chekhov's *The Seagull*. Most reviewers agreed that they were not yet ready for full-length plays.

They set their sights even higher for the next season. They moved to the Broadway area, settled in at the 700-seat Comedy Theatre on Forty-First Street, east of Broadway, and for two seasons alternated between bills of one-acts, O'Neill's *In the Zone*, Susan Glaspell's *Trifles*, some of their past successes, and long plays: Andreyev's *The Life of Man*, *Ghosts*, and *Mrs. Warren's Profession*. Moving into the commercial region was not all for the good. They assumed an unmanageable overhead, and their audience be-came less tolerant of their amateurish enthusiasm.

In the spring of 1918, the group announced that they were obliged to suspend operations. Too many of their company had gone to war. Cheney was not distressed by their collapse. "Their failure," he wrote, "does not bring us any sense of uneasiness over the future. The group that takes their place—and one will—should profit by their two mistakes. If it thus avoids the self-imposed financial handicap, and if it seeks first of all the best available artist-director."[25]

If the Washington Square Players lacked an artistic director, as Cheney suggested, the Provincetown Players did not. Their theatrical adventure originated in the mind of their leader, George Cram "Jig" Cook, and they were led by him through their first incarnation.

Cook was born in Buffalo, Iowa, a suburb of Davenport, in 1873, went to the University of Iowa, moved on to Harvard where he developed a life-long passion for Greek, taught briefly at the University of Iowa and at Stanford, and in 1903, returned to his native home to become a farmer. After an unhappy marriage which terminated in 1905, he met Susan Glaspell who had just returned from Paris. They lived briefly in Chicago where he met Floyd Dell and Maurice Browne and where he saw the Irish Players. Glaspell once wrote, "Quite possibly there would have been no Provincetown Players had there not been the Irish Players. What he saw done for Irish life he wanted for American life."[26] They then moved to Greenwich Village where they met John Reed, Max Eastman, Hutchins Hapgood, and others, and joined in the lively discussions about art, politics, and literature that were held at Polly's, at the Washington Square Bookstore. There was plenty to talk about: Isadora Duncan's startling new dances, *The Masses* and *The New Republic* crusading against social injustice, *The Little Review* printing installments of *Ulysses*, the Armory show of the new cubism, Steiglitz's discovery of the art of the camera, the lectures of Emma Goldman, Harriet Monroe's new magazine *Poetry*, the publication of *Sister Carrie* and *The Spoon River Anthology*.

In April 1913, Cook and Glaspell were married and took the Fall River boat to Provincetown for their honeymoon. In the summer they discovered that Provincetown was the summer outpost for the Greenwich Village crowd, so they returned the following year, bought a house, and the next summer, 1915, organized the Provincetown Players.

During their winter in New York, they had sampled the theatre and found it dull and lifeless. Nothing had moved them until they saw *Jephthah's Daughter* at the Neighborhood Playhouse. "It was full of a strong inherited religious feeling," Glaspell wrote, "it had a tribal religious feeling that was still a living thing to some of the Jews of Henry Street. That night, before the glowing grate in Milligan Place, we talked of what the theatre might be" (Glaspell, p. 250). The only other exciting theatrical experience had occurred two years earlier, when they saw John Reed's Paterson strikers' pageant at Madison Square Garden.

Glaspell and Cook had toyed with a short play spoofing psychoanalysis, and that summer when the Cooks discovered that Hutchins Hapgood's wife, Neith Boyce, had taken time out from her novel writing to try a play, Cook decided that a play-acting group might be a first step toward forming a "Beloved Community of Life-Givers."

Probably nothing more than the prospect of good fun drew the Province-towners together for their performance in the Hapgoods' rented house. Jones was on hand to help with the setting, as he had been for the Washington Square's initial effort. Boyce's *Constancy* was performed on the Hapgoods' balcony with the audience in the living room. For the Glaspell-Cook *Suppressed Desires*, audience and actors exchanged places. The bill was then repeated in Mary Heaton Vorse's studio in an old fish-house, and before the summer was out another program occupied the fish-house: Jig Cook's *Change Your Style* and Wilbur Daniel Steele's *Contemporaries*. "Thus ended the first season of the Provincetown Players," Glaspell wrote, "who closed without knowing they were the Provincetown Players" (Glaspell, p. 251).

The next summer they knew who they were. The fish-house was transformed into the Wharf Theatre, and John Reed put together a constitution and a set of resolutions. Although all members were to have a voice, the strong voice was that of Cook. His "sublime, gallant, crazy theatrical faith," his love of Greece, his dream of a "beloved-community" drew the others around him. "One man cannot produce drama," he once said. "True drama is born only of one feeling animating all the members of a clan" (Glaspell, p. 252).

In their second season, their first in the Wharf Theatre, they did some dozen programs between 1 July 1916 and 2 September. They revived *Constancy* and *Suppressed Desires*, offered new plays from the Hapgoods, Steele, Glaspell, Reed, and *Bound East for Cardiff* and *Thirst* from a newcomer. Susan Glaspell has described their meeting with O'Neill:

So Gene took "Bound East for Cardiff" from his trunk, and Freddie Burt read it to us, Gene staying out in the dining-room while the reading went on.

He was not left alone in the dining-room when the reading had finished.

Then we knew what we were for.

The sea has been good to Eugene O'Neill. It was there for his opening. There was a fog, just as the script demanded, fog bell in the harbor. The tide was in, and it washed under us and around, spraying through the holes in the floor, giving us the rhythm and the flavor of the sea while the big dying sailor talked to his friend Drisc of the life he had always wanted deep in the land, where you'd never see a ship or smell the sea. (Glaspell, pp. 253–54)

When they returned to New York in the fall, they took the Provincetown Players with them, rented an old mansion at 139 MacDougal Street, next door to the Washington Square Bookstore, converted the ground floor dining room into a stage and the living room into the house, and to inform their patrons about what to expect, they issued a circular which read in part:

The present organization is the outcome of a group of people interested in the theatre. The impelling desire of the group was to establish a stage where playwrights of sincere, poetic, literary, and dramatic purpose could see their plays in action, and superintend their productions without submitting to the commercial manager's interpretation of public taste.[27]

They opened on 3 November 1916, with *Bound East for Cardiff*, *The Game* by Louise Bryant (O'Neill was in love with her, before and after she was married to John Reed; she was later married to Ambassador William C. Bullitt), and *King Arthur's Socks* by Floyd Dell (in which Max Eastman appeared). They continued with O'Neill's *Before Breakfast*, *Fog*, and *The Sniper*, revivals of one-acts they had done on the Cape, and new plays by Boyce, Reed, Glaspell, and some newcomers.

For the second season, they offered new plays by O'Neill, *Ile*, *Long Voyage Home* (published that year in Menken and Nathan's *Smart Set*), *The Rope*, new plays by Glaspell, Dell, and Maxwell Bodenheim, and presented their first long play, Cook's *The Athenian Women*, a serious drama based on Aristophanes' *Lysistrata*.

For the season of 1918–19, they moved to 133 MacDougal. Here the ground floor space had formerly been a stable. Apparently, it was still occupied by a pungent aroma of horses and manure, and imbedded on the north wall was a hitching ring, above which John Reed inscribed "Here Pegasus was Hitched." (This was the John Reed who was to achieve his fame as author of *Ten Days that Shook the World*, for his adventures in Russia, and as the only American to be buried in the Kremlin.) Although the stage was only slightly larger than their previous stage, it was a proper stage, and in the basement they found quarters for a workshop, storeroom, and dressing rooms.

They opened on 22 November 1918 with Edna St. Vincent Millay's *The Princess Marries the Page*, O'Neill's *Where the Cross is Made*, and *Gee-Rusalem!* by Florence Kiper Frank. The season included *Moon of the Caribees*, Glaspell and Cook's *Tickless Time*, Wilbur Daniel Steele's *Not Smart*, and John Reed's satire on the Versailles Peace Conference, *The Peace that Passeth Understanding*. It was a healthy season at the box office, partly because they no longer had competition from the Washington Square.

Although Cook's name still appeared as director, on the circulars and on the programs, he had become somewhat disenchanted. There was too much internal strife, and he was hearing too much skepticism about his directorial and acting abilities. He saw little hope for his visions of a "beloved community," and he was distressed when O'Neill gave his *Beyond the Horizon* to a Broadway manager.

During this low period he wrote, "I once promised to let this theatre die rather than let it become another voice of mediocrity. I am now forced to confess that our attempt to build up, by our own life and death, in this alien sea, a coral island of our own, has failed. . . . We give this theatre we love good death; the Provincetown Players end their story here" (Glaspell, pp. 309–10).

However, in the Provincetown summer of 1920, his spirits were rejuvenated, his old enthusiasm returned, when O'Neill read him *The Emperor Jones* and asked him to direct it. (O'Neill was then living in an abandoned life-saving station, the interior of which had been decorated by Robert Edmond Jones and which was later to be occupied by Edmund Wilson.)

Cook returned to New York obsessed with *The Emperor Jones* and resolved to install a plaster dome in the theatre. He regarded it as a necessity for the proper rendering of the play. At first, the other Provincetowners dissented, but Cook's powerful insistence finally prevailed. The skydome was built, a good share of it by Cook's hand, and he engaged a new designer, Cleon Throckmorton, to do the settings. It was a triumph for Cook as a director and producer, and it initiated one of their strongest seasons, with O'Neill's *Diff'rent*, a new play by Cook called *The Spring* and closing with *The Hairy Ape*. During that season and later in the 1920s, the productions were praised for the remarkable designs of Cleon Throckmorton, another disciple of the New Stagecraft. Heretofore the Provincetown scenes, many of them devised by Zorach and by Nordfeldt, had been distinguished only by their simplicity and unobtrusiveness.

Cook's rejuvenation was short lived. One day, in the spring of 1922, Glaspell found him sitting alone in the theatre. "The curtain was up," she wrote, "the blue light he loved was on the dome. We sat there together, in that place to which he had given so much of himself, and through which so much of him was realized. At last he spoke. 'It is time to go to Greece,' he said" (Glaspell, p. 311).

In Greece he returned to writing poetry, took on the costume and manners of the natives, and when he died in 1924, "the government decreed that one of the great fallen stones from the Temple of Apollo be moved from its place to be used as a headstone" (Glaspell, p. 444).

After a year's hiatus, 1922–23, the Provincetown reopened under the direction of Macgowan, Jones, and O'Neill, and during the next six seasons, offered new one-acts by O'Neill as well as his *All God's Chillun Got Wings*, *Desire Under the Elms*, productions of *The Spook Sonata*, *The Dream Play*, *The Hand of the Potter* by Theodore Dreiser, and Paul Green's *In Abraham's Bosom*, and finally closed partly a victim of the stock market crash, on 14 December 1929, with Thomas H. Dickinson's *Winter Bound*.

The imprint of these fervent years, of this incredible decade, can be seen in the 1920s and in the years that followed at the Provincetown, at the Theatre Guild, in the Little Theatres throughout the land, in the colleges and universities, in the off- and off-off Broadway theatres, in the communal enterprises of the 1960s, and probably most notably in the new regional theatres, and in the universal acceptance, both in the commercial and noncommercial theatre, of the New Stagecraft and of the notion that all theatre artists must speak with one voice in bringing the playwright's text to life. It was a remarkable time.

Notes

1. David Edward MacArthur, "A Study of the Theatrical Career of Winthrop Ames from 1904 to 1929," Ph.D. diss., Ohio State University, 1962, p. 127.

2. Walter Prichard Eaton, *At the New Theatre and Others* (Boston, 1910), pp. 15–16.

3. F. Laruiston Bullard, "Boston's Toy Theatre," *The Theatre* 16 (March 1912), 84.

4. Quoted by Bernard Frank Dukore, "Maurice Browne and the Chicago Little Theatre," Ph.D. diss., University of Illinois, 1957, p. 1.

5. Maurice Browne, *Too Late to Lament* (Bloomington, 1956), pp. 116–17.

6. Maurice Browne, "The New Rhythmic Drama, Part II," *The Drama*, no. 17 (February 1915), 156–57.

7. Maurice Browne, "The New Rhythmic Drama, Part I," *The Drama*, no. 16 (November 1914), 629.

8. Maurice Browne, "Lonely Places," *Theatre Arts Magazine*, 5 (July 1921), 209.

9. George P. Baker, "From a Harvard Diary. Notes Made in the Eighties," *Theatre Arts Monthly*, 17 (July 1933), 515.

10. Mary Caroline Crawford, "Harvard University's School for Playwrights," *The Theatre*, 15 (May 1912), 154.

11. George P. Baker, "The 47 Workshop," *The Century*, 101 (February 1921), 425.

12. George P. Baker, "The Forty-Seven Workshop," *Quarterly Journal of Speech Education*, 5 (May 1919), 192.

13. John Mason Brown, "The Four Georges," *Theatre Arts Monthly*, 17 (July 1933), 538.

14. Gertrude Lynch, "Sumurun," *The Theatre*, 16 (February 1912), 54.

15. Arthur Ruhl, "A New Kind of Stage Magic," *Collier's*, 47 (10 February 1912), 33.

16. Kenneth Macgowan, "America's First Exhibition of the New Stagecraft," *The Theatre*, 21 (January 1915), 28.

17. Ruth Gottholdt, "New Scenic Art of the Theatre," *The Theatre*, 21 (May 1915), 248–49.

18. *Essays of E. B. White* (New York, 1977), p. 225.

19. "The Exhibition of American Stage Design at the Bourgeois Galleries," *Theatre Arts Magazine*, 3 (April 1919), 89.

20. Robert E. Jones, *The Dramatic Imagination* (New York, 1941), p. 127.

21. *Theatre Arts Magazine*, 1 (November 1916), 1.

22. *Theatre Arts Magazine*, 1 (August 1917), 167.

23. *Theatre Arts Magazine*, 1 (February 1917), 96.

24. Walter Prichard Eaton, *The Theatre Guild: The First Ten Years* (New York, 1929), pp. 20–21.

25. *Theatre Arts Magazine*, 2 (Summer 1918), 138.

26. Susan Glaspell, *The Road to the Temple* (New York, 1927), p. 218.

27. Robert Karoly Sarlos, "The Provincetown Players: Experiments in Style," Ph.D. diss., Yale University, 1966, p. 75.

The Chosen Ones:
The Founding of
the Group Theatre———————

On 8 June 1931, twenty-eight actors, three directors, with some wives, children, and a few friends left from the front of the Theatre Guild on 52nd Street in New York City for a barn and some cottages in Brookfield, Connecticut, to work on Paul Green's play, *The House of Connelly*. They were young. They had come from diverse ethnic, social, religious, and economic backgrounds, but they were now embarked on a common adventure to which they were "devoted." On the forty-fifth anniversary of their departure, the actress, Phoebe Brand, commented: "Nobody has that kind of devotion today." They felt they were the "chosen ones." They were to become the Group Theatre.

What had brought them together was a unique vision that had been articulated in a series of talks given late Friday nights after the curtain had fallen on the shows most of them were playing in. From November 1930 to May 1931, first in apartments belonging to some of them—where on one occasion chairs had to be rented from an undertaker to accommodate the growing crowd—and then in Steinway Hall, they and others had listened to Harold Clurman's fervent, fanatical oratory. "You would hear people say, 'Come and hear Harold talk,' " Ruth Nelson remembers. "It went all around town. All the youngsters were there." The inspirational force is vividly recalled by everyone who attended.

Harold Clurman, who with Lee Strasberg and Cheryl Crawford founded the Group Theatre, recorded the essential themes of these talks in *The Fervent Years*, his invaluable memoir. He had chosen, he wrote, "an almost metaphysical line which . . . emphasized the theatre's reason for being." The view he expounded to his avid audience of young performers was that a true theatre depended on "a unity of background, of feeling, of thought, of need, among a group of people." His objective was to define an approach to life "common to all members of the group" and "to establish a theatre in which our philosophy of life might be translated into a philosophy of theatre."

In exploring the founding of the Group Theatre, I have tried to find among those who took off together that June day in 1931 those links of "background, feeling, thought, and need" that brought them together. They were an extraordinarily diverse collection of individuals. Indeed, Stella Adler felt that the difference in "the personalities and background of the people in the Group Theatre was shocking." "An oddly assorted crew," Morris Carnovsky remembers them as they departed for Connecticut. "We must have regarded each other quizzically the first time . . . wondering what potency, what magic, was going to summon us into some semblance of unity."

To trace the "magic" that brought these colorful, individualistic artists to commit themselves to a collective endeavor, an act uniquely expressive of the 1930s, one has to follow a complex development in which personality, talent, theatrical ideals, social forces, and national identity are intermingled. Part of the tale of these interrelationships in the making of this American theatre is what this essay tries to tell.

The process begins in the late 1920s when the giddy joyride of the jazz age slowed down and a reassessment of contemporary American experience began to take shape. The "random rebelliousness" of the early half of the decade began to be replaced by a new concern for economics and politics. It was a period of transition from the "self-discovery and self-expression" of the early 1920s and the "social discovery and social experience" of the early 1930s. The execution of Sacco and Vanzetti in 1927 had radicalized many young artists. The pressure to participate in the social conflicts of American society undermined the earlier aloofness, detachment, and aestheticism of the artistic community. When Waldo Frank, who was one of Clurman's literary heroes in the tradition of Emerson and Whitman, "likened the contemporary American world to a jungle," and pointed out in his *Rediscovery of America* that "America needs groups," his call must have fallen on receptive ears.

The first coming together of some of those who were to become the Group Theatre occurred in 1928. Clurman and Strasberg, then fellow actors in the Theatre Guild, had been exchanging ideas about theatre. Between scenes, on walks, or over salami and eggs, they criticized Broadway and projected an ideal that they found themselves talking about as "our theatre." They decided to take some steps toward its realization by inviting a few actors—among them Morris Carnovsky, Franchot Tone, and Sanford Meisner—to work on a play entitled *New Year's Eve*, which the author, Waldo Frank, had permitted them to use. They had no immediate production plans. They rehearsed in the Riverside Drive studio of a well-to-do real estate broker, Sidney Ross, whom they were trying to interest in supporting a theatrical adventure. What they devoted themselves to was the exploration of the text as an aid to the actors' personal artistic growth, something almost completely neglected in regular productions even by the Theatre

Guild, the most artistic of the Broadway institutions. "The rehearsals themselves would constitute a schooling," was the way Clurman put it. The craft of the actor would be probed along the lines several of them had been learning from Richard Boleslavsky and Maria Ouspenskaya at the American Laboratory Theatre. Here the systematic study of acting developed by Konstantin Stanislavsky was first introduced to America along with the ideal of the theatre as a laboratory for an ensemble of players. With this new understanding of acting, they saw that they could go well beyond mere technical improvements in the skills of the actors to an intimate linking of the actor as artist and as human being with the inner life of the characters and the overall vision projected by the playwright. The actor who was required to live a role on the stage could only do so fully, they believed, if that role grew out of the actor's own life and contemporary concerns. As Clurman and Strasberg saw it, actor and playwright, directors and designers were all to work out of a common impulse. Some day, perhaps, a new theatre would come out of this vision, but for the moment the new practice was all that was promised. To this offer, Franchot Tone responded: "If you can do what you say, it'll be fine."

Later some of the same people rehearsed Padraic Colum's fantasy, *Balloon*, as part of this on-going exploration. They dreamed of going off to the country during the summer to pursue their investigations, but they were unable to find any backing for their venture. Yet they had made a start. In 1929, some of the same people plus others—Cheryl Crawford on the production team, Ruth Nelson, Eunice Stoddard, Luther Adler, and William Challee in the cast—were involved in a production of a Soviet play, *Red Rust*, offered as a special event for Theatre Guild subscribers. Clurman, at that point a playreader for the Guild, had suggested the play to Theresa Helburn for the project, which was called a Theatre Guild Studio, modeled, one supposes, on the studios of the Moscow Art Theatre. *Red Rust*, directed by Herbert Biberman, like their other early shows was a self-contained production, but the participants were feeling their way to their own sense of what they were after.

Four or five of them continued to meet informally to get to know one another and to bridge the isolation each felt. Clurman, ever the spokesman for their personal and artistic longings, identified their loneliness and lack of communication as theatre people with the greater separation among Americans generally. "People don't seem to talk to one another enough. We are separate. Our contacts are hasty, utilitarian or escapist. We must get to know ourselves by getting to know one another," he urged, and this was to become one of the basic themes of the Group Theatre.

Behind these efforts to group together lay even earlier experiences for the founders that established some of the unity on which they were to build their theatre. Clurman, Strasberg, and Crawford, as we have seen, worked together in the Theatre Guild. Clurman recalls seeing Lee Strasberg for the first time in a special performance of Pirandello's *Right You Are If You Think So* in 1925. This "intense-looking" young man with a "face that expressed keen intelligence, suffering, ascetic control," though "well cast" for the "typical Pirandello hero," in Clurman's view, "did not seem like an actor." As they got to know one another, he discovered that Strasberg was, indeed, an actor with a difference. Strasberg had already taken courses at the American Laboratory Theatre, to which he introduced Clurman, and had begun to try his hand at using what he was learning as a director at the Chrystie Street Settlement House on the lower East Side. His main fascination was with acting "upon which he seemed as concentrated as a jeweler over the inner mechanism of a watch." Clurman confessed, "I never dreamed there was that much to it."

Two major influences had shaped the ideas of the young Strasberg. He had joined the amateur Students of Art and Drama at the Chrystie Street Settlement House largely as a social activity. Introverted son of immigrant parents with no theatre in his background, he was in business as a manufacturer of ladies' hairpieces, "the human hair business," as he dubbed it. "I had no romantic ideas about myself as an actor and therefore would never have involved myself in any kind of professional activity in the hope of some ego gratification." It was reading Gordon Craig's *On the Art of the Theatre* that gave him "a sense of something worthwhile and something beyond myself. . . . Craig gave me a different conception, something to work towards, which somehow excited me."

To Craig's elevated synthesis of the theatre arts was added the spell of the performances of the Moscow Art Theatre, which came to New York in 1923. "It was not just the fine acting of the top people that was important to me," Strasberg recalls of the Art Theatre. "It was that everybody on the stage was equally real, not equally great, but equally real. When they had to come on the stage and spit, when they had to come on and hand you something, when they had to come in with a message, whatever they did, it had the same reality as Stanislavsky, Kachalov, Moskvin, or anyone else. This led me to the realization that they must have something special that they do, because all of the actors were doing it, not just the outstanding actors. Therefore it seemed to me there was something that every actor could do. What was that? That was the Stanislavsky system." Strasberg sold his business to his partner, enrolled in the Clare Tree Major School of Theatre, but soon left it for the newly organized American Laboratory Theatre. From there he went to the Theatre Guild where he had his first professional experience.

The "catalytic agent," as Clurman recalls, bringing Strasberg and himself "together with the thought of forming a theatre of our own" was the presence of Jacques Copeau in New York in 1927. Copeau, who had inspired an earlier generation of theatre innovators when his Vieux-Columbier company had performed in New York in 1917, was returning to direct his dramatization of *The Brothers Karamazov* with the Lunts for the Theatre Guild. Clurman knew and admired the work of Copeau which he had observed in Paris while attending the Sorbonne and writing a thesis on French drama. He offered to attend the Guild rehearsals to assist Copeau "when his English went dry," and wrote an article on Copeau which was used by the Guild for publicity. In turn, Clurman invited Copeau to a dress rehearsal of a production of Copeau's own play, *The House Into Which We Are Born*, then being directed by Lee Strasberg at the Chrystie Street Settlement House. Although Strasberg hardly exchanged a word with their distinguished visitor, Copeau's presence, his precepts, and his practice heartened the hopes of these two young men that the theatre they had been projecting in their conversations might become a reality.

Clurman's experience in practical theatre was fairly limited at this point. He says that he had acquired "a passionate inclination for the theatre" at age six when he was taken to see the great Jewish actor, Jacob Adler, as Uriel Acosta and Shylock. This passion was nurtured during his early years by frequent visits to this uniquely vital Yiddish theatre on the East Side immigrant section of New York, where his father was a doctor. However, his path to theatre participation was indirect. From Columbia University he went to Paris to study at the Sorbonne. Despite his admiration for Copeau and Pitoëff, he felt that theatre lacked the "significant contemporaneity" of the other arts he was enjoying with his good friend, Aaron Copland. Yet when he returned from his European liberal education looking for something to do, he eventually turned to the theatre, although his interests, then as now, "ranged beyond the theatre." His first job was as an extra in the Provincetown Theatre where Stark Young's *The Saint* was being produced by the newly reorganized triumvirate of Robert Edmond Jones, Eugene O'Neill, and Kenneth Macgowan. Here he was "touched" by the spirituality of Jones, who with Young was directing the play, but felt that Jones made no real contact with the performers. They had to call in Richard Boleslavsky to pull the production together.

After much persistent effort, Clurman was taken on as an extra by the Theatre Guild. He and Strasberg thus worked in various Guild productions, including the famous Rogers and Hart musical take-off, *The Garrick Gaieties*. They had small roles or served as stage managers. This left them time to share their growing interest in a different idea of theatre.

One who listened with especial attention to Clurman's expostulations was Cheryl Crawford. She was then "third assistant stage manager" on the production of Franz Werfel's *Juarez and Maximilian*, in which Clurman was playing several bits including a Mexican peon slouching in front of an adobe hut. Although on stage he didn't say much more than "Ugh," off stage he filled Cheryl's ears with his ideas for a theatre he and Strasberg were dreaming of. "I was very taken with it and overwhelmed by it," she recalls. She had come to theatre through acting, directing, and producing as a student at Smith College. Although no one in her "nice, normal midwestern family" in Akron, Ohio, had been in theatre, there was enough theatricality to spark her interest. Her mother had gone to the Emerson School of Elocution, her father was given to declaiming Shakespeare at the dinner table, and a stock company in Akron provided some first theatre occasions. A stint one summer in Provincetown, Massachusetts, with some of the original Players and then study at the short-lived Theatre Guild School had turned her into a professional, working for the Theatre Guild.

She recalls being very happy at the Guild where she became a stage manager, assistant to the producers, and even casting director. "But this guy, Harold Clurman, kept picking at me all the time and saying, 'This isn't what you really want to do, is it?' And he finally convinced me that it wasn't." She turned down money and advancement at the Guild because she decided that "Harold was right and Lee was right and the Theatre Guild was not really what I wanted to have in theatre at all."

With her executive ability and shrewd practical know-how, it was Crawford who convinced Clurman and Strasberg to move from talk to action. She suggested that they find actors who might be chosen to work in the permanent company of which they had spoken. She would find help at the Guild and elsewhere once people and plans were decided on. Clurman was to talk to potential members, "excite their enthusiasm, and generate the momentum that would transform what had been a somewhat vague program into a going concern." Thus, the Friday night gatherings began at which, as someone once quipped, Harold Clurman "talked the Group Theatre into existence."

Not everyone among the several hundred who came responded to the call to join a theatre expressing a collective vision and based on collective artistic and personal action. "Some were bored and baffled" by Clurman's curious "synthesis of Jeremiah and Walt Whitman." One auditor asked, "Is it a religion?" Clurman replied, "Yes." That person never came back, and the fiery proselytizer learned a lesson.

Ruth Nelson tells the following anecdote about Katharine Hepburn that captures the feel of the period, the people, and the conflict engendered by the occasion. "Katie Hepburn went to the meetings. She was a good friend of Eunice Stoddard's. [One of the original members of the Group who, like Nelson, had studied at the American Laboratory Theatre.] I had a little car, a little broken down Ford Roadster with a rumble seat. I used to go around and collect people Saturday night and we'd go up to Eunice's house. She lived in a brownstone house of her parents on 65th Street. We would go up to the third floor, which was her bedroom with a lovely fire glowing, and lie on the floor and talk about the theatre. I remember one night Katie Hepburn said: 'Well, I'm not going to join the organization. I've decided against it.' 'Why, Katie, how can you even think that way?' She said, 'I don't know. I just feel that I have to do it alone.' I'll never forget that night."

Robert "Bobby" Lewis, another of the original members, recalls that after one of the meetings in Steinway Hall when Hepburn was asked if she would like to join this theatre, she said: "Not a group, that's all right for you people, but, you see, I'm going to become a star." Lewis credits the honesty and self-knowledge we have come to associate with Hepburn rather than vanity for this remark.

Some who were already established performers did want to join. Stella Adler, for example, had been on the stage from the age of two in the company of the "acting Adlers." Her father, Jacob Adler, was the great star of the Yiddish theatre, and her mother Sarah and her several brothers and sisters all appeared with him here and abroad in a repertoire that included Shakespeare, Tolstoy, and Ibsen. Stella had played in vaudeville and on Broadway, but, as she reports, well before the founding of the Group Theatre, "I had searched for the craft of acting. . . . There was something in the air that said there was one step further that the actor could go. He could go further in using his experience and in formulating an approach that would give him a greater sense of craft in a subjective, experiential, personal way." This search brought her to the American Laboratory Theatre. It was here that she met Lee Strasberg and Harold Clurman, whom she was to marry, after a tempestuous romance that lasted through the decade of the Group Theatre. He has described her as "poetically theatrical . . . with all the imperious flamboyance of an older theatrical tradition—European in its roots—she was somehow fragile, vulnerable, gay—eager to add knowledge to instinct, spiritually vibrant. . . . " This special quality she exuded seemed to carry with it the whole tradition of her father's theatre. Jacob Adler's bold emotional acting was intended "not to amuse an audience . . . but to awaken the deepest emotions of their souls." He gave himself to roles that would express both the longings of the Jewish immigrants on the East Side and the high mission that he saw for art. In the early years of the century, the Yiddish theatre in America, as many observers have remarked, was offering major plays from the world repertoire performed by remarkable actors before a vibrant audience. For these newcomers to the "Golden Land," theatre was "a center of social intercourse . . . where the problem of their life, past and present, could be given a voice; here they would get to know and understand one another." It was surely in part this personal heritage that made Stella Adler responsive to Clurman's appeals just as it had been this very tradition that had originally inspired Clurman's own enthusiasm for theatre.

Morris Carnovsky was another who was well on his way to success when he opted for the Group Theatre. Son of immigrant parents, he too recalls the inspiration he drew from Yiddish stars like Jacob Adler when they came on tour to his native St. Louis. These "astonishingly versatile performers . . . who played with a sweep of emotion" for their special audience stirred his interest in theatre. After completing college, Carnovsky went first to Boston to the Copley Theatre where he learned "a genteel sort of behavior rather than acting." He left this behind for New York where in the next ten years, "propelled by instinct and desire, I acquired proficiency of a sort as I went from beard to beard." Six of those years were spent with the Theatre Guild. Here Carnovsky "encountered the good plays which were the Guild's great contribution" and he played fine parts in these plays as a young character actor. Although he found the acting "a cut above the acting I was accustomed to," he was "impatient in a nagging, vague way. I wasn't apparently learning anything that would nail itself down to my desire and spirit. I was possessed by idealism, even intolerance. The breeze that filled my sails . . . came from France and Russia. The names of Jacques Copeau and Konstantin Stanislavsky vibrated in the air like the harp of Memnon, irresistible and mysterious. Even without fully realizing what they pretended . . . we were drawn to them as to a promised land. It was that impulse, of course, that finally emerged as the inspiration for the Group Theatre."

Equally idealistic but coming from a totally different milieu, Franchot Tone also preferred what the Group promised to success mainly with the Theatre Guild. Son of the president of the Carborundum Company of America and like Carnovsky a Phi Beta Kappa college graduate, he was a witty, debonair man who might have played in light comedies but chose to associate himself with theatres where his intellectual concerns with economics and politics were expressed. His first New York appearances were in productions of the New Playwrights' Theatre, organized by John Dos Passos, John Howard Lawson, and Mike Gold in 1927 to stage radical plays about modern industrial life. In Lawson's *International*, the young Tone played the American hero, described as a kind of "adult Rover Boy," who "takes a stand with the exploited classes in the revolution that follows a war touched off by his own father, a reactionary business man." Seeing him in this part, Clurman invited him to participate in the first attempts to start a group, despite the fact that he found Tone "rather stiff in his role." Tone acted in the several projects of Clurman and Strasberg while playing roles in conventional productions. When invited to go off with them to Brookfield, he, like Carnovsky, was under contract to the Theatre Guild. Both were released in a gesture of support by the Guild for the revolt that was shaping up among its own young people. Tone's very upper-class parents, reflecting an old prejudice, were happier to see him in the leftish Group Theatre than in show business.

Margaret Barker, who had come to Clurman's talks with Tone, felt torn between the attractions of becoming a star and the alternative of becoming an artist who would be an instrument for a larger, communal meaning. She had acted with Tone in the *Age of Innocence* for Katharine Cornell's company and was now playing the ingenue in Cornell's highly successful production of *The Barretts of Wimpole Street*. It was, as she observed, "probably the most exciting and wonderful part an ingenue could have had at that time." She discussed the choices with Tone and others. She questioned him: "If we are asked to be part of this theatre, what would your answer be?" He responded: "If you want to be a good actress, then come with the Group. If you want to be a star, then don't." Cheryl Crawford discussing these issues with Barker over dinner one evening said: "If you want to play neurasthenic ingenues for the rest of your life, stay in *The Barretts of Wimpole Street*. If you want to be an actress, come with the Group."

How important and how trying the decision to join the Group was comes out in her recollection of the impact of Clurman's talks on her. Daughter of a dean of Johns Hopkins Medical School, she had gone to Bryn Mawr, the distinguished women's college, in the upper-middle-class tradition. She felt that in his talks Clurman "was tearing down all my romantic notions," but we felt "we had to find something. We weren't really sure what our values were, but we had enough of a common view of what we wanted theatre to be or what our theatre values were that we could come together. Harold in his strange, stuttering, overemphatic way really molded the whole group that winter."

When the time came for her to make the final decision, she went to talk with Katharine Cornell at her house one night after the show. "We talked till three or four in the morning. She asked me all kinds of questions and I talked about . . . all kinds of esoteric things that Harold had talked about that I didn't really understand. She said to me, 'Beanie, I think if I were ten years younger, it's what I'd want to do.' " Barker sent a telegram at once to say that she would join the Group.

For some, like Sanford Meisner, there was little sense that joining the Group was an "alternative to Broadway." He had been working with Clurman and Strasberg in the projects prior to the actual beginning of the new organization. For him, as he says, "it was just kind of a spontaneous move in one direction. I never had a choice, actually. I had no decision to make. Fortunately—because if it had been a decision between, you may say, the commercial theatre and the Group Theatre, it would have been too bad. If I had decided in favor of the commercial theatre, I would have been in my father's fur business years ago. I wouldn't have made it in the commercial scene. Not because of my own temperament as much as because of the way the commercial theatre operates—the type casting, the working in terms of fixed clichés."

Sandy Meisner introduced his friend Bobby Lewis, like him a trained musician, to the circle out of which the Group was to come. He, too, felt that he would not succeed as a lead actor in the commercial theatre. At the time of Clurman's talks, Lewis and Meisner were playing together at the Provincetown Theatre in Maxwell Anderson's *The Gods of Lightning*, a drama about the Sacco and Vanzetti case that was reshaping the awareness of the decade. Lewis had been an apprentice with Eva Le Gallienne's Civic

Repertory Theatre from which other Group Theatre actors had started. His delightful story of how he first met Clurman and Strasberg, who were to change the direction of his life, contrasts the intensity of their attitude to acting with the casualness of most performances. They had come to see their friend Sandy, and, says Lewis, "they saw me, too. They came backstage after the show. I don't remember what Harold said, but I'll never forget what Lee said. Lee looked at me and said: 'What were you trying to do?' I didn't know what the hell he meant. All I was trying to do was to give the best performance I knew how, and you know, I thought I was pretty good. I had gotten good notices and everything, but I could see they hated it." Yet they invited Lewis to the meetings in Steinway Hall, and he went.

When he was chosen to be one of the twenty-eight, he reports that "Cheryl Crawford asked me for ninety dollars to pay for the food for the summer. I didn't have ninety dollars, and nobody in my family had ninety dollars, and none of my friends had ninety dollars. But I knew that this was going to be the most important thing in my life." He asked the one rich man he knew to "invest" ninety dollars in his life. He did, but Lewis' salary with the Group remained so small that the man died before he could earn enough to pay him back.

This sampling from the lives of some of the original members suggests what they shared even before they committed themselves to the Group Theatre. Most had been associated with schools and theatres that stood in opposition to the Broadway "show shop." The Theatre Guild, the Provincetown Players, the New Playwrights' Theatre, the Civic Repertory Theatre of Eva Le Gallienne, the American Laboratory Theatre, and even the old Yiddish Theatre of the East Side were all organizations in which significant plays, artistic performances, community audiences, and contemporary relevance were espoused. They were associated with the artistic impulse of the earlier "new movement" that had introduced the major modern European theatre artists to America and then had encouraged the new significant American drama of O'Neill and others. Despite his criticism of some of these theatres, Clurman later acknowledged: "I was lucky in that the first people I met in the theatre world were exceptional. They were men and women of the theatre rather than mere 'show folk'." It is good to remember, by the way, that it was George Cram Cook, founder of the Provincetown Players, who had popularized the idea that a great theatre had to be based on the unity that sprang from "one shared fund of feelings, ideas, impulses."

Those who joined the Group had had the same idols—Craig, Copeau, Stanislavsky, and Boleslavsky. Some were already working in accordance with the "system" that was to shape their craft as actors and to provide perhaps the strongest binding element in their life as a group. Stella Adler observes: "We had a basic togetherness because we had this identical craft. It held us together. It made it hard to go to outside theatres where each person played differently, inspirationally. The craft fascinated the actors." The fascination had already begun to work before the Group Theatre was officially in existence.

They liked the same kinds of performances, those of the European Art Theatres they were lucky enough to see in the early 1920s—Max Reinhardt, The Moscow Art Theatre, Duse—and unique American stars like John Barrymore, Jeanne Eagels, or Jacob Ben Ami. What they did not like was the "Great White Way." Ruth Nelson recalls her first exposure to professional shows when she came to New York from California in 1927. "There were sixty-three commercial theatres running at the time. I went to the theatre every night. I couldn't get enough, and for the most part I was bitterly disappointed. It was not until I went to the Provincetown Playhouse and saw *In Abraham's Bosom* with Rose McClendon that I saw theatre that meant something to me. The theatre was filled with ladies and gentlemen, being awfully dear and oh so glamorous. I just couldn't abide it; it didn't interest me. I don't know where I got this from. But I had a very passionate notion of what the theatre should be and what I saw usually wasn't that."

Those chosen by the Group or those who chose the Group—the selection process really worked both ways—just did not fit the "Oh so glamorous" idea of theatre. Perhaps this anecdote about how they chose Clifford Odets, who was later to be their special playwright, will suggest the qualities they were looking for. "I remember this peculiar man named Clifford Odets who didn't say very much," Clurman recalls. "I felt he was a pretty bad actor. He never agreed with me because he thought he could do anything if he put his mind to it. . . . One night he wanted to walk with me and said: 'You know, I've heard ten lectures of yours and now I'm just beginning to understand what you're talking about. . . . ' When we had to decide, Lee Strasberg asked me: 'What about this Odets fella?' I said: 'Lets have him.' So he said, 'Why?' I said: 'Something is cooking with that man. I don't know what it is, whether it's potato pancakes or what it is, but what's cooking has a rich odor, a fragrance, something is going to develop from that man.' "

Although the fragrance was rich and something very important did develop from the young Odets, the chosen ones were hardly obvious theatrical types. The troupe was to transform the image of the American actor. Sandy Meisner felt that of the twenty-eight, only two might have made it on Broadway. Yet the professional theatre was their milieu unlike the amateur clubs of the workers' and peoples' theatres that were then emerging. Among theatre people they seemed somehow very untheatrical. Stella Adler, with her great personal beauty and theatrical upbringing, found herself an outsider in the crowd. In talking of Lee Strasberg, she set him down as a "fanatical, unsocial personality—untheatrical—and that made a big difference to people who had a certain theatrical flare. I had a flare. I didn't belong there."

It is hard to pin down what was so different about them. In notes made for *The Fervent Years*, Clurman himself wondered how the Group "got such peculiar, different people." Odets, for example, whom his best friend Clurman called a "peculiar duck," confessed that he "always felt homeless." His writings, he told an interviewer, were "very painful attempts to not only find my identity—not only to locate myself—but to write down the nature of neurotic illness, to try to come to some clear, objective sense of myself and my inability to handle and deal with life. They also had in them considerable ambition, which simply means a desire to be a significant writer." The Group's idealistic objectives, as Clurman has suggested, would, in themselves tend to attract "people under pressure of some kind, troubled, not quite adjusted people, yearners, dreamers, secretly ambitious."

Theresa Helburn of the Theatre Guild called them "fanatics." Going against the mainstream, on and off Broadway, they seemed somehow almost "un-American." On the fourth of July of their first summer together at Brookfield, for example, Franchot Tone, who was terribly ambivalent about his place in the company, started shooting off fireworks early in the day. He was alone in his celebration. When Carnovsky, who was playing Mozart on the victrola, as was his wont, came out and shouted: "Franchot, for God's sake, I can't stand the noise," Tone yelled back, "I can't stand your noise. . . . I am an American."

The Group, however, thought of themselves as uniquely American. Their interest was in American life; all their plays were to be new, native dramas; their whole reason for existing was to respond to what was happening to America and to themselves in the early years of the Great Depression. From the point of view of some of Tone's society friends or that of show business or even that of dominant American culture, what they were doing may have seemed un-American—and in the 1950s many were to be blacklisted on that charge—but they were, in fact, acting on a profound but often obscured impulse in American life.

It was the Depression that made it possible for this curious collection of young people to listen to that "different drummer" that has provided the rhythm for many American idealists. The need for collective responsibility became their theme in opposition to the ruthless individualism usually touted as the American way. It was the Depression that in many ways made the whole founding of the Group Theatre possible, for it did two things of crucial importance. It all but eliminated the possibility of the economic success that was the essence of the conventional American dream, and at the same time it stirred another dream. This one grew out of a reawakened national consciousness that led to a zeal for change so that as Odets was to say in *Awake and Sing*, "Life shouldn't be printed on dollar bills."

The Crash of 1929 and the failure of the economy to recover in the following two years reduced most of them and their families to hitherto unknown hardship. Clurman's father, for example, lost all his money in the stock market debacle. Those who had had little, now had less. Phoebe Brand's father was jobless and she recalls that she "didn't have any money at all." She didn't have carfare but walked the twenty blocks to the theatre in New York and the twenty blocks back. "We scrounged. I used to look through old purses to see if I could find five pennies to go downtown." Some did not themselves experience the devastating poverty that was settling on the land; indeed, some of the members of the Group came from well-to-do homes. In their very range, Clurman felt, they comprised "a perfect mirror of the Depression." Wherever they came from, they could not avoid the ugly Hoovervilles, the pathetic apple sellers, the long bread lines right on Broadway. "The world around you just wouldn't leave you alone," was the way Morris Carnovsky put it.

The more immediate economic facts of show business also could not be avoided. While some gave up jobs to join the Group, the prognosis for theatre, always a sensitive barometer not only of the audience's taste but also of its available cash, was grim. Each season from 1929 on, the number of productions on Broadway dropped. In 1929, there were some 249 shows, in 1930–31, there were 190, in 1932, half the theatres were closed, and by 1939 the number had been reduced to 80 shows. The boom that had made the expansive, varied theatre of the 1920s possible, that had, indeed, made their own beginnings in the art, little experimental theatres possible, was over. Sandy Meisner explains what in part drew him to the Group. "What else was there? There was no money. There was no making a good living. When the Depression eased up and people had somewhere to go that was more lucrative, they went."

The Group did not offer much in the way of economic security, but it was something. For the summer at Brookfield, they were just to get room and board, and some, like Lewis, obviously, even paid for their keep. In New York, each actor was to be paid as long as any Group Theatre production was running. The scale was based on the actor's need and his usefulness to the ensemble. The salaries ranged between $30 and $140 a week for the season. Morris Carnovsky and Franchot Tone, still under contract to the Theatre Guild, got their Guild salary of $300 a week, but this was later reduced for greater equality in the company. The directors got $50 a week and a share of the $1,500 director's fee for each show. In order to pay these salaries and to mount their first production, Cheryl Crawford scrounged for contributions. The major funding came from the Theatre Guild under whose auspices they were to do their first show; among other contributors were Maxwell Anderson, Edna Ferber, and Eugene O'Neill.

A great deal more than economic determinism, however, was involved in the founding of the Group, although this aspect cannot be overlooked. As they were organizing themselves that spring and summer of 1931, there was little discussion of the Depression or of politics. Ruth Nelson captures the mood of these young people and—judging from studies of the early days of the Depression—the mood of many in the country. "We didn't really know the Depression was on. We always lived on nothing. I could put aside

10. The Group Theatre, Brookfield, Connecticut, summer 1931. Photograph by and courtesy of Ralph Steiner.

twenty dollars a week and take care of groceries and all the bills. We didn't know there was a depression; we were inspired with the theatre."

It was through their idea of theatre, through their way of working, through the renewed idealism of the time that they became most fully aware of themselves and of their era. While many in the 1930s came to art through their social awareness, the Group came to "social consciousness through their art." Their theatre, Clurman told them in his talks, had to say something not only in individual productions but in a series of productions that would mark its whole career. "A theatre could not be one thing one day, another thing an other day." It had to have variety, but had to convey "some sense of life which is typical of it as a collective." Clurman wanted their theatre to have the same sort of "conscious sense of life" he identified in all the other arts. Theatre with a meaning, he was to feel, was one of the Group's unique contributions.

That meaning, however, was not a simple slogan or even a philosophy. It was to come out of the kind of people they had chosen and how they were to work together. Morris Carnovsky reveals the road they traveled to the kind of social awareness and commitment that was to mark their theatre:

We were ruthless in tearing ourselves apart in order to build ourselves up again. . . . If we were finished actors when we came to it, the Group unfinished us. It forced us to examine all that we were and had attained in the light of a harsh insistence on basic truth. "Be afraid to lie," says Michael Chekhov, and we took these words literally. By examining ourselves anew we were compelled to become painfully aware of the world we lived in. For it was not only ourselves that seemed out of touch with reality and with truth, but the very world that made us. We of the Group can never forget that we were born as a group in the Thirties, at the time of the Great Depression. We saw visible signs of it all around us, and since the experience of being a Group actor was intimately and organically bound up with the world we lived in, it followed with varying intensities of belief, that through our work we must effect, even change, that world.

For these mostly middle-class young people, a number of them children of immigrants or native idealists, the Group offered a collective life in place of the now-impossible and also rejected dream of individual success. As artists they would no longer be condemned to the usual isolation; they would have, for a while at least, a home. "People were so good to one another," Phoebe Brand reminisces, helping out with food, clothing, and money. Later in the worst days of 1932–33, most of them were to live together in an old brownstone on West 55th Street. It was sometimes known as "Groupstroy," on the Russian collectivist model, or more familiarly and realistically, as the Group "Poorhouse." The intimacy of their life-style, their rehearsal process, and the resulting productions were to intensify both their collective identity and the conflicts engendered by working in this way in a theatre and a society that remained highly individualistic.

The whole process was to be a painful one. Later Clurman was to say that "we are the only theatre which recognized the possibility of pain and failure in the course of our work." Stella Adler when asked what she recalled most vividly about the Group experience, replied: "Trouble, conflict, lack of peace and quiet." The conflicts they were personally living through were to become the major themes of their plays. They were living a uniquely American experience that highlighted "the tragedy of choice" among crucial competing values. The ambivalence that many felt about this tension is captured in a joke Clurman once told. A Jew says to God, "Are we the chosen people?" When God says, "Yes," the Jew responds, "Then choose somebody else."

Yet the rewards, both immediate and long run, were to be great. Despite her pained recollections, Stella Adler acknowledged the profound advantages, especially during the Depression. "The aspect of togetherness; the security of not just wandering into a production. . . . It was that kind of inspired moment where the actor responded to the social situation, to the group quality of not being alienated or alone." Ruth Nelson, who felt her personal career suffered in the Group Theatre, could yet say when it was over: "Working together with a group of like-minded people, working for a common goal outside of themselves, going together, suffering, and having joy together; it was a life experience that was very deepening and enriching. Nothing can compare with it."

Working together engendered a vital creativity in them all. Mordecai Gorelik, who contributed the important scenic images for many of their productions, had many differences with the leaders and the organization, of which he was never made a regular member. "Why did I want to be part of the Group if I had these many quarrels with them?" he wondered recently. "Well, the work was unique. It was the only place in America where there was organic theatre created. The Group productions were important statements to the audience and they were made by everybody working on the production. My designs for the Group were never just added to the play; they grew organically as part of the whole consideration of the direction of the play."

The plays themselves were part of this "organic" approach. It is important to recall that the play choices and later their own playwright, Clifford Odets, came after the Group was formed. Clurman had not lured them by promising specific parts or even specific plays. Those choices would come later. They were not going to be like the Theatre Guild, which Clurman criticized because "they had no blood relationship with the plays they deal in. They set the plays out in the show window for as many customers as possible to buy. They didn't want to say anything through the plays, and plays said nothing to them, except that they are amusing . . . or that they were 'art'."

Once they decided to go ahead with their organization, Cheryl Crawford convinced the Theatre Guild to give them Paul Green's *The House of Connelly* to work on. During the summer rehearsals at Brookfield, full of that special combination of conflict, tension, and loving creativity that was to mark their life together, they called on Paul Green to rewrite the ending of his play. At their urging, he turned his tragedy of Southern plantation life into an up-beat drama of potential social change since it was their objective "to affirm life." Thus, when *The House of Connelly* opened on 23 September 1931, at the Martin Beck Theatre as the first Group Theatre production, it spoke with their collective voice. However, that must remain part of the larger story of their relationships to authors, to backers, to audiences and critics as well as to one another during the ten years of their extraordinary existence as a theatre.

Here we have only been concerned with how they got started. As they packed wives, children, victrolas, and radios into a caravan of cars—and even got Bobby Lewis and his cello into Margaret Barker's rumble seat—Clurman's impassioned rhetoric must have been ringing in their ears. "We are people who want to act, but today there are a number of interferences with this simple human desire to act, to present fiction with our bodies. Therefore we have to fight for our theatre. Our theatre is one clear, strong, definite expression of the meaning of our life, which is also the life of our families, of our city, of our state, of our United States, of our world."

A Note On Sources

The essential document of the Group Theatre is Harold Clurman's *The Fervent Years*, originally published in 1945 by Alfred Knopf. The basic information about the people, the chronology, and the history of the theatre comes from this invaluable theatrical and cultural history. Central as Clurman's book is to any study, it is one man's view of what was a group endeavor. In my research, I have undertaken to find out what the experience meant in the lives of the other members. *Reunion: A Self-Portrait of the Group Theatre*, originally a special issue of the *Educational Theatre Journal*, 1976, is a collection of interviews I have published from my researches which I hope will result in a study of the careers of the major members of the Group Theatre.

In this paper on the founding of the Group Theatre, those quotations in the early section attributed to Clurman come mainly from *The Fervent Years*. Most of the quotations from other participants and many from Clurman are in *Reunion* or come from unpublished interviews and sources. The main papers of the Group Theatre are in the Theatre Collection, Library of the Performing Arts, Lincoln Center, New York.

I am grateful to the National Endowment for the Humanities for its assistance in my on-going research on the Group Theatre.

Bibliography

Adams, Cindy. *Lee Strasberg, Imperfect Genius of the Actors Studio*. New York: Doubleday, 1980.

Berkson, Michael A. "Morris Carnovsky: Actor and Teacher." Ph.D. diss., University of Illinois, 1975.

Brenman-Gibson, Margaret. *Clifford Odets: American Playwright; The Years from 1906 to 1940*. New York: Atheneum, 1981.

Clurman, Harold. *All People Are Famous*. New York: Harcourt, Brace, Jovanovich, 1974.

Clurman, Harold. *The Fervent Years*. New York: Alfred Knopf, 1945.

Chinoy, Helen Krich. *Reunion: A Self-Portrait of the Group Theatre*, reprinted from *Educational Theatre Journal*, December, 1976, Drama Book Specialists.

Chinoy, Helen Krich, and Toby Cole. *Actors on Acting*. New York: Crown, 1980.

Chinoy, Helen Krich, and Toby Cole. *Directors on Directing*. New York: Bobbs-Merrill, 1963.

Crawford, Cheryl. *One Naked Individual*. New York: Bobbs-Merrill, 1977.

Garfield, David. *A Player's Place: The Story of the Actors Studio*. New York: Macmillan, 1980.

Gasper, Raymond D. "A Study of the Group Theatre." Ph.D. diss., Ohio State University, 1955.

Goldstein, Malcolm. *The Political Stage*. New York: Oxford University Press, 1974.

Hethmon, Robert H., ed. *Strasberg at the Studio*. New York: Viking, 1975.

Himelstein, Morgan Y. *Drama Was a Weapon*. New Jersey: Rutgers, 1963.

Lewis, Robert. *Method or Madness*. New York: Samuel French, 1958.

Murray, Edward. *Clifford Odets: The Thirties and After*. New York: Frederic Ungar, 1969.

Williams, Jay. *Stage Left*. New York: Scribners, 1974.

Willis, Ronald A. "The American Laboratory Theatre, 1922–1930." Ph.D. diss., University of Iowa, 1968.

Don B. Wilmeth   **11**

The Margo Jones Theatre ──────────

It has been more than thirty years since the first performance of the
Margo Jones Theatre in Dallas in 1947 and more than twenty since the
organization collapsed in 1959, four years after Margo Jones's untimely and
tragic death at the age of forty-one.[1] No other regional theatre of the past
fifty years had more influence on the movement toward decentralized
professional theatre than did this small arena playhouse in Dallas.[2] In the
best sense, Margo Jones fought the battles and pointed the way for many,
long before it became fashionable to have a professional theatre in your own
urban backyard.

The Margo Jones Theatre, which began officially as Theatre '47 in June
1947, made a number of significant contributions to the American theatre.
It was the first professional nonprofit repertory theatre in the United States
to use arena staging as its sole method of production (at least until after
Margo Jones's death), although arena staging as a production medium in the
United States dates from 1925, when Gilmore Brown and Ralph Freud
created The Playbox, an adjunct to the Pasadena Playhouse, and began to
become popular after Glenn Hughes founded the Penthouse theatre in 1940
at the University of Washington. None, however, had been successful at
operating a professional arena stage until Miss Jones's effort. The Margo
Jones Theatre, moreover, was unique in presenting primarily new scripts
and classics in a city 1,500 miles from New York City. Discounting the
arena staging method used by the theatre, this distinction alone would be
reason enough to include the operation prominently in the annals of the
American stage.

The moving force behind the creation of this theatre, Margo Jones, was
the managing director of the theatre until her death in 1955. There is no
doubt that the success of the Dallas endeavor was largely due to her energy
and enthusiasm. A native Texan, Jones was obsessed with the theatre and
"prone to sudden vast enthusiasm that in a pinch became messianic convic-

tions."[3] Somewhat prematurely perhaps, she was called "The Margaret Webster of this American generation."[4] Fortunately, despite her idealism, she possessed an uncanny talent for raising money. George Sessions Perry, Texas author and close friend of Margo Jones, has left a vivid description of this side of her personality:

[T]rim as a ballerina, jumping with ideas, [she] has a way of rolling up her sleeves and getting things done. She is that unusual item, a genuine priestess of the theatre who can, in its behalf, also squeeze eleven dimes out of a dollar.[5]

John Rosenfield, the late drama critic for the *Dallas Morning News*, noted that "no one was ever disposed to turn Margo Jones down in anything. She was modest in her requests and courteous about them."[6] After the theatre had survived half of its first season, he wrote in his column on New Year's Eve 1947 that she had the kind of persistence that could "conquer worlds or steel plants," and could accomplish about anything. An interviewer once observed, "Her energy and enthusiasm for the theatre rise up and over-whelm one. There are no single impressions, but masses of them."[7]

Margo Jones described herself as an optimist, adding that anyone who planned to go into theatre work needed to be one. She believed that if a person had "talent and stamina," there would be a place for him or her in the theatre despite statistics on unemployment. She constantly stressed the impor-tance of a positive attitude. The word "discouragement" went out of her vo-cabulary when she went into the theatre; in its stead, she substituted the word "problems," which to her were interesting because they had to be solved.

Although Margo Jones ran her theatre "somewhat more autocratically than Catherine of Russia," as Rosenfield pointed out, she still believed strongly in the creativity of theatre artists. Her enthusiasm and positive attitude were an inspiration to those with whom she worked. As director of her theatre in Dallas, she always gave the actor a chance to be as creative as possible within the framework of her interpretation of the play.

She revered the playwright and in turn the playwright idolized Miss Jones. William Inge, typical of those who owed much to Margo Jones, expressed the playwright's adoration: "I probably loved Margo. She was always willing to give of herself to the writers she believed in. She could always find time to encourage one, to help him believe in himself again."[8] Her greatest desire was to create beautiful theatre, largely by discovering new playwrights, and to shout to all the world the need for professional theatres all over the country. She believed that every city with at least seventy-five thousand people should have a theatre of its own, a profes-sional theatre that could produce the best drama in the most imaginative way. Thornton Wilder, writing to Jones on 19 January 1950, called her a "Divining Rod for American drama . . . a fighter, a builder, explorer, a mixer of truth and magic."[9]

To the critic, she was one who never bickered over critical comment, and she avoided arguments except in the fine fun of bullfest. Rosenfield attested to this in the *News* of 31 July 1955: "To know that anybody was seriously angry with her caused her more pain than any issue involved." She expressed her own attitude in a letter to her parents, Mr. and Mrs. R. H. Jones, on 25 May 1951: "It's impossible to have friction if one pays no attention and really doesn't mind. People have been so good to me and written so many kind things that the other little remarks simply fade away."

Brooks Atkinson, an early encourager of Margo Jones's talent, summed up her personality: "Everyone agreed on one thing about Margo Jones. She was a dynamo. She was a vivid woman. She energized everyone and everything she came in contact with."[10] Indeed, it was Margo Jones's ebullience, her capacity to get things done in a hurry, her hunches, and inspiring leadership that made possible her success in Dallas.

Despite successful forays into the theatre world outside her home state of Texas, including the co-direction of Tennessee Williams' *The Glass Menagerie* in Chicago and New York, stints at the Pasadena Playhouse and the Cleveland Playhouse, and the direction of two plays on Broadway (*On Whitman Avenue* by Maxine Wood in 1945 and Maxwell Anderson's *Joan of Lorraine* with Ingrid Bergman in 1946), her dream always, first and foremost, was to establish a permanent professional theatre in Texas.

After serving as an assistant director to the Federal Theatre project in Houston in 1935, Margo Jones became director of the Houston Community Players for six years, beginning with the 1936–37 season.[11] It was during her work in Houston that she became interested in producing new scripts, the first of which was seen during the 1938–39 season: *Special Edition* by Harold Young, the city editor of the *Houston Post*. In 1940, she produced a new musical by Cy Howard entitled *Howdy, Stranger* and in the 1940–41 season, a musical by Howard and Robert Shannon, *Going Up*. It was also during her association with the Houston Community Players that she was first introduced to arena staging. In the spring of 1939, as a member of the executive committee of the National Theatre Conference, she attended the first national convention of the Confederacy of American Community Theatres in Washington, D.C. There she saw a production of a Rachel Crothers' comedy by the Blue Room Players of Portland, Oregon, a group formed by a disciple of Glenn Hughes, the director of theatre at the University of Washington. It was performed in a hotel ballroom without scenery and with the spectators sitting in chairs on four sides. On her return to Houston, Margo Jones initiated a series of performances at various hotel ballrooms "in the round."[12]

With the outbreak of World War II, it became difficult to maintain the Houston Community Playhouse. Subsequently, she became an instructor in drama at the University of Texas in Austin from 30 October 1942 to June 1944. During this period, she directed a number of original scripts, both at the university and at the Pasadena Playhouse and the Cleveland Playhouse, and was drawn more and more to the discovery and production of new plays.[13] She was also conceiving a plan to manage a professional repertory theatre of her own dedicated to the new play. In August 1944, she wrote to Gilmore Brown describing her conception and initial actions. Since the State of Texas had no theatre then presenting an entire season of plays, other than colleges, she pledged to establish her theatre in her home state. A chance meeting with John Rosenfield led her to choose Dallas as its site.

In her book, *Theatre-in-the-Round* (p. 52), Jones explains that Dallas filled all her requirements:

It is practically in the middle of the country; it is in a new, fresh, rich, pioneering part of the nation, it is a city already rich in theatre tradition; it had always been a good road town; there were many sincere theatre lovers there who were anxious to help; I had gone to school near Dallas [Texas Women's University in Denton] and had worked there; it was my home territory; Dallas at that moment was without a theatre of any kind and wanted one very badly. It was a logical choice for me.

In order to pursue her dream, Margo applied to the Rockefeller Foundation for a grant. Funding for a ten-month period was given, according to David Stevens, then Director of Humanities for the Rockefeller Foundation, "based on what we presume to be an essential study plan for contact with important places, rather than to sustain the operating plans of the Dallas theatre, except indirectly."

After extensive travelling throughout the country, investigating theatre operations and consulting with experts, and reading and re-reading plays and books on the founding of theatres and recent movements in the theatre (she was most taken by Robert Edmond Jones's *The Dramatic Imagination* and Sheldon Cheney's *The Art Theatre*), Jones was more determined than ever to establish her ideal theatre.[14] Officially, the theatre was founded in 1945, although problems in raising funds and locating an adequate theatre space, plus the interruption in 1944 caused by her involvement with *The Glass Menagerie*, postponed for a time an opening date.[15]

For a span of two years, before any performance in her Dallas theatre, the organization passed through its most trying period. It was a time of consequential decisions. From February 1945 to May 1947, the organization was officially chartered, a theatre building was located (a small stucco, glass, and brick air-conditioned building which had been constructed in 1936 at a cost of $110,000 by the Magnolia Petroleum Company as a miniature theatre for the projection of motion pictures and the display of exhibits on the State Fair ground), a financial campaign was terminated, and all pre-opening plans were completed.[16]

Margo Jones's theatre, which was to be called Theatre '45 and to change yearly "into infinity" (inspired by a pre-Nazi and pre-war experimental theatre in Prague), was founded with the following aims: to create a civic-sponsored, permanent, professional, repertory theatre, with a permanent staff of the best young artists in America; a theatre that would be a true playwright's theatre; a theatre that would give the work of young playwrights a chance to be seen; a theatre that would provide the classics and the best new scripts with a chance for good production; a theatre that would be financially solvent without depending on extensive subsidies; and a producing organization that would help break down the centralization of the American theatre. Margo Jones was amazingly successful in each instance.

Formed as a civic nonprofit organization, the theatre was able to obtain community support from the beginning. This was first illustrated in 1945, when $40,000 was contributed by Dallasites to the young project. It was necessary, however, at various times during the history of the Margo Jones Theatre, especially after its founder's death, to accept contributions from Board members in order to meet small deficits or to pay for needed building expenses.

The theatre's board, composed of local leaders, gave Miss Jones a free hand and unquestioning support. They allowed her to make all decisions affecting the operation of the theatre. During her management, the Board never interfered with its operation. After her death in 1955, however, the Board began to take on more power and to give less to the managing directors. Succeeding directors had less freedom in creating policies that were in accordance with their own theatre philosophies. The Board felt that the theatre could continue basically as it had under Margo Jones, although they gradually changed the policies until few of the original aims were left. The result was that there were no clear-cut policies.[17] As a series of managing directors came and went, less emphasis was placed on the production of new scripts and more was placed on popular successes. The theatre's organization was no longer unique. In view of the unstable conditions at the Margo Jones Theatre (its new name after her death) from 1957 through 1959, created by weak leadership, it seems reasonable to conclude that the years of true significance and influence were those of Miss Jones's management and the first two years thereafter.

Margo Jones intended her operation to become permanent, and after the 1949–50 season, there was little doubt that the organization had proven its stability. As a permanent, professional theatre, it offered unusual opportunities for young theatre artists. It provided stability for the actor and technician alike, and a proving ground for their talents. In the latter capacity, the theatre was very successful. Actors and technicians who gained training at the Margo Jones Theatre discovered that their experience was a boon to their professional careers. Young actors found their work there so helpful to their careers that few stayed for more than one or two seasons. The list of actors who later gained substantial professional reputations or at least continued to work in professional theatre with some degree of success is a lengthy one. Of the 300-plus actors who worked there, the following could be singled out as typical: Jack Warden, Tod Andrews, Mary Finney, John Hudson, Peggy MacCay, Peter Donat, Rex Everhart, Ray MacDonnell, Clu Gulager, Charles Braswell, Larry Hagman, Rosemary Harris, George Mitchell, and Louis Latham. Others, already established before coming to Dallas, added valuable experience to their training. Only a few actors returned for a second season, although a nucleus always came back. A small number of actors who worked there four or more seasons were such familiar figures to Dallas playgoers that they became household names. There were fewer changes in the production staff. Several staff members were with the arena theatre throughout its history. A complete change, in fact, did not occur until the organization moved out of its original home into a converted motion picture theatre (the Maple Street Theatre) in 1959–60, its final season.

Jones intended her theatre to operate as a repertory company and attributed her success to the practice of allowing each play a limited run, regardless of popular acceptance. Only two plays had extended runs, Owen Crump's *Southern Exposure* in 1950 and Lawrence and Lee's *Inherit the Wind* in 1955. Her original system was to repeat after the opening basic run of each play each of the plays that had preceded it and then to devote the last few weeks of the season to a repertory festival of the season's most popular plays. After the first year, plays were rarely repeated during the season, but the season did conclude with a repertory festival on nine occasions. Only once was a play performed during two seasons. Since the acting company changed each year, it was almost never possible to carry productions over from one season to the next. After Miss Jones's death, the repetition of plays during the season and the repertory festival at the end were all but eliminated. This was caused first by the conditions immediately after her death, which made it impossible to obtain a permanent company for the 1955–56 season. Later, guest stars could not be retained or brought back after the original run and repertory repeats were impossible. This also eliminated one of the theatre's significant features—a permanent company without guest stars.

Margo Jones's major aim was to create a true playwright's theatre, dedicated to the production of new plays and classics. She made a point to read at least one new play a day and kept detailed notes on all scripts read. During its twelve-year existence, her theatre produced 133 plays, eighty-six of which were new, approximately 65 percent of the total. During Margo Jones's management, 70 percent of all the plays produced were new plays.

The selection of a play was based on its quality and, admittedly, its appeal to Margo Jones, who felt that in a theatre like hers, which was nonprofit, she could afford to take chances on new scripts, even if they were unsuccessful, in order to encourage the playwright and to give him or her an opportunity to see the play in rehearsal and performance. Not even Miss Jones's most

11. Margo Jones and an unidentified cameraman. From the collection of Don B. Wilmeth.

ardent admirer attributed perfect taste or infallible judgment to her play selection. There is no doubt that upon occasion she made very poor selections and seemed to reflect less than ideal judgment. Furthermore, in rehearsals, she was often unable to correct or shape a script. This was also her greatest directorial weakness. However, in surveying her productions, one finds that only a small handful were complete failures. The least popular new plays at the box office were Vivian Johannes' *Skaal* (1949), Sari Scott's *An Old Beat-Up Woman* (1949), Shirland Quinn's *Here's to Us* (1948), Edward Caulfield's *The Blind Spot* (1952), William McCleery's *A Play for Mary* (1950), Anna Marie Barlow and S. Brooke White's *Cold Christmas* (1955), Gene Radano's *The World Is Yours* (1955), and Carl Oglesby's *Season of the Beast* (1958). The Dallas critics were least receptive to these, and also to Barnard C. Schoenfield's *The Summer of Fancy Dress* (1955), Patricia Joudry's *The Sand Castle* (1956), Violet Welles's *The Spring Affair* (1956), and Samuel R. Golding and Norbert Faulkner's *The Most Fashionable Crime* (1957). It should be noted that a large number of these were produced after Margo Jones's death. On Broadway for the same period, approximately 78 percent of the total productions of new scripts were failures at the box office. One must remember, though, that the Dallas audience tended to be less critical of a new play than the New York audience, and certainly an entirely different scheme of economics was involved.

Among the most popular plays at the Margo Jones Theatre were Loren Disney and George Sessions Perry's *My Granny Van* (1950), Owen Crump's *Southern Exposure* (1950), Frank Duane and Richard Shannon's *Walls Rise Up* (1951), A. B. Shiffrin's *The Willow Tree* (1951), Irving Phillip's *One Foot in Heaven* (1951), Rosemary Casey's *Late Love* (1953), Lawrence and Lee's *Inherit the Wind* (1955), Dorothy Parker and Ross Evans' *The Coast of Illyria* (1949), John Vari's *Farewell, Farewell, Eugene*, Richard Reich's *The Tin Cup* (1957), and Paul Vincent Carroll's *The Devil Comes From Dublin* (1957). Eleven of the plays that had premiere productions at the Margo Jones Theatre were later produced on Broadway: William Inge's *The Dark at the Top of the Stairs* (produced in Dallas in 1947 as *Farther Off From Heaven*); Tennessee Williams' *Summer and Smoke* (1947); Joseph Hayes's *Leaf and Bough* (1948); Crump's *Southern Exposure*; *Twilight Park* (*The Willow Tree*); *Late Love*; *Inherit the Wind*; *Farewell, Farewell, Eugene*; Eleanor and Leo Bayer's *Third Best Sport* (1956); and Katherine Morrill's *A Distant Bell* (produced in Dallas in 1958 as *And So, Farewell*). This was an average of almost one a year for the life of the theatre. At least half of the other plays had later productions elsewhere. The operation was, in any case, a true showcase for the young playwright and helped to introduce some of America's most successful playwrights, such as Tennessee Williams, William Inge, Ronald Alexander, Joseph Hayes, Sigmund Miller, Jerome Lawrence, and Robert E. Lee, as well as several European plays by such significant authors as Sean O'Casey (*Cock-A-Doodle Dandy*, 1950), Bridget Boland (*The Prisoner*, 1956), Paul Vincent Carroll (*The Devil Comes From Dublin*), James Bridie (*Mr. Gillie*, 1956), and Maura Laverty (*Tolka Row*, 1956).

It is notable that the production of new plays became more than experimentation and drew an enthusiastic audience. Playgoers were always aware that they might see a poor play, but the prospect of a completely new theatrical experience lured them. They accepted the new play, according to Rosenfield, with a strange blend of interest and tolerance.[18]

The production of classics (both those plays over fifty years old and later those termed "modern classics" by the management) was also a major aim of Margo Jones. These were almost invariably popular and contributed culturally and educationally to the community. Ten plays by Shakespeare; eight by Bernard Shaw; three by Molière; two each by Henrik Ibsen, Oscar Wilde, and Anton Chekhov; and one each by Oliver Goldsmith, August Strindberg, Richard Brinsley Sheridan, Ben Jonson, and Royall Tyler were presented. Modern plays by Somerset Maugham, Tennessee Williams, Lynn Riggs, Eugene O'Neill, Agatha Christie, Ring Lardner, Terence Rattigan, and Jean Giraudoux were produced. Shakespeare, Molière, Ibsen, and Shaw were always very popular with both the public and the critics. Of the classics, only *Othello*, the last production at the Margo Jones Theatre (in the former Maple Street Theatre), was unsuccessful. The only other classic that was not well received by both the critics and the patrons was *The Glass Menagerie* (1957). Among the most popular classics were *Hedda Gabler* (1947), *She Stoops to Conquer* (1949), *The Importance of Being Earnest* (1948), *Twelfth Night* (1948), *Ghosts* (1950), *The Father* (1952), *The Merry Wives of Windsor* (1954), *Misalliance* (1955), and *School for Wives* (1956).

Margo Jones believed that any type of play could be produced effectively in the arena theatre. Certainly, the productions listed above support this contention. She admitted that certain plays were more effective than others in this configuration, but said that with imagination any play, no matter how complex the production problems, could be staged in arena either by using simultaneous settings or by changing settings between scenes or acts. She found that many staging problems could be solved by simplifying the settings, and that if the dialogue or the actor could suggest a piece of scenery or property, the audience would believe that it was there. She felt that the lack of theatrical illusion was compensated for by the intensified audience participation and the demand on the imagination created by the intimacy of the theatre.[19] Except on rare occasions, her audience accepted the arena convention completely. As the most celebrated home of central staging in the 1940s and 1950s in the United States, the Margo Jones Theatre inspired many organizations to emulate its staging methods.

During the first four seasons, the critics praised the theatre for its imaginative productions, singling out especially the contribution of costumes and properties. For several years thereafter, both the costumes and properties were commonplace. From 1953 until the move into the Maple Street Theatre, more attention was given to the settings, but an examination of production pictures shows clearly that the imaginative level of the first few seasons was never achieved again.

From the very beginning, Margo Jones believed that a professional theatre outside of New York could sustain itself financially with little or no subsidy. Since her theatre was established as a nonprofit organization, it never attempted to build profits. The unusual financial solvency of the operation was due to Margo Jones's ability to gain economic support from Dallasites, to the interest aroused in the Dallas playgoer for the production of new scripts, and to the relatively low production costs in the arena theatre. Margo Jones never considered arena the ideal theatre form, but she found it advantageous to continue in the small theatre rather than to build a larger, conventional playhouse. While in the arena, the organization was able to depend solely on ticket sales for operating expenses, until the administration of Aaron Frankel in 1958–59. Unlike Miss Jones and her assistant and immediate successor Ramsey Burch, Frankel was unable to keep the business and artistic operations separate. The move into the Maple Street Theatre in 1959 had as one of its aims the separation of artistic and business responsibilities, but this move came too late to be effective. The additional production costs in the proscenium theatre proved to be more than the organization could support with ticket sales alone, and it suspended operations.

Margo Jones believed passionately in the decentralization of the American theatre and hoped that the Dallas operation would be the first of twenty such theatres across the United States. Today, the reality has far surpassed her dream. More than any other American director and visionary of her generation, however, she tried to fulfill this dream. Her only effort at starting another theatre like the Dallas operation, in San Francisco, failed, but Brooks Atkinson said that Miss Jones's "vision, skill, and vitality stimulated, not only her audience, but resident theatres in other parts of the country."[20] Although numerous resident professional repertory theatres were founded during her lifetime, many of which were directly influenced by the Margo Jones Theatre, this movement has today tripled her expectations. Two of the most stable and long-lasting regional theatres, the Alley in Houston and the Arena Stage in Washington, D.C., credit Margo Jones with direct and immediate influence. A letter in the Margo Jones Collection at the Dallas Public Library from Zelda Fichandler, founder and director of the Arena Stage, says that Margo Jones was a vital source of encouragement to that group; Nina Vance, director of the Alley Theatre, acted under Margo Jones in Houston and continued the tradition of arena staging in Houston. In 1969, the Alley moved from its small arena theatre into a new large plant. Margo Jones was eager to foster theatre wherever it might happen. Before her death, she became an original member of the planning board for the Dallas Theatre Center, which opened after her death under Paul Baker's direction and is still going strong, carrying forward Margo Jones's interest in and support of young playwrights, most notably in their production of Preston Jones's *Texas Trilogy* (1973–74).

Of the total number of professional regional theatres founded in the United States since 1945, it is impossible to know exactly how many have been directly (or indirectly) influenced by Margo Jones's first attempt at decentralizing the modern professional theatre. Her pioneer effort, however, clearly contributed mightily to this movement. More and more, as Margo Jones would have wished it, significant new plays are coming from the regional theatres. Fortunately, this special contribution of Margo Jones has not been completely forgotten, and will, one hopes, be remembered for many years to come. In 1961, Jerome Lawrence and Robert E. Lee initiated the "Margo Jones Award" to ensure such continuous recognition. The award is meant to honor the producing manager of an American or Canadian theatre whose policy of presenting new dramatic works continues most faithfully the tradition and vision of Margo Jones. In 1964, an award was added for the university that had done the most to help new playwrights. The principles of the Margo Jones Theatre are being kept alive through the award in her name.

In reality, the Margo Jones Theatre itself is not dormant—at least the name is once more attached to an actively producing theatre facility. On 22 January 1969, Southern Methodist University in Dallas presented a dedicatory performance of *Othello* to open the new Margo Jones Theatre, made possible through the generosity of a $200,000 gift donated by Miss Jones's constant supporters, Mr. and Mrs. Eugene McDermott. By presenting *Othello*, the Margo Jones Theatre's last production in 1959, Southern Methodist attempted to create a kind of continuity with the original Margo Jones Theatre. The new theatre is a sixty-foot square space, twenty-one feet high, with a wrap-around control deck at the height of thirteen feet. It is, as Miss Jones would have wished, a flexible stage able to "adapt itself to the special qualities of each play." As part of the Owen Fine Arts Center on the campus of Southern Methodist, it is a constant reminder to the Dallas playgoer that Margo Jones is very much a part of their cultural heritage.

The significance of the original Margo Jones Theatre is clear. As a successful professional repertory theatre dedicated to the new playwright it had no equal during its life and few, until recently, have succeeded in matching its accomplishments. During twelve years, 1947 through 1959, the Margo Jones Theatre produced more new plays than any other playhouse in the history of the contemporary American theatre. It was also the first professional theatre to use arena staging as its principal method of production. In both capacities, Margo Jones and her theatre were true pioneers in the movement to decentralize the American professional theatre.

APPENDIX:
Plays Produced by the Margo Jones Theatre

Key to Directors. R.A., Ronald Alexander; R.B., Ramsey Burch; B.B., Bill Butler; J.D., John Denney; M.E., Michael Ellis; A.F., Aaron Frankel; W.B.H., W. Broderick Hackett; S.J., Spencer James; M.J., Margo Jones; J.M., James McAllen; J.S., Jonathan Seymour; H.S., Hall Shelton; M.S., Milton Stiefel.
[a]First performance anywhere.
[b]First performance in the United States.
[c]First professional production.

AUTHOR	TITLE	DIRECTOR	OPENED	NO. OF PERFORMANCES
Theatre '47 (Summer)				
William Inge	*Farther Off From Heaven*[a]	M.J.	6/3/47	14
Martyn Coleman	*How Now, Hecate*	M.J.	6/10/47	14
Henrik Ibsen	*Hedda Gabler*	M.J.	6/24/47	14
Tennessee Williams	*Summer and Smoke*[a]	M.J.	7/8/47	14
Vera Mathews	*Third Cousin*[a]	M.J.	7/22/47	13
Theatre '47–'48				
Henrik Ibsen	*The Master Builder*	M.J.	11/3/47	16
Tennessee Williams	Three Short Plays: *The Last of My Solid Gold Watches*, *This Property Is Condemned*, *Portrait of a Madonna*	M.J.	11/17/47	16
Vivian Connell	*Throng O'Scarlet*[a]	M.J.	12/1/47	19
Shakespeare	*The Taming of the Shrew*	M.J.	12/15/47	24
Manning Gurian	*Lemple's Old Man*[a]	M.J.	12/29/47	16
Oscar Wilde	*The Importance of Being Earnest*	M.J.	1/12/48	37
Joseph Hayes	*Leaf and Bough*[a]	M.J	1/26/48	24
Barton MacLane	*Black John*[a]	M.J.	2/9/48	16
Theatre '48–'49				
Molière	*The Learned Ladies*	M.J.	11/8/48	34
Shirland Quinn	*Here's to Us!*[a]	M.J.	11/29/48	24

AUTHOR	TITLE	DIRECTOR	OPENED	NO. OF PER FORMANCES
Shakespeare	*Twelfth Night*	M.J.	12/20/48	34
Vivian Johannes	*Skaal*[a]	M.J.	1/10/49	24
Tom Purefoy	*Sting in the Tail*[a]	M.J.	1/31/49	30
Anton Chekhov	*The Seagull*	M.J.	2/21/49	24
Oliver Goldsmith	*She Stoops to Conquer*	M.J.	3/14/49	24
Dorothy Parker and Ross Evans	*The Coast of Illyria*[a]	M.J.	4/4/49	32

Theatre '49–'50

Bernard Shaw	*Heartbreak House*	M.J.	11/7/49	27
Sari Scott	*An Old Beat-Up Woman*[a]	M.J.	11/28/49	24
Shakespeare	*Romeo and Juliet*	M.J.	12/19/49	36
Loren Disney & George Sessions Perry	*My Granny Van*[a]	M.J.	1/9/50	36
Sean O'Casey	*Cock-a-Doodle Dandy*[b]	M.J. & J.S.	1/30/50	24
Henrik Ibsen	*Ghosts*	M.J.	2/20/50	24
Muriel Roy Bolton	*The Golden Porcupine*[a]	M.J.	3/13/50	29
Owen Crump	*Southern Exposure*[a]	M.J.	4/3/50	44

Theatre '50–'51

Oscar Wilde	*Lady Windermere's Fan*	M.J.	11/6/50	24
William McCleery	*A Play for Mary*[a]	S.J.	11/27/50	24
Shakespeare	*The Merchant of Venice*	M.J.	12/18/50	31
Edward Caulfield	*An Innocent in Time*[a]	S.J.	1/29/51	32
A. B. Shiffrin	*The Willow Tree*[a]	M.J.	1/8/51	36
Sigmund Miller	*One Bright Day*[a]	M.J.	2/19/51	24
Bernard Shaw	*Candida*	M.J.	3/12/51	24
Frank Duane & Richard Shannon	*Walls Rise Up*[a]	M.J.	4/2/51	44

Theatre '51–'52

Alden Nash	*The Sainted Sisters*[a]	M.J.	11/5/51	32
Irving Phillips	*One Foot in Heaven*[a]	R.B.	12/3/51	43
Shakespeare	*A Midsummer Night's Dream*	M.J.	12/23/51	27

AUTHOR	TITLE	DIRECTOR	OPENED	NO. OF PER FORMANCES

Theatre '51–'52 (continued)

AUTHOR	TITLE	DIRECTOR	OPENED	NO. OF PERFORMANCES
Ronald Alexander	*A Gift for Cathy*[a]	R.B.	1/21/51	29
Edward Caulfield	*The Blind Spot*[a]	M.J.	2/11/52	27
August Strindberg	*The Father*	R.B.	3/10/52	24
Edward Justus Mayer	*I Am Laughing*[a]	M.J.	3/31/52	24
Vera Marshall (Mathews)	*So In Love*[a]	R.B.	4/28/52	27

Theatre '52–'53

(Three weeks of repertory during the season are not included.)

AUTHOR	TITLE	DIRECTOR	OPENED	NO. OF PERFORMANCES
Vivian Connell	*Goodbye, Your Majesty*[a]	R.B.	11/3/52	27
Shakespeare	*Hamlet*	R.B.	11/24/52	24
Robin Maugham	*The Rising Heifer*[a]	R.B.	12/22/52	27
Eugene Raskin	*The Last Island*[a]	M.J.	1/12/53	24
John Briard Harding	*Uncle Marston*[b]	R.B.	2/9/53	24
Rosemary Casey	*Late Love*[a]	R.B.	3/2/53	29
Lesley Storm	*The Day's Mischief*[b]	M.J.	3/30/53	24
R. B. Sheridan	*The Rivals*	R.B.	4/20/53	25

Theatre '53–'54

AUTHOR	TITLE	DIRECTOR	OPENED	NO. OF PERFORMANCES
Burgess Drake	*The Footpath Way*[b]	M.J.	11/2/53	24
Harry Granick	*The Guilty*[a]	M.J.	11/23/53	24
Alejandro Cansona (Tr. by Ruth Gillespie and Elizabeth Cubeta)	*Happy We'll Be*[c]	R.B.	12/14/53	26
Sari Scott	*Oracle Junction*[a]	R.B.	1/4/54	24
Samson Raphaelson	*The Heel*[a]	M.J.	1/22/54	30
Milton Robertson	*A Rainbow At Home*[a]	R.B.	2/15/54	24
Ira Wallach, David Baker, Sheldon Harnick	*Horatio*[a]	M.J.	3/8/54	30
T. Williams	*The Purification*[c]	M.J.	3/29/54	25
and Jean Giraudoux (Tr. Arthur Nations and Marc Masotti)	*The Apollo of Bellac*[c]			
Shakespeare	*The Merry Wives of Windsor*	R.B.	4/19/54	29

AUTHOR	TITLE	DIRECTOR	OPENED	NO. OF PER FORMANCES
Theatre '54 (summer)				
Ronald Alexander	*The Inevitable Circle*[a]	R.A.	6/8/54	24
John S. Rodell	*The Brothers*[a]	R.B.	6/29/54	24
Reginald Denham and Conrad Sutton-Smith	*A Dash of Bitters*[a]	M.J.	7/20/54	24
William Case	*Sea-Change*[a]	R.B.	8/10/54	24
Ben Jonson	*Volpone*	R.B.	8/31/54	24
Theatre '54–'55				
Albert Dickason	*Marry-Go-Round*[a]	R.B.	11/8/54	24
Shakespeare	*As You Like It*	M.J.	11/29/54	24
Edward Hunt	*The Hemlock Cup*[a]	R.B.	12/20/54	24
Jerome Lawrence and Robert E. Lee	*Inherit the Wind*[a]	M.J.	1/10/55	44
Charles Robinson and Jean Dalrymple	*The Feathered Fauna*[a]	R.B.	1/31/55	24
Bernard C. Schoenfield	*The Summer of Fancy Dress*[a]	R.B.	2/21/55	24
Bernard Shaw	*Misalliance*	R.B.	3/14/55	31
Stephen Gray	*Ghost of a Chance*[a]	R.B.	4/4/55	24
Frederick Jackson and Irving Phillips	*La Belle Lulu*[a]	R.B.	4/25/55	24
Theatre '55 (summer)				
Bernard Shaw	*Pygmalion*	R.B.	6/13/55	16
Greer Johnson	*Whisper to Me*[a]	M.J.	6/27/55	16
Joseph Hayes	*The Girl From Boston*[a]	R.B.	7/11/55	16
Anna Marie Barlow and S. Brooke White	*Cold Christmas*[a]	R.B.	7/26/55	15
John Vari	*Farewell, Farewell, Eugene*[a]	R.B.	8/8/55	16
Theatre '55–'56				
Ferenc Molnar	*Somebody*[b]	R.B.	11/7/55	24
Gene Radano	*The World Is Yours*[a]	J.M.	11/28/55	24

AUTHOR	TITLE	DIRECTOR	OPENED	NO. OF PER FORMANCES

Theatre '55–'56 (continued)

Bernard Shaw	*The Dark Lady of the Sonnets; The Man of Destiny*	R.B.	12/19/55	24
Neal Roper	*Love is a Tutu*[a]	R.B.	1/9/56	24
Maura Laverty	*Tolka Row*[b]	J.M.	1/30/56	24
Molière	*The School for Wives*	R.B.	2/20/56	24
James Bridie	*Mr. Gillie*[b]	J.M.	3/12/56	24
Patricia Joudry	*The Sand Castle*[a]	J.M.	4/2/56	24
Violet Welles	*The Spring Affair*[a]	R.B.	4/23/56	24
Eleanor & Leo Bayer	*Third Best Sport*[a]	R.B.	5/14/56	24

Theatre '56 (summer)

Joel Climenhaga	*The Marriage Wheel*[a]	R.B.	6/4/56	16
Jacinto Benavente (Tr. Arthur Nations)	*Love Goes to School*[b]	J.D.	6/18/56	16
Bridget Boland	*The Prisoner*[b]	R.B.	7/2/56	16

Theatre '56–'57

Albert Mannheimer and Frederick Kohner	*Stalin Allee*[a]	R.B.	11/5/56	24
Shakespeare	*Macbeth*	R.B.	11/27/56	24
S. I. Abelow and Robert Canedella	*The Small Servant*[a]	H.S.	12/18/56	24
Don Liljenquist	*Woman Is My Idea*[a]	R.B.	1/8/57	24
Richard Reich	*The Tin Cup*[a]	H.S.	1/29/57	24
Somerset Maugham	*The Circle*	R.B.	2/19/57	24
Elinor Lenz	*Second Wind*[a]	H.S.	3/12/57	24
Samuel R. Golding and Norbert Faulkner	*The Most Fashionable Crime*[a]	R.B.	4/2/57	24
Anton Chekhov	*Uncle Vanya*	R.B.	4/23/57	24
Tennessee Williams	*The Glass Menagerie*	H.S.	5/14/57	24

Theatre '57–'58

| Paul Vincent Carroll | *The Devil Comes From Dublin*[b] | R.B. | 10/29/57 | 24 |

AUTHOR	TITLE	DIRECTOR	OPENED	NO. OF PER FORMANCES
Lynn Riggs	*Roadside*	R.B.	11/19/57	24
Bernard Shaw	*Androcles and the Lion*	R.B.	12/10/57	24
Kate Farness	*Heat of Noontide*a	R.B.	12/31/57	32
Katherine Morrill	*And So, Farewell*a	R.B.	1/21/58	24
Molière	*The Doctor in Spite of Himself*	R.B.	2/11/58	24
Carl Oglesby	*Season of the Beast*a	R.B.	3/4/58	16
Harry Granick	*The Hooper Law*a	R.B.	3/25/58	24
William Walden	*A Waiter Not Named Julius*a	R.B.	4/15/58	24

Theatre '58–'59

AUTHOR	TITLE	DIRECTOR	OPENED	NO. OF PER FORMANCES
Sheridan Gibney	*Penelope's Web*a	A.F.	11/3/58	24
Robert Penn Warren	*Willie Stark: His Rise and Fall*a	A.F.	11/25/58	25
Kurt Weill and Arnold Sungaard	*Legends and Fables: Down in the Valley*	A.F.	12/16/58	24
James Thurber	*Fables in Our Times*a			
Bernard Shaw	*The Millionairess*	A.F.	1/6/59	24
Ruth & Augustus Goetz	*The Heiress*	W.B.H.	1/27/59	24
Royall Tyler	*The Contrast*	M.E.	2/17/59	24
Eugene O'Neill	*The Moon for the Misbegotten*	W.B.H.	3/3/59	24
Agatha Christie	*The Mousetrap*	W.B.H.	3/24/59	24
Ring Lardner	*Triangle: The Tridget of Greva*			
Bernard Shaw	*Overruled*	W.B.H.	4/14/59	24
Terence Rattigan	*The Browning Version*			

Theatre '59–'60

AUTHOR	TITLE	DIRECTOR	OPENED	NO. OF PER FORMANCES
Kenneth Cameron	*Physician For Fools*a	B.B.	10/6/59	24
Bella & Samuel Spewack; Cole Porter	*Leave It to Me*	B.B.	10/27/59	24
Warren Tute	*A Few Days in Greece*	M.S.	11/17/59	24
Shakespeare	*Othello*	M.S.	12/8/59	9

Notes

1. Margo Jones died 24 July 1955. The cause of death according to the death certificate and an autopsy report was "Accidental inhalation of carbon tetrachloride fumes causing liver necrosis and acute interstitial pneumonitis, as well as acute renal failure." This bizarre turn of events occurred as a result of an after-hours art session with two friends, during which Jones had spattered paint around her apartment in the Stoneleigh Hotel. The next day the rug and sofa were cleaned with carbon tetrachloride, the fumes of which Jones subsequently inhaled while reading scripts in the apartment (whose room air conditioner permitted no outside ventilation). Apparently, she drank several beers during the day which increased the effect of the fumes.

2. For a history of theatre in Dallas, see John Williams Rogers, *The Lusty Texans of Dallas* (New York, 1951), pp. 205–22; Jackson Davis, "A History of Professional Theatre in Dallas, 1920–1930," Ph.D. diss., Louisiana State University, 1962; David Stephens, "Local Thespians Once Brought Dallas Fame," *Dallas Times Herald*, 25 May 1957; Stephens, "Dallas Little Theatre Once Soared, Then Evaporated," *Dallas Times Herald*, 26 May 1947; and John Rosenfield, "Done First in Dallas," *Dallas Morning News*, 23 April 1959. By the time Margo Jones established her theatre, even the internationally recognized Dallas Little Theatre, winner of three Belasco cups, had expired. See John Rosenfield, "Texas Regional Theatres," *Southwest Review*, 40 (Spring 1955), 183.

3. Murray Schumach, "A Texas Tornado Hits Broadway," *New York Times Magazine*, 17 October 1948, p. 19.

4. Fitzroy Davis, "A Texan Shows Enthusiasm for Round Theatres," *Chicago Sunday Tribune*, 24 June 1951.

5. George Sessions Perry, "Darndest Thing You've Ever Seen," *Saturday Evening Post*, 224 (1 March 1952), 112.

6. John Rosenfield, personal interview, 23 January 1964.

7. Denny Cralle, "Dallas Theatre '48 Owes High Professional Status to Margo Jones' Work," *Christian Science Monitor*, 18 November 1948.

8. Letter, William Inge to author, 9 January 1964.

9. Letter, Margo Jones Collection, Dallas Public Library. This collection has been my major source for data used throughout this essay. The files of this collection contain endless amounts of information relating the Margo Jones Theatre to its activities in Dallas: production data on each play (letters, photographs, newspaper clippings and reviews, and programs); scripts of the plays produced; correspondence with playwrights, actors, and play agents; personal correspondence of Margo Jones; organization material (special programs and brochures); and business materials (accounts, ledgers, and statements).

10. Brooks Atkinson, brochure for "The Margo Jones Award," 1961.

11. All biographical data are taken from a biographical sketch compiled by Margo Jones in 1944, now in the Dallas Public Library, or are drawn from her book (mostly ghost-authored by Theodore Apstein), *Theatre-in-the-Round* (New York, 1951).

12. For an account of Houston theatre, see Jack H. Yocum, "History of Theatre in Houston, Texas, from 1936 to 1954," Ph.D. diss., University of Wisconsin, 1954.

13. New plays directed in this period included Theodore Apstein's *Sporting Pink, Choice of Weapons,* and *Velvet Touch*; Tennessee Williams and Donald Windham's *You Touched Me*; and Williams' *The Purification*.

14. Margo Jones's notes on first few weeks' progress after reception of the Rockefeller grant (in Margo Jones Collection). She also comments on Mordecai

Goreliks' *New Theatres for Old*, Kenneth Macgowan's *Continental Stagecraft*, P. P. Howe's *The Repertory Theatre*, Percy Mackaye's books on civic theatres, Sarah Bernhardt's *The Art of the Theatre*, and Irving Pichel's *Modern Theatres*. Miss Jones clearly saw her quest as part of the art theatre movement.

15. Jones, already a close friend of Williams, had read *The Glass Menagerie* under its original title, *The Gentleman Caller*, and was eager to be involved in its production. She co-directed the play with Eddie Dowling.

16. Some twenty-five existing structures were considered and a request to build a theatre was turned down by the Civilian Production Administration so that "the construction of homes for veterans of World War II may proceed as rapidly as possible" before the final structure, then owned by Gulf Oil Company and located at Grand and First Avenues, was settled upon. The building, leased for free in exchange for free publicity, was adapted for arena staging by the installation of a series of stepped platforms for seats in a space about 35 feet by 40 feet at a cost of $3,000. The seats were donated by the parents of Jennifer Jones; the capacity was limited to 198. The playing area was in the shape of a trapezoid, measuring 24 feet by 20 feet. A detailed account of the physical plant, funding for the theatre, and a season-by-season analysis can be found in my doctoral dissertation, "A History of the Margo Jones Theatre," University of Illinois, 1964.

17. Miss Jones' attitude toward a theatre board was expressed in a letter to Maria Stebbins (of the San Francisco Theatre Association), 13 October 1947: "You have to have a Board for there must be civic representation when you go after civic money and they're very important from a public relations point of view. . . . some of them can be very helpful—few have time to. . . . A Board *must never* be in a position to dictate the policy—if so you'll have a non-professional attitude and it is impossible to get the job done in a non-professional way."

18. John Rosenfield, "More Iconoclasm at Theatre '56," *Dallas Morning News*, 14 January 1956.

19. Her ideas of arena staging are fully explained in her book, *Theatre-in-the-Round*, still a standard source on the subject after thirty years.

20. Brooks Atkinson, brochure for "The Margo Jones Award," 1961.

12

The Stratford Festival and the Canadian Theatre

Tyrone Guthrie hailed the Stratford Festival he helped found as "a symbol of a new spirit in Canada"[1] that "established technical precedence"[2] in the theatrical world. The first season, 1953, was a summer of superlatives. Herbert Whittaker of the *Toronto Globe and Mail* (14 July 1953) called the opening "the most exciting night in the history of Canadian theatre." Arnold Edinborough prophesied that the Festival would become "as momentous for Canada as the founding of the Old Vic was for England, or the Abbey Theatre for Dublin."[3] A commemorative book was aptly entitled *Renown at Stratford*.[4]

The superlatives have continued season after season, with non-Canadians in general being the more effusive. *New York Times* critic Walter Kerr judged the Festival Theatre "the only new theatre of any consequence on the American continent."[5] Kerr's successor, Clive Barnes, considered Stratford "unquestionably the best classic repertory company in North America,"[6] and described one season as "one of the most important theatre events in the world."[7] Samuel Hirsch of the *Boston Herald* (8 June 1966) was unequivocal: "Suffice to say that the acting company is the finest ensemble on our continent and the Festival Theatre is itself an object for pride and admiration." The Stratford Festival has been saluted as one of "the three top companies of the English-speaking world."[8]

Statistics also help tell the Stratford success story.[9] Sixty-eight thousand people (96 percent of capacity) attended the first six-week season that had been extended a week to accommodate them. In contrast, the 1979 season lasted twenty-six weeks and attracted over five hundred thousand spectators. The box office grossed almost five million dollars, a more than twentyfold increase. In 1953, eighty people had helped produce the two plays in the tent theatre; in 1979 close to seven hundred, many of them full-time employees, were needed to mount fifteen plays in three theatres.

In Stratford co-founder Tom Patterson's words, the Festival's open stage "influence[d] theatrical production throughout the world."[10] It inspired many other thrust stages including those in the Guthrie Theatre, Minneapolis, and the Chichester Festival Theatre and the Crucible Theatre, Sheffield, in England. The Vivian Beaumont Theatre in New York and the Olivier Theatre in London's National Theatre are modifications of the Stratford plan.

Yet in spite of its achievements, the Stratford Festival found itself, particularly in the 1970s, increasingly at odds with the rest of Canadian theatre. International acclaim had come at the price of nationalistic antagonism. The Festival had become isolated from, rather than an intrinsic part of, the Canadian theatre.

The Stratford Festival was the cornerstone in Tyrone Guthrie's vision of a Canadian theatre, a "distinctive national style ... of acting, producing, writing [and] criticizing plays ... founded on the study of the classics." For Guthrie, "evolving a distinctively Canadian comment on the classics" was the way to develop "any satisfactory native dramatic style," not the "writing and producing of realistic comedies of Canadian life." Train actors by letting them "grapple with some of the great Shakespearean roles" in a world-class theatre and eventually, Guthrie felt sure, a national theatre would emerge.[11]

The nationalists who led the so-called alternate theatre movement in the early 1970s had a seemingly irreconcilable vision of a theatre, a vision which emphasized Canadian plays and national concerns. The Stratford Festival was the enemy: a monolithic symbol of cultural colonialism impeding the growth of the real Canadian theatre. The history of the Stratford Festival's relations with the rest of Canadian theatre, the subject of this essay, helps explain how this probably inevitable schism occurred.

Tyrone Guthrie accepted Tom Patterson's offer to come to Canada, because he saw the chance he "had long dreamed of"[12] to build a stage that promised "a fresh advance in Shakespearean production." His career in England had stalled; he was seeking a new challenge. As his biographer James Forsyth explains, Guthrie regarded the Stratford offer as "the one that must not get away."[13] His own dream came first; a Canadian theatre could come later.

Ironically, national considerations helped realize Guthrie's international dream. Stratford-native Tom Patterson had been impressed with opera and theatre in Europe and could not accept that being Canadian meant being uncultured. Patterson reasoned that "Canadians might very well be as talented, as discriminating and energetic as Europeans, and they were certainly richer" (Guthrie, *A Life*, p. 282). Guthrie believed Stratford "symbolized Canada's desire for mature, and, if possible, distinguished artistic expression" (*A Life*, p. 299). The public was eager to support "a conspicuous endeavour"[14] which "attempted to put artistic standards ahead of any and every other consideration, and which set out to show that Canadian artists could achieve in this professional sphere standards of which they need not feel ashamed" (Guthrie, *Renown*, p. 26). Stratford's success became "a matter of national prestige," because it "coincided with a great surge of national prosperity, which . . . inspired a great surge of national self-confidence."[15]

To capitalize on this national spirit, Guthrie insisted that "the project must be demonstrably a Canadian one, carried out not merely by Canadian initiative, and with Canadian finance, but by Canadian actors" (*A Life*, p. 284). His first auditions had confirmed there were "several Canadian actors who could play leading roles with credit by any standard" (*Renown*, p. 29). The Banff School of Fine Arts, Hart House Theatre at the University of Toronto, the Dominion Drama Festival, and theatres such as the New Play Society, the Canadian Repertory Company in Ottawa and the Montreal Repertory Company had produced many fine performers who had achieved distinction in Canadian Broadcasting Corporation radio dramas and who were ready for the challenge of Stratford.

However, Guthrie was also aware that there was no Canadian actor "whose mere name on the bills provides for the public some guarantee of status, some indication that the goings-on will be worth the price." He hoped that perhaps "in even so short a time as five years" the Stratford Festival might be able to help Canadian performers acquire "that sort of status and prestige" (*Renown*, p. 30). In the meantime, Guthrie strongly recommended that the new Festival secure "an actor of the highest quality and international fame" to "attract sufficient attention," sell tickets, and provide credibility (*Renown*, p. 7).

Tom Patterson managed to obtain from England Alec Guinness and Irene Worth to star in the first Stratford Festival, with Douglas Campbell and Michael Bates in support. The presence of Guinness attracted "leading drama critics from New York, who . . . wrote enthusiastically of what they saw." Guthrie realized the importance of that: "Canadians, very understandably and through the modesty of inexperience, lack self-confidence in artistic judgment. . . . Now finding the New York critics out-singing even the local newspaper in praise set the seal upon artistic success and ensured the prosperity of the new Festival" (*A Life*, p. 299).

Guthrie modestly described his 1953 productions of *Richard III* and *All's Well That Ends Well* as "not bad" (*A Life*, p. 300), comparing the Canadian company favorably to those at the Old Vic and the English Stratford. The Canadian productions, however, "seemed livelier and fresher because of the design of the theatre" (*A Life*, p. 300). The open stage was Guthrie's most significant contribution to the Festival. In fact, no Stratford production has ever attracted as much international attention as has its stage. Guthrie admitted the stage "intrigued and excited simply by its novelty," but was convinced the plays of Shakespeare for which the stage was designed could "best be presented by getting as near as possible to the manner in which the author envisaged" them being performed (*A Life*, p. 301). The Stratford stage embodied two characteristics of the Elizabethan playhouse: "the physical relation between actor and audience," and the "practical features" of the stage.[16]

The tent theatre could seat fifteen hundred people around three sides of the stage, which was at the focal point of the auditorium and designed to emphasize the actor. With the furthest spectator only forty-six feet from the stage, as Guthrie's assistant Cecil Clarke described, "the feeling of intimacy . . . [was] quite remarkable."[17] The stage was formal, symmetrical, and, to use Guthrie's term, "functional," offering actors "standing places, seats and things to lean against, where they needed them, . . . [and] neither too much space nor too little."[18] Three steps surrounded the stage which had a small balcony at the back supported by pillars, reachable from the stage level. Five major entrances (plus the aisles) from both the front and the back encouraged smooth rapid transitions between scenes. It was a stage, concluded Alice Griffin in *Theatre Arts* (September, 1954), that "mercilessly spotlight[ed] the flaws in a poor production as well as provide[d] exciting opportunities for a good one." Modifications, particularly in 1962 and 1975, did little to radically alter the stage Guthrie had conceived.

Guthrie and his designer Tanya Moiseiwitsch established a Stratford tradition by using lavish, colorful costumes and properties for visual effect. Three highly experienced technicians, Cecil Clarke, Ray Diffen, and Jacqueline Cundall, arrived from England to oversee the technical areas of the Festival and ensure high production standards. Canadians assisted, but had not, in Guthrie's opinion, had the opportunity to "get the experience which would qualify them to undertake these tasks" (*Renown*, p. 30).

Guthrie's arrival had not been entirely selfless, nor was his eventual leavetaking in 1955. He was conscious of perceptible nationalist dissatisfaction. As James Forsyth has described, "Out of what had initially been a post-war movement towards a form of national theatre, he had channelled that wave of enthusiasms—and the resources of talent and money raised—into a regional success with a seasonal theatre just serving a summer festival. Nobody could deny that he had thereby set exemplary standards for the whole nation in the quality of direction, design and playing, but even so. . . . And Guthrie shared in this 'but' too" (Forsyth, p. 252). *Toronto Star* critic Nathan Cohen had begun to argue that "there is no such thing as a Canadian style of doing Shakespeare, and won't be for a long time."[19] Guthrie had reached much the same conclusion by 1954: "I don't know how far it may be possible to interpret a classical play in a distinctively Canadian way" ("Long View," p. 166). Nonetheless, Guthrie remained convinced it was vital for Canadians to "assimilate classical works of art as part of their own heritage, not just regard them as imports" ("Long View," p. 167). Guthrie answered criticism that "a Festival which offers no encouragement to Canadian authors has no right to consider itself a Canadian institution" by pointing out that Canadian playwrights would benefit from better trained

12. *The Merchant of Venice*, Stratford Festival, 1955, directed by Tyrone Guthrie, designed by Tanya Moiseiwitsch, with Frances Hyland as Portia and Donald Harron as Bassanio. Courtesy of Stratford Festival Archives.

actors, a more receptive audience and from example; "any dramatist of quality, no matter how revolutionary, how 'original', his work may be, can learn valuably from the classics of dramatic literature" ("Long View," pp. 165–66).

Whatever the developments in Canadian theatre, Guthrie insisted that "Stratford's claim for survival . . . [should remain] an annual programme of Shakespearean productions at a standard that commands respect." In the process, the Festival would help develop indigenous talent, "not merely to learn technique, but to compare standards and to learn how to criticize one's own and other people's work." While eventually, he predicted, it would "be possible to do without the importation of artists from abroad," he hoped that process would "not be speeded up by chauvinistic pressure." Guthrie envisioned a Stratford Festival "which is perceptibly, but indefinably, Canadian; which is able to manage without assistance, but which, nevertheless, considers that some outsiders, not from Britain exclusively, give richness and variety to a company which has no fear that its Canadian-ness is so thin and weak as to be ruined by a little dilution" (*Renown*, pp. 27–30).

Tyrone Guthrie remained as Artistic Director for only three years, although he returned occasionally to direct. His chosen successor was Michael

Langham, a young English director first brought out to stage *Julius Caesar* in 1955. Some nationalists denounced the appointment of another Englishman: Guthrie himself had predicted a Canadian would eventually take control. However, in Langham's opinion, very few of the theatre people who protested "yet seemed equipped to shoulder the heavier responsibilities"[20] of directing, designing, or heading production departments. Besides, Langham claimed, as long as Stratford remained a festival devoted to Shakespeare, "its task was to reveal as recognizably as possible the world of [his] plays, which is commonly the entire field of human experience," and not "the purely national scene." Indeed, Langham conceded he could not even define a uniquely "Canadian version of a classic" (Langham, pp. 9–10). Under Michael Langham, who as Artistic Director from 1956 to 1967 consolidated much of Guthrie's work, Stratford remained a theatre that was international first and national second.

Yet Michael Langham's audacious opening production of *Henry V*, starring Christopher Plummer from Montreal, was acclaimed precisely because it did emphasize a distinctively Canadian theme. He had done "what a native Canadian might have balked at even if he thought of it (which is unlikely),"[21] and turned the play into a battle between two cultures, English and French, happily and harmoniously united at the end. To reinforce his message, he cast Quebec actors such as Gratien Gelinas, Guy Hoffman, and Jean-Louis Roux in the French parts. As Langham recalled later, "It was plain common sense to use French Canadian talent like this, for its involvement could help realize some of the national identity which Stratford was instinctively beginning to seek" (Langham, p. 7).

The new permanent theatre opened in 1957 with Christopher Plummer appearing as Hamlet. Architect Robert Fairfield of Toronto managed to retain much of the feeling of his original tent design in the circular building that brought together under one roof full workshop facilities, administrative offices, a rehearsal room, and audience amenities. By adding a balcony, Fairfield ensured that none of the 2,200 spectators were more than sixty-five feet from the stage.

Michael Langham described the company he inherited as "very uneven in skill and quite diverse in approach," containing much talent that was "with few exceptions (mostly non-Canadian) . . . raw and confused in expression" (Langham, p. 6). He molded this talent into a strong Canadian company bolstered regularly by notable imports such as Paul Scofield, Julie Harris, Siobhan McKenna, Jason Robards, Jr., Eileen Herlie, Tammy Grimes, and Martha Schlamme. In Langham's farewell season, 1967, Zoe Caldwell, in her second visit, played Cleopatra to Alan Bates's Antony. Langham advanced the careers of Canadians Christopher Plummer, John Colicos, Donald Davis, Kate Reid, Frances Hyland, Tony Van Bridge, Leo Ciceri, Toby Robins, Pat Galloway, Douglas Rain, Martha Henry, Bruno Gerussi, and Stratford's perennial leading man, William Hutt. Most of Langham's many excellent character actors originally were or eventually became Canadian, including Eric Christmas, Hugh Webster, William Needles, Amelia Hall, Eric House, Joseph Shaw, Bernard Behrens, Mervyn Blake, Mary Savidge, Powys Thomas, and Max Helpman.

Tyrone Guthrie envisioned a Canadian theatre growing out of Stratford; under Michael Langham it happened. In 1954, Tom Patterson and Douglas Campbell founded the Canadian Players, a small band of mostly Stratford performers who mounted long winter tours throughout Canada and parts of the United States doing Shakespeare and modern classics by writers such as Brecht and Shaw. The success of the Stratford Festival also helped spur the government into finally accepting the Massey Commission recommendation that a Canada Council be formed to subsidize and encourage theatre across the country.

If the Stratford Festival could "command the service of the most serious and talented of the Canadian actors for a few weeks in the summer," Guthrie felt that was the most useful thing it could do "for them, for itself and for the Canadian public" (*Renown*, p. 28). What would these actors do for the rest of the year? Once again Guthrie had an answer: they should form "an attachment to a particular environment," because that was "vital for their health as artists; and . . . no less vital for the health of the community" ("Long View," pp. 170–71). In many ways, the regional theatres that sprang up across Canada in the late 1960s were created in Stratford's own image: they were international in outlook and favored a balanced repertoire of important classical and modern plays from other countries that would attract large and diverse audiences.

In a 1952 radio talk, Guthrie stated that Canadians would never have a flourishing theatre until they began "to feel that a serious theatre is not merely an amenity—but a necessity" (Forsyth, p. 231). John Hirsch, who in 1959 founded the Manitoba Theatre Centre in Winnipeg with Tom Hendry, had a similar belief in the importance of theatre to a community. Under Hirsch, the Manitoba Theatre Centre, a model for many regional theatres in North America, practically became a western Stratford. To raise standards, Hirsch brought in the finest talent available, talent that tended to congregate each summer at the Stratford Festival, including, for example, Winnipeg-native Douglas Rain, Zoe Caldwell, Donald Davis, and Kate Reid.

The Stratford-Manitoba Theatre Centre link strengthened when John Hirsch began directing at the Festival in 1965. Then the following year, Hirsch and Langham concluded a more formal arrangement to open two productions in Winnipeg the winter before their Stratford runs, thereby splitting costs and keeping a strong company together longer to the benefit of both theatres. One of the two, Strindberg's *Dance of Death* featuring Jean Gascon and Denise Pelletier, was a critical success. However, the problems with the other, American William Kinsolving's *Nicholas Romanov*, were so great they led to the termination of the accord. This "Stratford-size" production, in Winnipeg critic Ann Henry's phrase,[22] expired in the old cramped Dominion Theatre in spite of accomplished acting and striking designs. The Stratford Festival treated the Winnipeg engagement as a tryout, just what the Manitoba Theatre Centre had insisted not happen. Michael Langham cancelled *Nicholas Romanov* and replaced it at Stratford with a hastily written play, Michael Bawtree's *The Last of the Tsars*, to salvage the costumes and properties of the Russian Revolution. Stratford's first attempt at establishing a winter home had failed, as would later efforts to locate in Montreal.

Lengthening Stratford seasons prevented many Festival actors from accepting winter engagements by the late 1960s. Stratford was losing direct contact with the burgeoning regional theatre movement, which had once depended so heavily on Stratford talent. For example, after working at the Festival, young Toronto director Leon Major had founded the Neptune Theatre in Halifax in 1963. Stratford helped inspire the Shaw Festival at Niagara-on-the-Lake, and many of the actors featured there were Stratford veterans. In 1963, Norman Campbell directed *The Mikado* at Stratford, with Alan Lund choreographing. Two years later, Lund's production of *Anne of Green Gables*, written by Campbell and another Stratford alumnus, Donald Harron, became a fixture of the infant Charlottetown Festival. Christopher Newton went from Stratford after the 1968 season to found Theatre Calgary.

Canadians gradually began assuming limited artistic responsibility at the Stratford Festival itself. George McCowan was Langham's co-director on *Henry IV, Part I* in 1958; Marie Day assisted designer Tanya Moiseiwitsch. Langham had been so impressed with the work of Jean Gascon, the director of Montreal's Théâtre du Nouveau Monde, which played limited seasons in French at the Avon Theatre in 1956 and 1958, that he engaged him as George McCowan's co-director on *Othello* in 1959, with Robert Prévost of the Théâtre du Nouveau Monde as designer. McCowan and Gascon were the first Canadians to direct on the Festival stage, although Douglas Campbell, who had settled in Canada, did *The Winter's Tale* that same summer and continued to direct regularly thereafter. Another expatriate Briton, Brian Jackson, began as head of the properties department before designing first at the Avon, then, in 1960, at the Festival Theatre. Jackson and Desmond Heeley from England designed most major productions at Stratford during the Langham years.

Langham believed the Stratford Festival had to tour to test itself before unfamiliar audiences. In 1956, he took the company to the Edinburgh Festival, where it performed *Henry V* and *Oedipus Rex* to positive reviews. *Two Gentlemen of Verona* and Donald Harron's adaptation of Kleist's comedy *The Broken Jug* visited three Canadian cities during a six-week 1959 tour prior to a New York engagement. In the early 1960s, two popular Guthrie Avon Theatre Gilbert and Sullivan productions also played limited

New York seasons, as well as dates in London, Los Angeles, San Francisco, and Vancouver. It was Centennial year, 1967, before Langham succeeded in arranging a major tour of western Canada. Then that autumn the Festival presented two productions at Expo '67 in Montreal.

However, the Festival's most important tour was probably its 1964 visit to England when it presented three productions at the Chichester Festival Theatre. "The Canadians have come as missionaries to convert us by example to the true use of that apron stage," wrote George Seddon in *The Observer* (12 April). On an open stage resembling its own, the company was displayed to advantage. Bernard Levin in the *Daily Telegraph* (7 April) wrote just one of the many flattering reviews, praising Stratford for using "the awkward Chichester apron stage as well as it can be used."

"Disagreement over the appointment of a successor" (Langham, p. 11) led Michael Langham to remain as Artistic Director until 1967, with a sabbatical season off in 1965, when Douglas Campbell was in charge. During his last five years at Stratford, Langham attempted "a semi-transformation of the Festival" through achieving "operating continuity, involving the performance of contemporary plays, winter tours and eventually a winter home," and by relating "our work on the stage more vividly to the world around us" (Langham, p. 11). Neither objective was fully realized. The Festival did not get a winter home and produced few contemporary plays. Langham also found challenging modern interpretations were "quite strongly resisted by both the press and the middle-aged public of Ontario" (Langham, p. 12). In 1966, for example, his pessimistic anti-war *Henry V*, with none of the heroics and pageantry of his 1956 production, proved unpopular. Neither John Hirsch's staging of the first part of John Barton's *Henry VI* adaptation nor *Dance of Death* at the Avon had appeal enough to compensate, and attendance plummeted by almost twenty thousand from the year before despite a longer season. A lesson learned, in 1967 the Festival imported a star from England, Alan Bates, to play Richard III and cancelled plans announced in 1964 to complete the entire history cycle. However, not until 1968 did attendance finally pass the 1965 level.

In the 1970 Stratford souvenir program, Jean Gascon praised Michael Langham, claiming that during his "formative years . . . many of the promising artistic objectives of the [Festival] were crystalized." Yet under Langham the majority of directors and designers remained English. Canadian plays in particular were ignored. A *Globe and Mail* playwriting contest led to a Festival stage production of Donald Jack's *The Canvas Barricade* in 1962, the only Canadian play in Stratford's history to be performed on the open stage. The competition was not repeated. During Canada's Centennial, only one Canadian play, James Reaney's boyhood reminiscences of the Stratford area, *Colours in the Dark*, was scheduled. It was time for a Canadian artistic director, time for a new beginning.

In fact, Stratford appointed two Canadians, Jean Gascon and John Hirsch.

Langham supported such a move, having decided "at least two years before my term expired, the Festival had become too large and unwieldy for one man to give to all its varied undertakings the attention they merited" (Langham, p. 12). Both Gascon and Hirsch were former artistic directors of other theatres with extensive Stratford experience. However, they proved personally and professionally too incompatible to provide what Nathan Cohen called the "courage of management and . . . large clarity of artistic visions" needed to get the Festival "out of its cul-de-sac."[23] As Hirsch has acknowledged, "Although we like one another as human beings, we were really opposite in temperament, background and aspiration."[24] Gascon agreed: "The business of two artistic directors, looking back on it, was a mistake, causing a lot of friction and a split in the organization."[25]

John Hirsch resigned after the 1968 season, finally leaving one Canadian in sole charge of Guthrie's theatre. Yet under this Canadian, the Stratford Festival continued to drift further and further away from the mainstream of Canadian theatre. Nevertheless, Gascon could boast, "In my time, more than 90% of the whole organization was Canadian," because Canadians now had the required "know-how and the savoir-faire" (Shaw, p. 125).

Jean Gascon hoped to bring "a modern way of behaving, a kind of Gallic flair" to Shakespeare, instead of "seeing the plays the way in which they are traditionally seen" (Shaw, p. 125). He put on some of Shakespeare's less familiar plays, such as *King John*, *Cymbeline*, and *Pericles*, and widened the repertoire to include Jonson, Webster, Sheridan, Goldsmith, de Musset, and Ibsen. He was, however, only partially successful in meeting his three major objectives: to develop a self-contained Canadian company, expand operations year 'round, and establish a theatre for experimental and Canadian work.

"The star system should stop," Gascon believed. "The Company should sell, and not big names imported from England and elsewhere" (Shaw, p. 126). He took his leads from within the company, partly from necessity. With seasons now so long, well-known Canadians such as Christopher Plummer could not accept Stratford engagements. Kenneth Welsh played Hamlet and Lorenzaccio; Pat Galloway, the Duchess of Malfi and Lady Macbeth; William Hutt, King Lear and Tartuffe; and Douglas Rain, Mosca in *Volpone* and Iago. However, the company as a whole began to deteriorate as many of Langham's actors departed, some permanently, others for a season or more, without being adequately replaced. Tony Van Bridge left in 1967, Martha Henry and Douglas Rain in 1968, and even William Hutt for a year in 1969. Mervyn Blake recalled that "at one time, we did have a strong core of middle actors . . . a company's strength. Now we are no longer as strong. There are too many younger people."[26] Not until 1971 did Stratford general manager William Wylie feel that his and Gascon's policy not to bring in imports "but rather to let our junior members develop" was vindicated, with the Festival "re-establish[ing] solidity and a level of professionalism that we haven't had here in years."[27] Yet only 30 percent of the 1971 company returned the following season (Kareda, *Toronto Star*, 3 June 1972).

To help keep his company together, Gascon instituted an expanded touring policy that resulted in regular spring tours to places such as Montreal, Chicago, Ann Arbor, and the Guthrie Theatre in Minneapolis. *There's One in Every Marriage* appeared on Broadway. A seven-week European tour in 1973 culminated in a visit to Russia. *The Imaginary Invalid* went to Australia in 1974. International attention, however, failed to mask growing discontent within the company and among Canadian critics. Why was an organization now billing itself the Stratford National Theatre of Canada touring Europe (not Canada) without a single Canadian play in its repertoire? The Festival could not even claim that the two Shakespeare plays done in Europe had distinctively Canadian interpretations since one, *King Lear*, was directed by an Englishman. Stratford was representing not the Canadian theatre, only itself.

Stratford's short unhappy life as the National Theatre of Canada began in a formal way during the National Arts Centre experiment. The National Arts Centre, which opened in Ottawa in 1969, had a theatre equipped with an open stage and a flexible studio for experimental work. Finally, Stratford could have an appropriate winter home in the nation's capital. Gascon's seeming triumph lasted less than one year, from November 1969 to May 1970, although the Festival continued to stage productions from Stratford in Ottawa until 1972. During that one season, the company mounted two school tours, John Hirsch's children's play *Sauerkringle*, four Stratford productions, and, in repertory, Brendan Behan's *The Hostage* and Boris Vian's *The Empire Builders*. In the Studio, the company presented bills of short plays by Jean-Claude Van Itallie and Slawomir Mrozek, and James Reaney's *The Easter Egg*. Even with relying heavily on productions being planned for or already presented at Stratford, the company found itself dangerously overextended. Gascon had come to believe "you can't stretch yourself indefinitely without losing something."[28] He made a choice and put the Stratford Festival first. Out of ten evenings of theatre presented by the Stratford National Theatre of Canada, only two, Hirsch's children's play and *The Easter Egg*, were Canadian.

At Stratford, Gascon struggled to find a purpose for the Avon Theatre, which the Festival had purchased in 1963, trying a musical, new European plays, French farces, satires, Russian works, and operetta in succeeding seasons. He created the Third Stage as an economical home for less traditional offerings. Under his assistant, Michael Bawtree, programing was dominated by Canadian chamber operas and children's plays. The Third Stage did little to develop Canadian plays. Sharon Pollock's *Walsh* had been successful elsewhere, Betty Jane Wylie's *Mark* was quickly forgotten, and only the stage version of Michael Ondaatje's *The Collected Works of Billy the Kid* was produced at other Canadian theatres. The Third Stage meant third priority. Neither the Avon nor the Third Stage with their separate companies seemed intrinsic parts of an overall Festival plan.

Gascon needed a change and the company needed a change. As he said in a 1973 interview, "I need to be recycled in some way (Kareda, *Toronto Star*, 26 May 1973). His achievements notwithstanding, by the time he left after the 1974 season, Gascon's Stratford had become cut off from the exciting new developments in Canadian theatre. Alternate theatres such as Factory Theatre Lab and the Tarragon Theatre had opened in Toronto in the early 1970s, producing Canadian plays often with considerable success. Theatre Passe Muraille had moved to Clinton, Ontario, not far from Stratford to develop *The Farm Show*. Insistently, often stridently, dedicated nationalists attacked the Stratford and Shaw Festivals and the entrenched regional theatres for ignoring Canadian plays. Why, they argued, should Stratford receive $460,000 in government grants in 1972–73, the largest public subsidy of any theatre in the country, for producing Shakespeare for tourists, while the Tarragon Theatre was struggling to develop an indigenous Canadian theatre on $7,000?[29]

The appointment of a young English director, Robin Phillips, to succeed Gascon was considered the final insult by many nationalists and provoked protest nationwide. Several notable Canadian directors, including John Hirsch, met with some of the Stratford Board to express their "concern for the future of the theatre in Canada, and [their] conviction that the Stratford Festival must play a dominant role in that future." The directors acknowledged that "when Stratford was founded it began a new era in Canadian theatre, and we have benefited from its enterprise and courage." However, they claimed, "theatre in Canada has advanced to a direction that Stratford does not reflect," regrettably producing "two theatres in Canada—ours, and yours—one firmly national and the other imitatively international." The directors exhorted Stratford to take more seriously "its responsibilities as a *de facto* national theatre."[30]

Robin Phillips soon realized that "Stratford had lost its sense of purpose. It had lost sight of its role as part of the Canadian theatre community, its potential for training." He also felt "the organization had lost sight of the importance of the actor and of the writer. . . . Costumes were becoming more important than the spoken voice." The controversial Phillips proceeded to reorganize and revitalize the entire operation, almost doubling the number of productions between 1974 and 1978 and making a greater personal impact on the Stratford Festival than any director since Guthrie. He assumed complete control, claiming that "any organization that's worth anything is run by one man or one woman."[31] He appointed a Head of Design from England, Daphne Dare, and assigned her to renovate the Avon Theatre extensively, design simple permanent settings for both the Avon and Third Stage, and modify the Festival stage, making the balcony removable for the first time. Defying logistical problems, Phillips created one Stratford company; in three successive evenings, a performer could appear in Shakespeare at the Festival Theatre, a musical at the Avon, and a new Canadian play at the Third Stage.

Robin Phillips was the first Stratford Artistic Director to make a success of the Avon Theatre. In 1975, large audiences came to see his Young Company, fresh from the Festival's first Canadian tour in eight years, performing lively unconventional versions of *Two Gentlemen of Verona* and *Comedy of Errors*. Soon Phillips had turned the Avon into the busiest of Stratford's three theatres.

However, many of the problems with the Third Stage remained unsolved. For one thing, it was housed in a building not designed for theatre with no air conditioning and inadequate heating, that was "an inconvenience to the performers . . . and an actual health hazard to audiences." In 1975, Phillips used it for a potpourri of musical and dramatic productions, some Canadian, climaxed by *The Importance of Being Earnest*, featuring William Hutt as Lady Bracknell, one of Phillips' most popular productions, twice revived at the Avon. Phillips found such diverse programing unsatisfactory, but "the notion of using the Third Stage as a showcase for new Canadian work . . . [only] added a suggestion of castoffs."[32] He closed the Third Stage to the public in 1976 and 1977 to concentrate on building up the Avon.

The Third Stage reopened in 1978 with three Canadian plays and an evening of short works by Samuel Beckett. In 1979, the Third Stage saw its first Shakespeare, *Taming of the Shrew*, featuring many younger company members, in repertory with another Stratford first, a full-length improvisation (based on Lorca's *Yerma*), and another new Canadian script. An adaptation of Shakespeare's *Henry VI* plays and Patrick Garland's *Brief Lives* were the only productions scheduled for 1980.

Robin Phillips restored glamour to the Stratford Festival by importing stars, particularly Maggie Smith, Brian Bedford, and Peter Ustinov, supported by distinguished international performers such as Hume Cronyn, Jessica Tandy, Margaret Tyzack, Jeremy Brett, Kathleen Widdoes, and Patricia Conolly. Canadian stars such as Kate Reid, Roberta Maxwell, Gordon Pinsent, and Tom Kneebone also played Stratford seasons, some for the first time. The box office confirmed their impact: in Maggie Smith's initial Stratford season, attendance increased by over eighty thousand and gross receipts by over a million dollars. The stars brought back many international critics who helped increase the Festival's prestige. In 1977, former English critic Ronald Bryden called the predominately Canadian company "as strong a collection of talents as most that Britain's National Theatre or Royal Shakespeare Company could field today," and pointed out that Phillips had "shown what he was capable of achieving: a match for the best in the English-speaking world."[33] Robert Cushman, critic of London's *Observer*, wrote, "Mr. Phillips has, by almost universal consent, restored to

Stratford an excitement missing for close on twenty years."[34] Richard Eder, then *New York Times* critic, praised Phillips for showing "how exciting, human, and above all, alive the theatre can still be."[35]

Yet Phillips also gave distinguished Canadian talent the chance to excel. Martha Henry in particular received acclaim for a wide variety of roles including Isabella in *Measure for Measure*, Sister Jeanne in *The Devils*, Hecuba in Edward Bond's *The Woman*, and Beatrice in *Much Ado About Nothing*. English critic B. A. Young described her as "totally captivating" and compared her to Olivier in her "ability to change her physical shape at will."[36] To their long list of Stratford triumphs, William Hutt added the Fool opposite Peter Ustinov's King Lear, and Douglas Rain, Gloucester and Henry IV.

Alan Scarfe appeared as Othello, Bottom, and Benedick. Nicholas Pennell widened his range to include roles such as Oswald in *Ghosts*, Grandier in *The Devils*, and Iago. Richard Monette came from the alternate theatre to become a Shakespearean leading man, portraying Hamlet, Prince Hal, Romeo, and Henry V. Jack Wetherall, who, Phillips recalled, "had been here for years and never opened his mouth,"[37] ended up as Orlando to Maggie Smith's Rosalind. Marti Maraden played most of Shakespeare's ingenues including Juliet, Ophelia, and Miranda. Domini Blythe acted Desdemona and Strindberg's Miss Julie. Stephen Russell joined the company in inconsequential parts and had the opportunity to work his way up to Hotspur, Richard II, and Henry VI. Phillips gave his young actors extra experience by producing two versions of *Hamlet* and *Henry V* and three of *Richard II* by changing principals. For Ronald Bryden, much of Stratford's new quality came from "the striking improvement in young actors . . . who two seasons ago promised little more than promise" (Bryden, p. 58). In 1978, Phillips issued agreements guaranteeing fifty performers parts for three years to emphasize the importance of his acting ensemble.

Robin Phillips tried to bridge the gulf between Stratford and the rest of Canadian theatre. Realizing his own lack of Canadian experience, he accepted his position only after being promised a year not only to familiarize himself with the Festival but to travel extensively in Canada seeing plays and meeting theatre people. As his Literary Manager, Phillips appointed Urjo Kareda, former critic of the *Toronto Star*. Phillips established an advisory board for each of the three Stratford theatres, later blended into one body, consisting primarily of directors and actors both within the company and across the country. He willingly opened the Festival to new talent from the alternate theatres. For example, in the summer of 1976 while Maggie Smith and Jeremy Brett, as Cleopatra and Antony, were starring on the Festival stage, so too were alternate theatre veterans Jackie Burroughs and Nick Mancuso in Bill Glassco's production of *The Merchant of Venice*.

Nor were playwrights neglected. As a 19 October 1978 press release stated, "During the past three years, the Stratford Festival has demonstrated a most positive commitment to Canadian playwrights, both initiating projects which have borne immediate results and also creating new programs designed to develop over a longer time period." Part of Urjo Kareda's job, said the release, was "to help specifically in the development of scripts and work with playwrights." Jessica Tandy starred in Larry Fineberg's adaptation of Constance Beresford-Howe's novel *Eve* at the Avon in 1976. Vancouver writer Sheldon Rosen's *Ned and Jack* was produced at the Third Stage in 1978; a year later it was revived in a revised form at the Avon.

Under a policy that "European classics scheduled for production at the Stratford Festival would be presented in specially commissioned new adaptations by Canadian playwrights" (19 October 1978 press release), John Murrell adapted *Uncle Vanya* and *The Seagull* (and had a new play commissioned), Tom Cone adapted *Servant of Two Masters* (and had his own *Stargazing* performed at the Third Stage), and Larry Fineberg adapted *Medea*.

Robin Phillips' efforts, however, were not always accepted in good faith. As *Toronto Star* critic Gina Mallet observed, "British praise for Phillips has also insulated him from having to come to grips with the criticism levelled at him here. Negative criticism can be conveniently put down to nationalist sour grapes."[38] Mallet particularly mentioned the suspicion that Phillips had somehow deliberately made look bad the several experienced Canadian directors (Eric Steiner, Marigold Charlesworth, Bill Glassco, and John Wood) who have had Stratford failures, usually on the difficult Festival stage. Phillips blamed inexperience for the problems encountered: "One understands the energy that wants to do it, but then really hurting mistakes are made and people don't want to come back."[39] One person successful in her first attempt at directing on the Festival stage, with *Othello* in 1979, was Frances Hyland, who could draw upon many years of experience acting on that stage. Phillips encouraged interested company members to try directing. Brian Bedford's production of *Titus Andronicus*, first seen in 1978, was successfully revived in 1980. Urjo Kareda served as co-director several times. Martha Henry, Alan Scarfe, Ted Follows, and Richard Monette directed at the Third Stage. Peter Moss, a Canadian, became a major Festival director within Robin Phillips' Stratford. After considerable experience in England, Moss went from an assistant to regular director on all three Festival stages. His productions of the two parts of *Henry IV* were considered highlights of the 1979 season.

Phillips, partly from necessity (he was unsuccessful in recruiting outside directors), and partly to economize, did much of the directing himself, which quickly led to the charge that the Festival was becoming a one-man show. In 1976, he directed or co-directed seven out of ten plays; within four seasons, he had directed more productions than Jean Gascon had in seven or Michael Langham in thirteen. Phillips' work load exacted the same toll of illness and creative exhaustion it had from his two predecessors. In 1978, two scheduled productions had to be cancelled for the first time. After the 1978 season, as Phillips explained, "I *had* to resign. I felt it was the only honest thing I could do. . . . It was tough just explaining that I did not have another job to go to, that I did not want to leave Canada. I just wanted to stop" (Cuthbert, p. 16). Instead, the Board persuaded him to take what became a very short sabbatical.

Phillips became convinced that the Festival needed a permanent winter home, preferably in Toronto, the largest and most active English-speaking theatre center in Canada. In 1979, he proposed a liaison between Stratford and the St. Lawrence Centre in Toronto. Both theatres would have separate administrations but share a pool of directors. Phillips believed Stratford at least required a team leadership to maintain standards and excitement year after year. Different members of the directorate would have the responsibility for planning and supervising each season, although all would direct regularly and consult on policy. Gina Mallet for one saw the merit in Phillips' plan: "Almost everyone who's watched the growing problems of the single artistic director of any major institution, agrees that directorates are the only way to go."[40] However, the St. Lawrence Centre link did not materialize and plans for a Festival directorate remain conjectural at best.

In general, the Stratford Festival has fulfilled most of its original stated aims and objectives. Primarily through its productions, Stratford has "promote[d] interest in, and the study of, the arts generally and literature, drama and music in particular," with special emphasis naturally on "Shakespearean culture and tradition."[41] As Tyrone Guthrie claimed, "A Classical programme is the indispensable training ground both for the practitioners and connoisseurs of any art" ("Long View," p. 158). Student performances, publications, special seminars, concerts, and musical performances of all kind, displays of costumes and properties, art exhibits, and sessions where audience members can meet the company have all helped enrich the Stratford experience.

When it was founded, the Festival pledged "to provide improved opportunities for Canadian artistic talent, [and] to advance the development of the arts of the theatre in Canada." Unquestionably, it has done much in both areas, but it is a matter of some debate whether it can or should do more. As early as 1958, Tyrone Guthrie could justifiably claim that "Success at this Festival has advanced the professional status of Canadian actors . . . and has won for several of them prominent engagements in New York and Hollywood" (*A Life*, p. 300). The same cannot be said for designers and directors, whose opportunities through the years have been limited. In 1954, Guthrie urged the Festival to "give opportunities for young directors to get their feet in the door, not necessarily by entrusting them with the responsibility for the main productions, but by putting them in charge of understudies' rehearsals, special performances and so on" ("Long View," pp. 189–90). Canadians have served as assistant directors, co-directors, workshop directors, and Third Stage directors, but few have been assigned major productions. Those that have, particularly Jean Gascon and John Hirsch, were experienced before coming to Stratford. In twenty-eight years, only George McCowan, under Langham, and Peter Moss, under Phillips, have developed noticeably within the Festival. More seriously, Stratford has not done enough to help groom its own future artistic leaders.

Late in 1979, the public learned that the Stratford Festival was in real danger of closing permanently at the end of the 1980 season. In 1979, a year in which box office revenues and corporate and individual contributions were at record highs, the Festival incurred a deficit of almost $650,000, only partially offset by a previous surplus of $400,000.[42] Far from being extravagant, the Festival could prove the cost of mounting a Shakespearean play on the main stage had not increased in seven years. The Festival simply could not break even with 14-percent inflation raising costs while the Canada Council was reducing its grant by 7 percent and the Ontario Arts Council keeping its unchanged. The Stratford Festival emphasized it paid the federal and provincial governments more than four million dollars in taxes alone in exchange for $750,000 in grants.

Stratford's warning failed to elicit any promises from politicians, but it did attract attention. In a lead editorial, the *Toronto Star* (11 December 1979) declared, "The Stratford Festival is too important to be allowed to die. . . . The festival is a great source of pride to Canadians. . . . Given the training the festival offers fledgling Canadian actors, the high level of entertainment it offers a vast audience and the large amount of money it earns for the government, it would be well worth $2 million a year in government grants to keep the festival alive." Considering its national and international prestige, and the fact it is a major Ontario tourist attraction, the economic mainstay of its region, injecting, by its own estimate, approximately twenty-five million dollars into the local economy each summer, no government would dare let the Festival close. It has earned that security.

However, fiscal restraint could kill Stratford creatively, reducing it to what Nathan Cohen called "just another summer theatre venture, with special overtones of snobbery."[43] Stratford needs to grow, adapt, and challenge itself by touring, establishing a winter home, and experimenting with film and television. All these costly initiatives are vital to keep the Festival from becoming artistically moribund.

Some critics have argued that since Stratford is what they call a "picnic theatre," it should be funded by government tourism agencies, not by arts councils. However, if Stratford has no artistic merit, it is doing much more harm to Canadian theatre by squandering so much precious talent than it is by taking an unfair share of grants. Besides, there is nothing intrinsically wrong with playing primarily for visitors, many from outside Canada. Tyrone Guthrie wanted the trip to Stratford to be a kind of pilgrimage, a time for people to forget everyday concerns and concentrate on the plays (*Renown*, p. 32).

In the last few years, the Stratford Festival has regained much of its former stature. It has changed, becoming much more responsive to the alternate theatre. The alternate theatre has also changed, opening itself up to classical and international work. Under its new artistic director, John Hirsch, Stratford is still primarily a classical theatre with an international outlook, but it encourages Canadian work at all levels. The alternate theatre is still primarily nationalistic, interested in Canadian plays, but it now has the self-confidence to display its Canadian work alongside plays from other times and places. Both Stratford and the alternate theatre have moved closer together; both can learn from each other; and, moreover, in this time of financial uncertainty, both need each other.

The Stratford Festival is no longer at the center of Canadian theatre the way it was in 1953. Nor is it any longer even our unofficial national theatre. It is, nonetheless, a vital, integral part of theatre in this nation, an indispensable element in the Canadian theatrical mosaic.[44]

Notes

1. "A Long View of the Stratford Festival," in *Twice Have the Trumpets Sounded*, ed. Tyrone Guthrie and Robertson Davies (Toronto, 1954), p. 155.
2. Tyrone Guthrie, *A New Theatre* (New York, 1964), pp. 72–73.
3. Arnold Edinborough, "A New Stratford Festival," *Shakespeare Quarterly*, 5 (1954), 50.
4. Tyrone Guthrie, Robertson Davies, and Grant Macdonald, *Renown at Stratford. A Record of the Shakespeare Festival in Canada, 1953* (Toronto, 1953).
5. Quoted in Shakespeare, *The Merchant of Venice*, ed. John Stevens (Toronto, 1970), p. xv.
6. Quoted in a Stratford Festival publicity release, 1971.
7. Quoted by Sid Adilman, *Toronto Star*, 9 June 1972.
8. Comment by Robin Phillips in a 29 October 1979 speech, distributed by the Festival.
9. Statistics from publicity booklet, *The Stratford Festival Story* (1979 edition).
10. "The Story of the Stratford Festival," in *The Merchant of Venice*, ed. John Stevens, p. x.
11. Guthrie, *Renown at Stratford*, p. 28.
12. Tyrone Guthrie, *A Life in the Theatre* (London, 1960), p. 286.
13. James Forsyth, *Tyrone Guthrie* (London, 1976), p. 222.
14. Grace Shaw, *Stratford Under Cover* (Toronto, 1977), p. 48.
15. *Globe Magazine* (Toronto), 14 June 1958.
16. Tyrone Guthrie, "Shakespeare at Stratford, Ontario," *Shakespeare Survey*, 8 (1955), 127.
17. Cecil Clarke, "An Open Stage at Stratford-on-Avon, Ontario," *Theatre Notebook*, 8 (1953–54), 43.
18. Guthrie, "Shakespeare at Stratford," p. 128.
19. Nathan Cohen, radio broadcast 24 July 1955, quoted in Wayne E. Edmonstone, *Nathan Cohen: The Making of a Critic* (Toronto, 1977) p. 229.
20. Michael Langham, "Twelve Years at Stratford," in *The Stratford Scene*, ed. Peter Raby (Toronto, 1968), p. 8.

21. Arnold Edinborough, "Consolidation at Stratford, Ontario," *Shakespeare Quarterly*, 7 (1956), 404.

22. Ann Henry, "Stratford Comes to Winnipeg," *Performing Arts in Canada* (Spring 1966), p. 33.

23. Nathan Cohen, "Stratford After Fifteen Years," *Queen's Quarterly*, 75 (Autumn 1968), 61.

24. Quoted in Grace Shaw, *Stratford Under Cover* (Toronto, 1977), p. 125.

25. Quoted in Urjo Kareda, "Stratford: An Uneasy Time," *Toronto Star*, 26 May 1973.

26. Quoted in Urjo Kareda, "Stratford: Turnover Strains the Company," *Toronto Star*, 3 June 1972.

27. Quoted in Don Rubin, "Return of Veterans Promises an Impressive Stratford Year," *Toronto Star*, 8 May 1971.

28. Quoted in a Stratford press release, April 1970.

29. Peter Hay, in *Canadian Theatre Review*, 2 (Spring 1974), 15.

30. Letter to the Stratford board, reprinted in *Canadian Theatre Review*, 3 (Summer 1974), 34–35.

31. Quoted in Art Cuthbert, "The Merchant of Stratford," *Centre Stage* (November 1978), p. 18.

32. *Stage One, The Future*, Stratford Festival booklet, [1977].

33. Ronald Bryden, "A Former Light Restored," *Macleans*, 11 July 1977, p. 56.

34. The *Observer*, 19 June 1977 (as quoted in *Stage One*).

35. *New York Times*, 26 June 1977 (as quoted in *Stage One*).

36. *Financial Times*, 14 June 1977 (as quoted in *Stage One*).

37. Quoted in Gina Mallet, "A Charming Despot," *Toronto Star*, 11 February 1977.

38. Gina Mallet, "Wherefore Are Thou, Stratford," *Toronto Star*, 12 May 1979.

39. "Charming Despot," *Toronto Star*, 11 February 1977.

40. Gina Mallet, "Festival Season Worthy," *Toronto Star*, 20 October 1979.

41. Aims listed in *The Stratford Festival Story* (1978 edition).

42. *Toronto Globe and Mail*, 30 October 1979.

43. Radio broadcast, 11 July 1954, quoted in Edmonstone, *Nathan Cohen*, p. 227.

44. For a summary of the controversial events involving the resignation of Robin Phillips from the Stratford Festival, and the appointment of John Hirsch as artistic director, see Boyd Neil's "Chronology," *Canadian Theatre Review*, 30 (Spring 1981), 25–33.

Ann Saddlemyer

13

Thoughts on National Drama and the Founding of Theatres _____

I would like to suggest in this essay some tentative, exploratory comparisons between Canadian and Irish theatre. They are tentative because, in comparison with the massive documentation on the development of Irish theatre, Canadian scholars are lamentably lacking in the nuts-and-bolts knowledge of the history of theatre and drama in their own country; they are exploratory because it is difficult, with this vacuum in our past, to stand back sufficiently from the contemporary explosion of plays and play-making to offer confident critical assessment of a national nature. However, parallels, both specific and general, there are; and, bearing in mind the young Samuel Beckett's warning to the Joyce industry, "Literary criticism is not bookkeeping," what I have learned about the one seems to provide insight concerning the other.[1]

I have recently been working on the collection, transcription, dating, and annotating of letters between W. B. Yeats, Lady Gregory, and J. M. Synge, the first directorate of Ireland's national theatre, the Abbey. Established by Yeats and Lady Gregory with the help of Edward Martyn some years before Synge became actively involved, the theatre achieved its first flowering during the period from 1904, when it moved into its own building, to Synge's death five years later. Rarely, except in time of extraordinary crisis (as distinct from the steady series of minor crises regularly spawned by theatrical activities) were three, or even two, directors in Dublin together; consequently, the correspondence is especially revealing both of the complexities of managing a theatre and of the delicacy of human relationships (always to be reckoned with in matters theatrical). Yeats wrote from Paris, London, Dublin, most often from Coole; Synge, who (Yeats once complained to Bernard Shaw) was sometimes "rather languid in his letter writing,"[2] sent messages from Paris, London, Kerry, Wicklow, Rathgar, and Kingstown. Often Lady Gregory wrote twice daily; frequently all three wrote to each other on the same day; and always, in a steady stream, came the yellow missives, addressed singly or jointly, from Yeats's patron and owner of the theatre building, the redoubtable Miss Horniman. This many-sided correspondence dealt with programing, lighting, costumes, staging, publication, promotion, touring, casting, critics, fund-raising, rehearsals, tantrums, salaries, resignations, dismissals, revisions, rejections, chanting, singing, speech-making—and, of course, with the plays themselves. Out of this unlikely, fortuitous, instinctive, frequently uneasy collaboration, we can discern some of those nuts and bolts—the aims, projects, achievements, and failures—that make up a national movement.

For from the beginning, this was Yeats's ambition: as early as 1893 he had written of his book of essays, *The Celtic Twilight*, "I have desired, like every artist, to create a little world out of the beautiful, pleasant, and significant things of this marred and clumsy world, and to show in a vision something of the face of Ireland to any of my own people who would look where I bid them."[3] Elsewhere, in 1892, reviewing a friend's play, "England is old . . . but Ireland has still full tables. Here in Ireland the marble block is waiting for us almost untouched, and the statues will come as soon as we have learned to use the chisel."[4] He urged his fellow writers to turn away from the influence of England and the desire to emulate works written for another people, out of another culture, rooted in foreign histories; he established literary societies (first in London, then in Dublin), planned a circulating "Library of Ireland," encouraged scholarship and critical/historical studies, compiled anthologies, lectured, and proselytized. The result of this literary nationalism would be, he believed, a truer, more honest, a richer art: "We should make poems on the familiar landscapes we love, not the strange and rare and glittering scenes we wonder at," he instructed a fellow poet, while apparently not always writing so familiarly himself. "One should love best what is nearest and most interwoven with one's life." "One's verses should hold, as in a mirror, the colours of one's own climate and scenery in their right proportion."[5] Inevitably, finally, this emphasis on a feeling of *place*, developed by his own highly visual sense and need for historicity (of both folk and faerie), led him by devious route through the west of Ireland to Lady Gregory. When he told her of his desire for a theatre for the plays he was writing, she asked the obvious question, "Why not in Ireland?" So all roads came at last together in Dublin.

The history of the early years of the Irish dramatic movement has been told frequently in memoirs, biographies, daily journals, newspaper articles, academic theses, and documentary histories. From these the discerning reader, isolating fact from partisan fiction, can trace the frequent metamorphoses—beginning with the Irish Literary Theatre (composed entirely of playwrights) on the one hand, and a group of players led by Frank and Willie Fay on the other; through the infusion of Maud Gonne's Daughters of Ireland (who had gained some performance experience in political/historical tableaux and some of whom, like Sara Allgood of the golden voice, stayed to perform while others went on to the larger arena still of the 1916 Easter Rebellion); which in turn formed, first, W. G. Fay's Irish National Dramatic Company, and, after that uneasy amalgamation, the Irish National Theatre Society with Yeats as president. To this group, Miss Horniman granted free use of the new theatre on Abbey Street, one time city morgue.

Although possessed of a stage, and riding the tide of nationalist fervor and thespian fever, Yeats was not content. "I am only certain of Lady Gregory, Synge and myself on a question of dramatic policy," he wrote in 1905 to his long-term friend and sometime foe AE (the poet George Russell).[6] To him he outlined what he hoped would be a final transformation into a limited company. With AE's help ("it requires a great deal of tact," he argued convincingly), he wished to persuade the diehard nationalists to give up their haphazard democratic method with its hours of fruitless discussion, and to become for the first time salaried professionals. (The money, supplied by the English Miss Horniman, was only incidental, as one actress explained when after much vacillation she refused to join at one pound a week.) AE, organizer of men, banks, and creameries, reluctantly agreed to help, and by late autumn Yeats was able to write to the actress Florence Farr (*Letters*, p. 463): "I have been kept all this while and am still kept by the affairs of the Theatre Society. We are turning it into a private Limited Liability Co. in order to get control into a few hands. If all goes well, Lady Gregory, Synge and myself will be the Directors in a few days and will appoint all Committees and have more votes between us than all the other Shareholders. . . . I am now entirely certain that we will make a great Theatre and get an audience for it."

"Players and painted stage took all my love," Yeats wrote in "The Circus Animals' Desertion," and certainly players required great care, for Yeats's theories of speaking and stage management—in reaction to the English tradition which, he felt, emphasized stage personality to the detriment of stage play—had long been developed through his experiments with chanting to the psaltery with Florence Farr. Although Synge was a reluctant convert, because he had himself been trained as a musician he took painstaking care over the speaking of his own difficult, rhythmic lines, even punctuating for rhythm and sound as much as for sense. In striving for the reality of a language rooted in fresh soil, Lady Gregory, too, with her "Kiltartan" dialect, demanded a new vocal range and inflection. Later Yeats was to admit, "I wanted all my poetry to be spoken on a stage or sung and, because I did not understand my own instincts, gave half a dozen wrong or secondary reasons" (*Essays and Introductions*, p. 529). Upon hearing Yeats give a reading in London, the author Stefan Zweig remarked, "more of a celebration of poems than spontaneous reading."[7] It was this very quality of celebration that Yeats sought in the speaking of his plays, and all were fortunate in Frank Fay's passion for verse-speaking, which had been transmitted to the early actors. Years later, Sara Allgood was still exercising her voice according to her first teacher's precepts.

So, too, with stage management; for the style of acting developed by Willie Fay demanded that very economy and simplicity the new plays required: movement so subordinated to voice that even the natural clumsiness of the actors contributed to the total effect of simplicity and stillness. Amateurism became an asset, unchannelled energy and basic love of storytelling directed toward the lines alone. "The actors must move," Yeats wrote in *Samhain*, "slowly and quietly and not very much, and there should be something in their movements decorative and rhythmical as if they were paintings on a frieze. They must not draw attention to themselves at wrong moments."[8] Although the oft-quoted example of Yeats's stage management— that the actors rehearse in barrels, moving only when poked with a long stick (not the only precursor of Beckett's dramatic methods)—did not take place, Lady Gregory frequently rehearsed the actors with books on their heads. Synge, even more cautious, wrote detailed stage directions as to every movement and facial expression in his plays. Even the farcical situations woven into their comedies were carefully controlled, actions and energy dictated by character, and an overall stage pattern of movement.

Stage design, too, became a home (one could almost say a cottage) industry. Although supported at various times by Robert Gregory, Charles Ricketts, and Gordon Craig (who allowed the use of his famous screens even before the Moscow *Hamlet* and designed masks for Yeats's early plays), much of the setting and costumes were designed or supervised by the triumvirate. Lady Gregory took an active role in costuming and building properties. "I have got a fine second hand coat for Frank Fay at a pawnshop," she writes exultantly over *The Pot of Broth* (which she and Yeats wrote together). She was equally conscientious over productions by other dramatists. "I am distracted trying to get Synge's properties together for staging *Riders to the Sea*. I luckily took the flannel myself to the Gort dyer, and found he was going to use Diamond dyes instead of madder, and only 2 lbs. arrived. No real Aran caps can be got so far, or tweed. . . . [Synge] has to deal with Aran Islanders, I with nuns, and I do think they might run a race backwards! However, yesterday 'An ass and car went into the country' and brought back the spinning wheel in triumph, and it has been sent off by the nuns, but the red petticoats aren't ready yet and the pampooties will have to be made in Dublin, and a good thing too, there is no object in bringing local smells into the theatre."[9] Two years later, Synge is suggesting that Molly Allgood be taught to spin, so that "there be no fake about the show." Letters contain detailed instructions for the blocking of plays, drawing of costumes, discussions (especially over Yeats's *Shadowy Waters* and Synge's *Deirdre of the Sorrows*) concerning colors of costumes, and a sharp awareness of any tendency in the actors to "gag" their lines or overdo make-up. Inevitably there were constant worries over theatre management, budgeting, advertising, and business matters. Checks required to be signed, and there are pathetic pleas from the business manager for salary funds. "We were very much taken aback when we heard from Miss Horniman that you were in London," writes Synge to Lady Gregory from Dublin, "as we had just sent cheques to Coole, and had no money for Dundalk." Nor were they always in agreement on planning: after one particular argument, Synge, who was often called upon to conciliate, wrote privately to Lady Gregory, "One moral from the story is that W.B.Y. must not be the person to deal *directly* with the actors, as he is rather too impetuous." On another occasion, Lady Gregory wrote in exasperation to Yeats, "I have felt that Synge would leave us to deal with all trouble," while Synge replied vehemently to Yeats, "I may have been wrong in what I decided but in such things one has to follow one's instinct." Lady Gregory and Synge objected, then reluctantly agreed, to a trial period when Miss Horniman and Yeats wished to "enrich" the company—and incidentally add some necessary discipline—by importing an English-trained Irish "star" for his verse plays and an English stage manager. Neither actress (Miss Darragh) nor manager (Ben Iden Payne) lasted for more than four months. Some months later, Synge in turn wrote a lengthy memorandum objecting to a reorganization along continental lines, suggested by Yeats and Lady Gregory. The strength of the movement, he insisted, is that it is local, speaking to ourselves in our own voices.

Perhaps the greatest continuing worry and cause for disagreement was the choice of program both at home and on tour. Lists of suggestions bounced back and forth between Coole and Dublin, a harassed Willie Fay sighing for speedier decisions on revisions, printers waiting for complete cast lists for programs, business manager holding up newspaper copy for the subscription list, that delicate balance between plays and playwrights meanwhile being weighed from all angles by the worried directors. A major crisis occurred when an overworked Willie Fay, aggrieved at his lack of control over the actors, resigned, taking his brother with him. Still, the theatre went on.

However, three playwrights, especially when performing such multiple roles, do not a theatre—and certainly not a national movement—make. "I have learnt much of Ireland as a reader for the Abbey Theatre," Yeats was to write in *On the Boiler* (his last platform-journal), "perhaps as much as a priest learns in the confessional" (*Explorations*, p. 445). One of their first moves on the formation of the limited company had been to do away with the democratic play-reading committee, reserving to themselves alone, as Lady Gregory put it, "this delicate and difficult matter, which requires culture, instinct and courage." (Rumor persisted for many years, though unfounded, that the real reason was the rejection of one of Yeats's early plays, submitted under an assumed name.) Again, business was carried out in a three-cornered fashion, each director making full notes on every play submitted, and frequently giving lengthy comments even when the play was rejected. Where Yeats concentrated on ideas, Lady Gregory analyzed characterization, while Synge tended to comment on structure. Often, after a play was accepted, more than one director worked closely with the author on revisions. Eventually, they wrote "Advice to Playwrights Who are Sending Plays to the Abbey, Dublin," which reads in part:

The Abbey Theatre is a subsidised theatre with an educational object. It will, therefore, be useless as a rule to send it plays intended as popular entertainments and that alone, or originally written for performance by some popular actor at the popular theatres. A play to be suitable for performance at the Abbey should contain some criticism of life, founded on the experience of personal observation of the writer, or some vision of life, of Irish life by preference, important from its beauty or from some excellence of style; and this intellectual quality is not more necessary to tragedy than to the gayest comedy. We do not desire propagandist plays, nor plays written mainly to serve some obvious moral purpose.

Careful attention should be paid to dialogue, and it was advisable to send a scenario together with one completely written act before writing a lengthy play.[10]

However, too frequently the dramatists did not appear, and those who did exhibited an increasing fondness for modern Irish life at the expense of the legendary and historical material the directors also recommended. To their chagrin, often the more popular plays were those the directors privately considered inferior—pandering to unthinking laughter (such as William Boyle's farces) or patterned too closely on the naturalist mode for that inner spark of magic they sought. Occasionally, too, mistakes were made: long before the fracas over O'Casey's *The Silver Tassie*, a play by Ezra Pound was rejected "on the grounds that the indecencies would cause a riot in Dublin;"[11] Yeats wrote some thousand words to Shaw explaining where he and Synge felt *John Bull's Other Island* should be cut, finally accepting the play despite Willie Fay's nervousness about casting; but, in the end, for lack of a Broadbent, the play was lost to the theatre. So, despite the occasional flash of dark genius from George Fitzmaurice, the competent craftsmanship of Lennox Robinson and others, the first decade of the theatre movement belonged, in theory and practice, to the directors.

There were further responsibilities, for plays once written must find as wide an audience as possible. Thus, the directors found themselves involved in publishing. The Abbey Theatre series was established by their former associate, George Roberts of Maunsel and Company, and Miss Horniman gave permission for theatre editions to be sold on performance in the theatre. In turn, that reading public must be enlarged and educated, and so there appeared a theatre journal—*Beltaine* was followed by *Samhain* (which also published one-act plays); when specific quarrels required an answer, Yeats invented *The Arrow*. When these did not suffice, there were always lectures, letters to the editor, and lengthy discussions through the newspaper columns. The addiction to polemicizing was primarily Yeats's, although he encouraged Lady Gregory to edit one heated exchange (*Ideals in Ireland*) and Edward Martyn another (*Literary Ideals in Ireland*).

In most cases, battles with the public, as with the players, were over conflicts of means more than ideals. After the Easter rebellion, Lady Gregory wrote to Yeats of Pearse and McDonagh, "who ought to have been on our side of intellectual freedom, and I keep wondering whether we could not have brought them into that intellectual movement. Perhaps those Abbey lectures we often spoke of might have helped." "It seems as if the leaders were what is wanted in Ireland, and will be even more wanted in the future—a fearless and imaginative opposition to the conventional and opportunist parliamentarians, who have never helped our work even by intelligent opposition." Always, for Lady Gregory at least, it was worth starting again—providing plays, players, and audience were in good faith and hence retrievable. She once suggested closing the theatre altogether for a while; "I have a desire to unload all the rubbish we have been taking on of late, and make a new start in better times." Yeats, on the other hand, revelled in a fight, and Synge provided him with ample fuel, remaining determinedly nonpolitical and uncompromising. After *The Playboy* riots, Yeats wrote to his New York supporter John Quinn: "It will take some time to measure the consequences of this dispute, but so far as I can judge it has done us good. It has been for some time inevitable that the intellectual element here in Dublin should fall out with the more brainless patriotic element, and come into existence as a conscious force by doing so. I think this has happened."[12] Despite her battles to give it a hearing, Lady Gregory disliked *Playboy* intensely, although she admired it as a work of art and did everything in her power to assist Synge. Of Yeats's struggles over this and Norreys Connell's *The Piper* barely a month later, she commented, "It may really be the turn of the tide, for we shall get respect anyhow for going on with what we think good work."

Why did they do it? What is it that, in Yeats's words, "compels a man to make his own cup bitter?"[13] Each had other responsibilities and interests: Synge suffered from ill health and was undergoing the strain of an unsatisfactory love affair; Yeats's activities, both personal and public, were so numerous that, fortunately, they are too familiar to require enumeration here; Lady Gregory had family responsibilities and was immersed in editing family journals, translating the sagas, and running Coole. None was wealthy and all three felt compelled to earn by writing. For Lady Gregory, the explanation was perhaps most simple: she believed in educating for Home Rule, in "restoring to Ireland its native dignity," in seeking and making public the tales of ancient Ireland and the simple wisdom of "the folk." The theatre was her platform, and she dreamed of a series of historical plays that would be performed by school children across the country. Synge sought in his wanderings through the west, in the twilights of Wicklow, and within himself, the union of natural with supernatural, passion with action, immediacy with eternity, spirit with the clay and worms. The theatre bodied forth that vision. And Yeats? "I had not wanted to 'elevate them' or 'educate them' as the words are understood," he writes in *Discoveries*, "but to make them understand my vision, and I had not wanted a large audience, certainly not what is called a national audience, but enough people for what is accidental and temporary to lose itself" (*Essays and Introductions*, p. 265).

Once, cataloguing his debts to critics, Ezra Pound categorized Yeats's contribution as "considerable encouragement to tell people to go to hell, and to maintain absolute intransigence" (*Letters of Ezra Pound*, p. 245). All three directors shared some of that arrogance. Yeats once asked Synge, "Do you write your plays out of love or out of hatred of Ireland?" and received the reply, "I do not know. I have often asked myself that same question. But whatever is the motive the work cannot be different."[14] Lady Gregory once bitterly commented, "We have certainly come across a good deal of the seamy side of human nature since we began this theatre. . . . I hope we may preserve our own integrity." In old age, Yeats was to write in *On the Boiler*, "The success of the Abbey Theatre has grown out of a simple conviction of its founders: I was the spokesman because I was born arrogant and had learnt an artist's arrogance—'Not what you want but what we want'—and we were the first modern theatre that said it." Then he added, almost as an afterthought, "Yet the theatre has not, apart from this one quality [of teaching players to understand the play and their own natures] gone my way or in any way I wanted it to go, and often, looking back, I have wondered if I did right in giving so much of my life to the expression of other men's genius" (*Explorations*, p. 414). Many times Synge felt the same and, in fact, was so disillusioned after the *Playboy* reception that he offered to give up his directorate. Yeats's reply was emphatic and to the point: "While we are busy fighting your battles is no time to talk of resigning." A few years later, Lady Gregory had to pull Yeats himself up sharply, refusing to allow his resignation but offering as a compromise to take full responsibility for rehearsals. When the Fays were threatening to leave and the players particularly unruly, she temporarily lost her usual optimism: "I don't think we have ever been at such a boggy place, no enemy to fight in the open, but the ground sinking under us."

But they also gained much, for all three learned their craft in the collaboration of common aims, devastatingly honest appraisal, and theatre practice. Dublin, as Lady Gregory expressed it, was also their laboratory. In 1906, Yeats wrote of the play that had perhaps gained most from that laboratory:

The Shadowy Waters . . . is to be judged, like all my plays, as part of an attempt to create a national dramatic literature in Ireland, and it takes upon itself its true likeness of a Jack-a-lantern among more natural and simple things, when set among the plays of my fellow-workers. . . . Nor is it only the stories and the country mind that have made us one school, for we have talked over one another's work so many times, that when a play of mine comes into my memory I cannot always tell how much even of the radical structure I may not owe to the writer of 'The Lost Saint' [Douglas Hyde], or of 'The Shadow of the Glen' [Synge], or more than all, to the writer of 'Hyacinth Halvey' [Lady Gregory]; or that I would have written at all in so heady a mood if I did not know that one or the other were at hand to throw a bushel of laughter into the common basket.[15]

Eighty years ago, the manifesto of the Irish Literary Theatre was first published. It read in part,

By the word 'literary' is meant production, which however much it may fall short of its aim, will at least be inspired by artistic ideas, uninfluenced by the purposes which under present conditions give us the production of plays on the regular stage—that of achieving an immediate commercial success. The Irish Literary Drama will appeal rather to the intellect and spirit than to the senses. It will eventually, it is hoped, furnish a vehicle for the literary expression of the national thought and ideals of Ireland such as has not hitherto been in existence.[16]

Not many years after Synge's death, Yeats wrote his famous open letter to Lady Gregory, announcing the failure of his dream, but the success of a theatre.[17] Privately, Lady Gregory agreed. "From the unmeasurable [it has] become concrete, has fallen from imagination to reason. . . . I dont [sic] see how we can keep it. I dont know if we can ever expand again. But I think of the early days when all seemed possible even a seventh day of creation. I dont wonder that you are looking to a new audience, one must find it somewhere or become barren." Yet Sean O'Casey was still to come, his "gift for characterization" spotted, in an early submission, by Lady Gregory. If Synge had lived, surely he would have insisted with her that *The Silver Tassie* remain in Ireland. If the Abbey had not remained open, despite all misgivings, would O'Casey have written at all? Never again would a phalanx of artistic belief be driven through the minor differences of three distinguished minds of such diverse experience and outlook. For without that privilege of trust, even as O'Casey studied his craft under the tutelage of some of Ireland's finest actors, the influence of the Abbey Theatre was waning. Perhaps Yeats's ambition was impossible, to bring "the imagination and speech of the country, all that poetical tradition descended from the Middle Ages, to the people of the town." "I thought we might bring the halves together if we had a national literature that made Ireland beautiful in the memory, and yet had been freed from provincialism by an exacting criticism, a European pose."[18]

It could be that the "exacting criticism," when it did arrive, condemned the Abbey as old-fashioned. Joyce certainly did: "The bloody nonsense that has been written about Ireland!—parish froth! I intend to lift it into the international sphere and get away from the parish pump."[19] Lennox Robinson, appointed director by Yeats (and in spite of Lady Gregory), tried to shore up from within. With Yeats's approval, he founded the Dublin Drama League, which performed, with Abbey actors and friends, on Sunday nights on the Abbey stage, playwrights the Abbey Theatre patent outlawed: Toller, Strindberg, Pirandello, Benavente, Schnitzler, in fact, that very international tradition Edward Martyn had tried, again and again, to establish. Eventually, a branch of the players group of the League established themselves as the New Players, and presented their productions in the little experimental theatre in the Abbey's catacombs, called the Peacock. Finally, in 1928, under the leadership of Hilton Edwards and Michael MacLiammoir—a partnership between an English actor/director and an Irish actor/playwright/designer—the Gate Theatre was born. Named after a successful internationally minded theatre in London, and an avowedly "alternate theatre" to the Abbey, for some years the Gate operated in the Peacock before finding its own home.

One could be forgiven for seeking an apt symbolism in this new wave forcing open the portals of an enshrined tradition, for the young new company became the Abbey's conscience, providing riches from both Ireland and abroad, expanding in the directions of both Gaelic theatre and European. It also offered the first production of a play that was to become an emblem almost as Chekhov's *The Seagull* became the trademark for the Moscow Art Theatre. For when the Gate produced Denis Johnston's *The Old Lady Says "No!"* in 1929, Irish theatre came of age. Written originally for the Abbey, revised several times after Yeats and Lady Gregory had both rejected it, this play (originally entitled *Shadowdance*) introduced more than expressionist form to Dublin theatregoers. A satirical medley of the ideas, phrases, and concepts of all the Irish romantics (including the great last three themselves), Johnston parodied the dream of Cathleen ni Houlihan and her dance of death while celebrating a new vision of Ireland. Meanwhile, the Abbey sunk once again into narrow realism, stifled even further by government insistence on bilingualism. During the 1940s, poet-dramatist Austin Clarke founded the Lyric Theatre in an effort to revive the verse drama no longer heard on the Abbey stage. In the 1950s, Alan Simpson, in his tiny Pike Theatre, introduced both Brendan Behan and Samuel Beckett to the English-speaking theatre. When the Pike was closed and Simpson arrested for offering the European premiere of Tennessee Williams' *The Rose Tattoo*, other groups filled the gap: today small theatres in Dublin, as elsewhere, offer a rich mixture of indigenous and foreign work while the Abbey steadfastly pursues its original mandate as "national theatre" shrunken in age and ambition, with occasional fits and starts of a former greatness; and the touring houses, which Yeats combatted, blandly continue to offer the same cross-channel fare.

Perhaps the most lasting legacy of the theatre of Yeats, Lady Gregory, and Synge is the audience itself. For the Gate and all that followed could not have survived without the zeal for performance and sense of play roused by those early days. Denis Johnston recalls the 1920s when the Dublin Drama League was first established: "nearly everybody in the city seemed to be either writing a play himself, or used to appear on the stage, and . . . it was quite impossible to draw a line between the Professional, the Performer who would be a professional whenever he could collect, and the considerable number of very good actors who never cherished any hope of collecting at all, but went on acting just the same."[20]

Nor was that amateurism, in the true sense of the word, confined to Dublin. The Abbey players had from the beginning toured the country, taking one-night "fit-ups" into small country towns some of whose inhabitants had never before seen a performance. Inspired by the first years of the movement, the Ulster Players established their own Literary Theatre, again a mingling of amateur, semi-professional, dramatist/directors, and—what the Abbey never achieved—actor/dramatists. Other companies in Belfast followed: during the 1950s in Dublin the only opportunity to see Yeats's plays was the annual visit from Belfast of the Lyric Players. Apart from a very few writers in Dublin—whose plays, like Hugh Leonard's, are produced in the Dublin Theatre Festival in London and New York (hardly ever at the Abbey)—the most experimental, exciting, intellectual, and literary voices in the theatre of Ireland are those of the North. No longer following models from Dublin and London, speaking with their own harsh, lyrical voice, playwrights such as Brian Friel (*Philadelphia Here I Come!*, *The Freedom of the City*, *Living Quarters*), Wilson John Haire (*Within Two Shadows*, *Lost Worlds*), and Stewart Parker (*Spokesong*) have inherited the mantle not only of the early Abbey founders but of Denis Johnston and the Gate as well: truth, beauty, pain, laughter, music, and play, their writing, as Yeats had said of that of Synge and Lady Gregory, "a victory as well as a creation." Writing of Ulster and the world now and as it has been, for their own people and to theatre international, they most truly represent the combination of which Yeats dreamed in 1934:

A nation should be like an audience in some great theatre—"In the theatre" said Victor Hugo "the mob becomes a people"—watching the sacred drama of its own history; every spectator finding self and neighbour there, finding all the world there as we find the sun in the bright spot under the burning glass.[21]

How, then, does Canadian theatre compare? "The danger," as Beckett again warns us, is in the "neatness of identifications" (Beckett, p. 3), but it is not difficult to acknowledge strong similarities between Canadian struggles toward a self-conscious emerging cultural nationalism and those stumbling, well-intentioned, exploratory and protective, occasionally ludicrous, yet gradually successful, attempts to carve out, while still defining, an independent indigenous theatre. Many Canadians have experienced with the same

13. Barry Fitzgerald as Boyle and Eileen Crowe as Juno in the Abbey Theatre's 1933 touring production of *Juno and the Paycock*. Courtesy of the Theatre Department, Metropolitan Toronto Library.

determination those very frustrations, concerns, and building block techniques described in the letters of the first Abbey Theatre directorate. Let us take a broader, more sweeping perspective still (ignoring for the moment the equally obvious differences between the two countries), and these comparative generalizations continue to hold: the long, slow struggle into self-awareness; a sense of apartness from Britain while dependent on her traditions and themes, leading to the warping of imagery, setting, even history in all literatures; the gradual blending of political and intellectual urges into forms of "literary nationalism"; "Miss Eire" and "Canada First" movements; Castle tableaux and Cuchulainoid spectacles of nineteenth-century Dublin, the historical pageants and masques of Canada; the search for indigenous heroes (Cuchulain, Cathleen, Pearse, Emmett, Walsh, the Donnellys, Riel, Ponteach, Macdonald), and local villains (the "Black and Tans," Wacousta); the compulsion to "educate" away from one culture and audience to another; and "To write for my own race/And the reality" (Yeats's "The Fisherman"). Relating even more directly to the theatre, both countries suffered (and gained) from familiarity with the travelling professionals: Dublin had for centuries served as the "second city" for English theatre, indeed had provided many of its greatest playwrights; the major touring companies of both London and New York began sweeping up into upper and lower Canada as early in the nineteenth century as travel made possible, and frequently well before there were adequate theatre spaces to greet them. Professed theatregoers, longing for the entertainment "back home," developed and encouraged amateur theatricals in the governing and military classes. History can boast not only that first marine masque of 1606, Marc Lescarbot's *Theatre of Neptune in New France*, but before that, "morris Dancers, Hobby Horsse and Maylike Conceits" on board Sir Humphrey Gilbert's ship in the harbor at St. John's.[22] Since 1819 when Parry's crew performed on shipboard somewhere within the Arctic Circle, and, in the 1840s, ships of the pax Britannica performed comedies off the coast of British Columbia, Canada has continued that marine tradition. For three centuries, "garrison theatre" maintained an uninterrupted commendable level of performance and repertoire. During the nineteenth century, also, resident stock companies, hastily assembled from available amateurs and semi-professionals, walked the boards with leading players from Britain and the United States; later, when "the Road" had proved financially viable and cities had responded by building worthy Opera Houses, the split between local and visitor (who became synonymous with "the professional") was intensified by stars bringing in their own supporting companies. The result in Canada, as it had been in Ireland, was a sense of insecurity (which was all too frequently synonymous with "lack of standards") both in form and content. Ulster playwright Stewart Parker recently remarked that the Abbey Theatre, with few exceptions, provided a revolution in content but not of form, leaving later playwrights with no tradition or total view; if one examines "consciously Canadian" plays from the poetic dramas of Mair and Heavysege to the contemporary plays of Gélinas, Denison, Davies, Coulter, French, Freeman, and others, a remarkable number of them are traditional in form and staging. David French's most recent play, *Jitters*, illustrates my point: a comedy dealing with the last days before a production opens, it makes effective use of such familiar devices as "play within the play," realistic settings in both, and dwells on the plight of the dramatist writing for critics who will compare him unfavorably with non-Canadian writers, his play performed by actors who care only for the response of a visiting Broadway producer—who at the last moment does not show up.

However, if the propaganda of "amateurism" had these drawbacks of conservatism, there were compensations that should not be overlooked. The Irish Literary Theatre of the 1890s, the three-year experiment of Lady Gregory, Yeats, and Martyn, while bringing over English players to produce original plays, was "subscription theatre" like that which has supported similar ventures throughout Canada; a willingness on the part of audiences to support the home team in its effort to create (or import, for that matter) theatre, the recognition of a need all the keener for the active tradition of "the Road" as well as the Garrison. It was this spirit that led Earl Grey to encourage the best in the dramatic arts early in the century, and the Earl of Bessborough (actively assisted by Vincent Massey) to establish the Dominion Drama Festival some twenty years later. (Rideau Hall, the Governor-General's official residence, has always been interested in drama, and the diaries of Lady Dufferin, who went so far as to have an assembly room converted into a theatre, provide an intriguing view of contemporary popular fare.) Some might say that gentle coercion from Ottawa remains a significant factor in directing the arts in Canada; but compared with the demands and objections Yeats had to deal with in Miss Horniman—who finally withdrew her subsidy altogether as protest against the "political" gestures she read into Abbey policy—the guidelines of the Canada Council, Wintario, and Heritage grants are innocuous indeed. When the Abbey directors officially handed over their "national theatre" to the Irish government, the irony of Miss Horniman's objections deepened: as civil servants, the actors were required to pass examinations in Irish.

This paternalism—whether arising from well-meaning patron/founders, or governmental good intentions—led in Canada also to an emphasis on "educating." One of the major aims of the Dominion Drama Festival was to improve the quality of staging, performing, and playwriting by the system of travelling adjudicators—imported from Britain and France. Yeats, too, depended upon visiting instructors for additional voice training, designing, and stage management. It could well be that the modest "Advice to Playwrights" distributed by the Abbey directors is primarily responsible for today's college and university theatre programs. When George Pierce Baker became head of the postgraduate Department of Drama at Yale, he wrote to Lady Gregory, "If it had not been for your visit to this country and my knowledge of what the Abbey Theatre had done with so little money, I doubt if the Harvard 47 Workshop could have come into being."[23] The tradition of playwriting workshops, and, indeed, resident playwrights, adapted easily to cultural nationalism, as did the pattern of Little Theatres, many of them inspired by the Abbey Theatre visits to North America. Shortly after Hart House Theatre opened in 1919, Yeats lectured from its stage on "A Theatre of the People"; but despite Massey's efforts, few Canadian playwrights appeared in those early years. Lady Gregory's ambitions had extended further than the playwright; she dreamed of introducing the children of Ireland to their national heritage through a series of folk-history plays, many of which (in addition to her "Wonder Plays") she herself wrote. Sarah Anne Curzon's *Laura Secord*, "written to rescue from oblivion the name of a brave woman, and set it in its proper place among the heroes of Canadian history," was published in 1887; she had already invaded university circles, figuratively if not literally, with her *Sweet Girl Graduate* in 1882, a blow for the admission of women to Canadian universities. In 1897, Catherine Merritt celebrated the United Empire Loyalists of Upper Canada in *When George the Third was King*. These, and many more, were aimed not only at burgeoning amateur groups, but also at schools. The tradition of theatre for and by children began long before the establishment of Young People's Theatres or "developmental drama" became a discipline; it moves from strength to strength, attracting more and more playwrights from Len Peterson, Henry Beissel, Eric Nicoll, and Victoria's Company One who have dramatized the legends of native peoples, to Carol Bolt, Robert Swerdlow, Paddy Campbell, Rex Deverell, Betty Lambert, Gwen Ringwood, Dennis Foon, the creations of British Columbia's Holiday Theatre, Nova Scotia's Mermaid, and James Reaney's Listeners' Workshops in London, Ontario. A recent checklist records over two dozen professional theatres devoted entirely to theatre for young people, while many more companies have adjunct school touring groups.[24]

Parallels, too, can be discerned in related publishing activities, both theoretical and historical. Yeats hammered out his dramatic aesthetic in *Beltaine, Samhain, The Arrow*, and *On the Boiler*, and in countless newspaper articles; Reaney began with *Alphabet* (devoted to "The Iconography of the Imagination") and moved on to *Hallowe'en*, "an occasional theatrical newsletter," while the NDWT company distributes "Teaching Kits" as school companions to its plays. Lady Gregory published *Our Irish Theatre*, a potpourri of events, recollections, letters, brickbats, and bouquets documenting the first fifteen years of the National Theatre; Yeats followed with *Discoveries, Autobiographies*, and reserved his most extravagant blessings and curses for *A Vision*. An early footnote in Reaney's *14 Barrels from Sea to Sea* invokes the spirit of Yeats and Lady Gregory and the making of a National Theatre; in this personal journal of the national tour of the Donnelly trilogy (the cycle itself a superb example of cosmic myth-making rooted in time and history), Reaney offers his guide to the heart of Canada, a playfully serious jigsaw puzzle of architecture, street signs, poetry, and people, mixed with recipes, birthdays, sunsets, gummy pavements, lit-crit, theatre-crit (and the lack of it), noise levels, ghosts, and the celebration of talk and story, country rather than town, garden over supermarket.[25] Throughout we are possessed, as Reaney's plays are, with a sense of place.

It was, more than anything else, this sense of *place* that led Vincent Massey with the establishment of Hart House Theatre, John Coulter of the Arts and Letters Club, Gwen Ringwood at the North Carolina Playmakers School and at home in western Canada, Herman Voaden with his "symphonic expressionism" based on the Group of Seven, Robertson Davies in his dialogue between Lovewit and Trueman for the Royal Commission on National Development in the Arts, to draw their own personal and national parallels with the Abbey Theatre movement. Most recently, an issue of *Canadian Theatre Review* published extracts from the journals of Alan Richardson of Compact Theatre, returned to Canada after an extensive period at MacLiammoir's Gate Theatre in Dublin; he alternates trenchant observations on the state of Canadian theatre and drama with passages from Yeats's diaries.[26] We can easily extend the list of more specific parallels: Michael Cook seeks among the fishermen of Newfoundland the folk material and accent Synge found in Wicklow and Aran; the trenchant wit and earnest fantasy of Canada's foibles in Robertson Davies' *Fortune My Foe* and *Question Time* echo Shaw's concerns in *John Bull's Other Island* (and, like Shaw, Davies glorifies theatre as "a temple of wholeness")[27]; Gwen Ringwood celebrates the eccentricity of character in her own version of Kiltartan; Reaney seeks in a true collaboration with a selected group of committed actors a form free of earlier restrictions, creating a flowing celebration of the heroic at play; the Abbey realists grew out of the same rich soil that nourishes so many of Bill Glassco's Tarragon playwrights—a finely honed, sometimes harsh, always truthful, concern with forcing us, now, to face ourselves; a group of concerned playwrights band together to create the cottage-industry-turned-big-business Playwrights' Co-op, while on the west coast Talonbooks expands, as does Quebec's Leméac, and Alberta's *NeWest Review* joins the field; political dissidents break away from parent companies to form cooperative activist units (Savage God, Codco, Catalyst, Globe, Théâtre d'aujourdhui); the enlightening impudence of John Gray's *Billy Bishop Goes to War* reflects the mature loving satire of Johnston's *The Old Lady Says "No!"*, taking its form from America's answer to the expressionist theatre of the 1920s, the musical; the original Alternate Theatres find themselves, as Ken Gass of Factory Theatre Lab has described it, struggling to find the Canadian middle road: "Meaningful experimentation on one hand, public acceptability on the other";[28] a recent interview with Martin Kinch, the harassed artistic director of Toronto Free Theatre, reveals some rueful admissions familiar to the first Abbey directorate: "The demands of being an administrator are absolutely crippling in terms of being a director and writer"; and of his theatre's present paradox: "We're trying to base ourselves on being Canadian. But release ourselves from being a service organization for Canadian playwrights. It's not that easy."[29]

Irish playwrights, now as then, find a ready echo in Canada, in lamenting a lack of incisive, constructive, inspiring criticism.

This was perhaps what the Abbey in middle age suffered from most. For after a generation of playmaking, Ireland had not provided one drama critic of any stature to match the necessary arrogance of the artist. With rare exceptions, Canadian playwrights could say the same. In part, this is inevitable given the geographical spread of our major theatre centers, our penchant for establishing centers devoted to theatres of other nations (Shaw, Shakespeare). There is something inward looking, enclosed, and defensive about the very names of many of our regional theatres (Bastion, Citadel), which make the names of Alternate Theatres appear vulnerable: Passe Muraille, Open Circle, Theatre Second Floor, Northern Light, 25th Street House Theatre (which is not even on 25th Street). Despite the many schools, workshops, and play centers stretching from Victoria to St. John's, Canadian theatre historians and scholars have tended to enter from another field, and consequently what little critical theory there is tends to be borrowed also. I would contend that our drama is not characterized by a garrison mentality, or its offspring, survival, nor even as more recently suggested, by "leaving home" (despite the number of plays dealing with this subject);[30] but rather by arriving, exploring, questioning, and, above all, by celebrating the discovery of *place*. An overridingly simple metaphor, perhaps, but inevitable, given the basic requirements of theatrical form. James Reaney concludes his contribution to *Stage Voices* by cataloguing the names of actual theatres where he has enjoyed "a good theatrical experience," reminding us, once again, that no matter how simple the lumber, costumes, and properties, a physical space and an audience are required. Given this space, "you hear the heartbeat and you try to give it head, guts, and limbs" (*Stage Voices*, p. 174). Above all, in Michel Garneau's words, "Theatre is that incredible place where poetry can be spoken" (*Stage Voices*, p. 294). (One is reminded here, as elsewhere, of the fine plays sponsored by the CBC, where poetry could be spoken to an audience across the country, united in a single action "Listeners' Workshops" also.)

It is this task of recollecting the heartbeat in a given space that leads to my final parallel, between the playwrights of contemporary Ulster and present-day Quebec. In both, we recognize the search for a separate political, cultural, and social identity within the universal search for geographic and historical identity; both are striving to express that search in their own accents, not that of standard English or Anglo-Irish or Parisian French, but in the tone and metaphors, texture and taste (as Synge would have it) of their own peoples. For both, in words uttered by an Ulster playwright and reinforced by Michel Tremblay in his cycle of "Les Belles Soeurs": "the subject is wished upon you, one is cursed by necessity to write of one's roots."[31] Perhaps it is this very urgency and compassion that create some of the best theatre in Canada today: not only in Quebec's Tremblay, Garneau, and

Gurik, but also in the earthy, simple, acute, naive, strong monologues of Antoine Maillet's Acadian *La Sagouine*, that woman of the sea, the scrubwoman, who speaks directly to us of life, and death, and everything in between. For these playwrights, as in individual works by Rick Salutin, Timothy Findley, Gwen Ringwood, Robertson Davies, James Reaney, John Herbert, John Gray, George Ryga, and Michael Cook, the key to national drama can be found in words discovered by Reaney (appropriately from a book on Eskimo masks): "not me in the world, but the world in me."[32] Or, to return one last time to Yeats, "character isolated by a deed/To engross the present and dominate memory."

Notes

1. This paper was prepared at the invitation of the Association of Canadian University Teachers of English for its meeting in Saskatoon on 23 May 1979; it represents more a report of "work in progress" than any definitive statement of comparison. See Samuel Beckett, "Dante . . . Bruno. Vico . . . Joyce," *Our Exagmination Round his Factification for Incamination of Work in Progress* (London, 1972), p. 4.

2. Bernard Shaw Papers, British Library, London. Quoted by permission of The British Library.

3. W. B. Yeats, "This Book," *The Celtic Twilight* (London, 1893). (Omitted from *Mythologies*.)

4. "The Rhymers' Club," *Letters to the New Island*, ed. Horace Reynolds (Cambridge, Mass., 1934), p. 148.

5. *Letters of W. B. Yeats*, ed. Allan Wade (New York, 1955), pp. 99, 104; "What is 'Popular Poetry'?," *Essays and Introductions* (London, 1961), p. 5.

6. National Library of Ireland, ms. 15,600.

7. Stefan Zweig, *The World of Yesterday* (London, 1943), p. 126.

8. W. B. Yeats, *Explorations* (London, 1962), pp. 176–77.

9. Lady Gregory, *Seventy Years* (Gerrards Cross, 1974), pp. 414–15. Unless otherwise stated, quotations from the letters are taken from my forthcoming edition of the correspondence of the first Abbey Theatre directors, to be published by Colin Symthe Ltd., Gerrards Cross.

10. Quoted in Lady Gregory, *Our Irish Theatre* (Gerrards Cross, 1972), pp. 62–63.

11. *Letters of Ezra Pound 1907–1941*, ed. D. D. Paige (London, 1951), p. 148.

12. John Quinn Memorial Collection; Manuscripts and Archives Division; The New York Public Library; Astor, Lenox and Tilden Foundations.

13. "The Irish Dramatic Movement: A Letter to the Students of a Californian School," in *The Voice of Ireland*, ed. William G. Fitz-Gerald (Dublin, 1923–24), p. 465.

14. A speech at the Court Theatre, London, quoted in "Some New Letters from W. B. Yeats to Lady Gregory," ed. Donald T. Torchiana and Glenn O'Malley, *Review of English Literature*, 4 (July 1963), 34.

15. Preface to *Poems 1899–1905* (Dublin, 1906), pp. xiii–xiv.

16. Henderson Press Cuttings 1899–1901, National Library of Ireland, ms. 7271.

17. W. B. Yeats, "A People's Theatre. A Letter to Lady Gregory," *Irish Statesman*, 29 November and 6 December 1919; reprinted with alterations in *Plays and Controversies* (London, 1925), pp. 199–218.

18. W. B. Yeats, *Autobiographies* (London, 1955), p. 102.

19. Quoted by Arthur Power in "James Joyce—The Internationalist," *A Bash in the Tunnel*, ed. John Ryan (Brighton, 1970), p. 181.

20. Denis Johnston, "The Dublin Drama League," an unpublished Radio Eireann talk (about 1947), Johnston papers, New University of Ulster in Coleraine, quoted by Christine St. Peter, "Denis Johnston's "The Old Lady Says 'No!' ": The Gloriable Nationvoice." Ph.D. diss., University of Toronto, 1979, p. 11.

21. Commentary on "Three Songs to the Same Tune," *King of the Great Clock Tower, Commentaries and Poems* (Dublin, 1934), pp. 36–38.

22. I am indebted to David Gardner for many of these details concerning marine theatre.

23. *Lady Gregory's Journals 1916–1930*, ed. Lennox Robinson (New York, 1947), p. 325.

24. *Checklist of Canadian Theatres* (Downsview, Ontario, 1979).

25. James Reaney, *14 Barrels From Sea to Sea* (Erin, Ontario, 1977).

26. Alan Richardson, "On Returning Home," *Canadian Theatre Review*, 21 (Winter 1979), 9–16.

27. *Stage Voices*, ed. Geraldine Anthony (Toronto, 1978), p. 79.

28. Ken Gass, "Toronto's Alternates: Changing Realities," *Canadian Theatre Review*, 21 (Winter 1979), 132.

29. Interview with Bryan Johnson, *The Globe and Mail* (Toronto), 19 May 1979.

30. Richard Plant, "Leaving Home: A Thematic Study of Canadian Literature with Special Emphasis on Drama, 1606 to 1977." Ph.D. diss., University of Toronto, 1979.

31. Stewart Parker during a panel discussion on "New Directions in Playwriting," Canadian Association for Irish Studies conference, Vancouver, B.C., 3 May 1979.

32. "A Letter from James Reaney," *Halloween*, in *Black Moss*, Series 2, Number 1 (Spring, 1976), 5.

L. W. Conolly

Bibliographical Survey _____

In this bibliographical survey I have tried to guide the interested reader to sources that provide extra information or commentary on the subjects dealt with in the essays in this book, or to sources that extend the subjects into new but related areas. I have avoided repeating the sources, primary or secondary, used in the essays, but I hope the connections between those sources and the ones I cite will be clear. I list nothing here, for example, on Irving (for which see Arnold Rood's essay), but I cite material on Sarah Bernhardt; nothing directly on the Group Theatre (Helen Krich Chinoy's essay), but books on the Federal and other noncommercial theatres; nothing on the Stratford Festival (Ross Stuart's essay), but sources on other important Canadian and American regional theatres. Throughout the survey I have kept in mind the subject of this book, Theatrical Touring and Founding, and its more precise manifestation, Commerce versus Art.

Like most of the essays in this collection, the bibliographical survey is concerned more with the theatre than with drama. The survey is necessarily selective; I have included a number of articles that seem to me to matter, but no theses or dissertations (for which see the Reference and Bibliography section below).

I should emphasize, too, that I have concentrated on the period from about 1880 to the present (i.e., the period covered by the essays). Thus, while the Boston theatre, say, of the late nineteenth and early twentieth century is of direct interest, its earlier history is not, and has, consequently, been omitted.

Reference and Bibliography

Some early works are still worth consulting. *Who's Who on the Stage, 1908. The Dramatic Reference Book and Biographical Dictionary of the*

Theatre, Containing Careers of Actors, Actresses, Managers, and Play-wrights of the American Stage, edited by Walter Brown and E. De Roy Koch (New York, 1908) provides useful information, as does the massive (41 volumes) *Dramatic Index . . . Covering Articles and Illustrations Concerning the Stage and Its Players in the Periodicals of America and England and Including the Dramatic Books of the Year,* published annually in Boston from 1910 to 1952. Also still useful are Blanch Baker's respected works, *Dramatic Bibliography: An Annotated List of Books on the History and Criticism of the Drama and Stage and on the Allied Arts of the Theatre* (New York, 1933), and *Theatre and Allied Arts: A Guide to Books Dealing with the History, Criticism, and Technique of the Drama and Theatre, and Related Arts and Crafts* (New York, 1952). Baker's coverage is international; specifically American theatre bibliographies are Don Wilmeth's excellent *The American Stage to World War I: A Guide to Information Sources* (Detroit, 1978), Carl F. W. Larson's *American Regional Theatre History to 1900: A Bibliography* (Metuchen, N.J., 1979), and Carl J. Stratman's *Bibliography of the American Theatre, Excluding New York City* (Chicago, 1965). Wilmeth's work is strengthened by intelligent annotation; Larson's is weakened by the absence of annotation; and the scope of Stratman's work (nearly 4,000 entries) makes it indispensable. Stratman includes theses and dissertations, but the best source for these remains Fredric M. Litto's *American Dissertations on the Drama and the Theatre* (Kent, Ohio, 1969), supplemented by the annual volumes of *Dissertation Abstracts International* (Ann Arbor, 1969–). For guidance on American theatre periodicals, Carl Stratman's *American Theatre Periodicals, 1799–1967* (Durham, N.C., 1970) is essential, and for American theatres, William Young's two-volume *Famous American Playhouses* (Chicago, 1973) remains important, despite some shortcomings. Over 200 critics are included in Albert E. Johnson and W. H. Crain's "Dictionary of American Dramatic Critics, 1850–1910," *Theatre Arts,* 13 (1955), 65–89, a list that is extended by Walter E. Rigdon's *Biographical Encyclopedia and Who's Who of the American Theatre* (New York, 1966), a solid and comprehensive guide. For Canadian theatre, the essential works are John Ball and Richard Plant's *Bibliography of Canadian Theatre History 1583–1975* (Toronto, 1976), and the *Supplement* (Toronto, 1979). Ball and Plant's coverage is admirably comprehensive, and includes French-Canadian theatre, though John E. Hare's "Bibliographie du théâtre canadien français," *Archives des lettres Canadiennes,* 5 (1976), 951–99 must also be consulted.

General Histories

Most general histories of theatre in North America deal to a greater or lesser extent with aspects of touring and founding. There are as yet few substantial histories of Canadian theatre. For the province of Quebec, Jean Béraud's *350 ans de théâtre au Canada français* (Montreal, 1958) is the major historical work, and there is a good survey by Alonzo LeBlanc, "La tradition théâtrale à Québec," *Archives des lettres Canadiennes*, 5 (1976), 203–38. Jean Hamelin's *The Theatre in French Canada, 1936–66* (Quebec, 1968) surveys Quebec theatre at mid-century, and Yerri Kempf's collection of reviews, *Les trois coups à Montréal: chroniques dramatiques 1959–64* (Montreal, 1965) covers a briefer period with the emphasis on Montreal. The early history of theatre in Montreal is dealt with in Franklin Graham's *Histrionic Montreal: Annals of the Montreal Stage, With Biographical and Critical Notices of the Plays and Players of the Century, 1804–1898* (Montreal, 1902; New York, 1969). For English-Canadian theatre history, there are two concise surveys and only one substantial history: Mavor Moore's "History of English Canadian Amateur and Professional Theatre," *Canadian Drama/ L'art dramatique canadien*, 1 (1975), 60–67, Ross Stuart's "Theatre in Canada: An Historical Perspective," *Canadian Theatre Review*, 5 (1975), 6–15, and Murray D. Edwards' *A Stage in Our Past: English Language Theatre in Eastern Canada from the 1790s to 1914* (Toronto, 1968).

The American theatre is better served. Daniel Blum's *Pictorial History of the American Theatre, 1860–1960* (New York, 1960) is an engaging and informative survey. More scholarly are Glenn Hughes's valuable *History of the American Theatre, 1700–1950* (New York, 1951), and Barnard Hewitt's documentary history, *Theatre U.S.A. 1669–1957* (New York, 1959). Walter Meserve's *Outline History of American Drama* (Totowa, N.J., 1965) includes the theatre as well as drama, as does Garff B. Wilson's textbook, *Three Hundred Years of American Drama and Theatre* (Englewood Cliffs, N.J., 1973). A collection of essays edited by Henry B. Williams, *The American Theatre: A Sum of its Parts* (New York, 1971) contains essays by several distinguished historians on a wide variety of theatrical subjects.

Theatrical Memoirs, Biographies, and Autobiographies

Many of the people directly involved in theatrical touring and founding have left accounts of their experiences. The major critics were based, of course, in New York, but one gets a broader perspective from *The American Theatre as Seen by Its Critics*, edited by Montrose J. Moses and John Mason Brown (New York, 1934), and a Canadian point of view is given in two books by Toronto critic Hector Charlesworth, *Candid Chronicles* (Toronto, 1925) and *More Candid Chronicles* (Toronto, 1928). Of the many collections of essays, memoirs, and reviews published by New York critics, the following can be recommended: Franklin Fyles' *The Theatre and Its People* (New York, 1900), Norman Hapgood's *The Stage in America 1897–1900* (New York, 1901), Brooks Atkinson's *Broadway Scrapbook* (New York,

1947), Stark Young's *Immortal Shadows* (New York, 1948), George Jean Nathan's *The Magic Mirror; Selected Writings on the Theatre*, edited by Thomas Quinn Curtis (New York, 1960), and John Mason Brown's *Dramatis Personae* (New York, 1920).

There are several comprehensive accounts of the actors and actresses who enjoyed successful careers in the commercial theatre on Broadway and on tour in the regional theatres of the United States and Canada. William Winter's three-volume *Shadows of the Stage* (New York, 1892–95) includes foreign as well as domestic stars. *Famous American Actors of Today*, edited by Frederic E. McKay and Charles Wingate (New York, 1896) has comments on and photographs of forty-two actors, while Lewis C. Strang deals with the actresses in *Famous Actresses of the Day in America* (Boston, 1899). The companion volume to this is Strang's *Famous Actors of the Day in America* (Boston, 1900). *Players of the Present* (New York, 1899) is a three-volume, illustrated biographical dictionary compiled by John Bouve Clapp and Edwin F. Edgett, and there are more illustrations in two large works, *The American Stage Today* (New York, 1910), introduced by William Winter, and Daniel Blum's *Great Stars of the American Stage* (New York, 1952). William Young's *Famous Actors and Actresses of the American Stage* (New York, 1975) is informative but uneven. The best history of American acting is Garff B. Wilson's *A History of American Acting* (Bloomington, 1966).

Valuable insights into the practices and values of Broadway and the road are gained from individual memoirs. The following are all useful: Clara Morris' *Life on the Stage* (New York, 1901); Rose Eytinge's *Memoirs* (New York, 1905) (good on the western states); Augustus Pitou's *Masters of the Show As Seen in Retrospection by One Who Has Been Associated with the American Stage for Nearly Fifty Years* (New York, 1914); John Drew's *My Years on the Stage* (New York, 1922); Daniel Frohman's *Memoirs of a Manager* (Garden City, N.Y., 1911), and *Daniel Frohman Presents* (New York, 1919); David Belasco's *The Theatre Through the Stage Door* (New York, 1919); Otis Skinner's *Footlights and Spotlights* (Indianapolis, 1924); James T. Powers' *Twinkle Little Star: Sparkling Memories of Seventy Years* (New York, 1939); Katharine Cornell's *I Wanted to Be an Actress* (New York, 1939); and Ethel Barrymore's *Memories: An Autobiography* (New York, 1955).

Somewhat more objective accounts of Broadway and the road can be found in studies of prominent theatre individuals. Marvin Felheim's *Theater of Augustin Daly* (Cambridge, Mass., 1956) is an excellent assessment of Daly's achievements, and Lise-Lone Marker's study of Belasco, *David Belasco: Naturalism in the American Theatre* (Princeton, 1975) is another scholarly assessment of a major Broadway figure, a better assessment, it should be said, than Craig Timerlake's earlier *The Bishop of Broadway: David Belasco, His Life and Work* (New York, 1954). Other major theatre businessmen are discussed by Daniel Frohman and Isaac F. Marcosson in *Charles Frohman, Manager and Man* (New York, 1916), Vincent Sheean in *The Amazing Oscar Hammerstein I: The Life and Exploits of an Impresario* (London, 1956), and Helen M. Morosco and Leonard P. Dugger in *The Life of Oliver Morosco, the Oracle of Broadway* (Caldwell, Idaho, 1944). Neither the Frohman nor the Morosco book is notably objective. Three biographies of important performers can be more warmly recommended: Archie Binns's *Mrs. Fiske and the American Theatre* (New York, 1955), Charles Edward Russell's *Julia Marlow: Her Life and Art* (New York, 1926), and Hollis Alpert's substantial critical study of John, Ethel, and Lionel Barrymore, *The Barrymores* (New York, 1964).

Broadway and Commerce

To understand the history of theatrical touring in North America, and to appreciate why theatres were founded to accommodate or resist the power of Broadway, one must perforce know something of New York's rich theatre history. In addition to the books mentioned in the previous section, most of which contain a good deal of information on New York, there are some useful histories. George Odell's fifteen-volume *Annals of the New York Stage* (New York, 1927–49) is essential for the early period (beginnings to 1894). Also useful for the eighteenth and nineteenth centuries is T. Allston Brown's *History of the New York Stage from the First Performance in 1732 to 1901, in Encyclopedic Form* (New York, 1903 and 1963). Ruth Crosby Dimmick's *Our Theatre Today and Yesterday* (New York, 1913) is brief, but it takes the history of New York theatre up to the First World War. *The New York Stage: Famous Productions in Photographs*, edited by Stanley Applebaum (New York, 1976), covers the period 1883–1939, and Allen Churchill's *The Great White Way* (New York, 1962) surveys the years 1900–1919. Brooks Atkinson's *Broadway* (New York, 1974) is a substantial and well-illustrated history, 1900–1974. The best comprehensive history of New York theatre is Mary C. Henderson's *The City and the Theatre* (Clifton, N.J., 1973).

The specifically commercial and economic aspects of Broadway have received considerable discussion, attracting several energetic apologists. M. B. Leavitt's *Fifty Years in Theatrical Management, 1859–1909* (New York, 1912), is an informative inside account, and Alfred Bernheim gives a spirited defence of commercialism and the syndicates in *The Business of the Theatre* (New York, 1932, 1964). The Theatrical Syndicate itself (1896–1916) is defended by Monroe Lippman in "The Effect of the Theatrical Syndicate on Theatrical Art in America," *Quarterly Journal of Speech*, 26 (1940), 275–82, while a disappointingly neutral position is taken by Steve Travis in "The Rise and Fall of the Theatrical Syndicate," *Educational Theatre Jour-*

nal, 10 (1958), 35–40. Milo L. Smith sides with Syndicate directors Marc Klaw and Able Erlanger in "The Klaw-Erlanger Myth," *Players*, 44 (1959), 70–75. A less partisan approach is adopted in two full-length and valuable studies of commercialism, Jerry Stagg's *A Half-Century of Show Business and the Fabulous Empire of the Brothers Shubert* (New York, 1968), and Jack Poggi's *Theatre in America: The Impact of Economic Forces, 1870–1967* (Ithaca, 1968).

In the Provinces

There is a large body of material on the theatre outside of New York, covering the early stock companies, the take-over by the road shows emanating from New York, and the founding of regional theatres largely independent of Broadway. There is space here to comment on only the more significant of the books and articles on provincial theatre in the United States and Canada.

There are a few interesting studies of touring as it was in the second half of the nineteenth century before New York took control of the road. Andrew F. Jensen has written on "Two Decades of Trouping in Minnesota, 1865–1885," in *Minnesota History*, 28 (1947), 97–119. Jefferson de Angelis and Alvin F. Harlow's *Vagabond Trouper* (New York, 1931) concentrates on trouping in California and Utah, and Alice Henson Ernst's *Trouping in the Oregon Country* (Portland, 1961) is mainly a history of frontier theatre. Philip C. Lewis' *Trouping: How the Show Came to Town* (New York, 1973) is, geographically speaking, more comprehensive, and the author was himself a trouper, but not, unfortunately, a scholar. His book is entertaining, but not entirely reliable.

The activities of stock and touring companies in the South have been well documented. John S. Kendall's *The Golden Age of the New Orleans Theatre* (Baton Rouge, 1952) surveys the New Orleans stage up to the 1880s, and Shirley Harrison traces the later battle between a New Orleans theatre manager and the Syndicate in "New Orleans: Greenwall vs. the Syndicate," *Players*, 46 (1971), 180–87. Joseph S. Gallegly's *Footlights on the Border: the Galveston and Houston Stage Before 1900* (The Hague, 1962), and Donald Brady's *The Theatre in Early El Paso, 1881–1905* (El Paso, 1966) document nineteenth-century Texas theatre (rather skimpily in Brady's case). James D. Kemmerling's "A History of the Whitley Opera House in Emporia, Kansas, 1881–1913," *Emporia State Research Studies*, 18 (1970), 1–72, Claire Eugene Willson's *Mimes and Miners: A Historical Study of the Tombstone Theater* (Tucson, 1935), and Lewis Maiden's "The Theatre in Nashville, 1876–1900," *Southern Speech Journal*, 29 (1963), 12–46, all extend our understanding of pre–World War I theatre in the South.

For the West Coast, Mary Katherine Rohrer's *History of Seattle Stock*

Companies (Seattle, 1945) is useful. San Francisco is exhaustively treated in the *San Francisco Theatre Research Monographs*, edited by Lawrence Estavan, a W.P.A. project published in twenty volumes between 1938 and 1942. A more concise history is Edmond McAdoo Gagey's *The San Francisco Stage* (New York, 1950). Los Angeles is not so well served, though Alan Woods's "Popular Theatre in Los Angeles at the Turn of the Century," *Players*, 48 (1973), 173–78, is a good starting point. Robert Todd's "The Organization of Professional Theatre in Vancouver, 1886–1914," *B.C. Studies*, 44 (1979–80), 3–24, is excellent for that West Coast Canadian city. Julia McCune Flory's *The Cleveland Play House: How It Began* (Cleveland, 1965) covers the years 1915–1927, and contemporary developments in the Canadian Midwest are examined in Ruth Walker Harvey's memories of her father's theatre in Winnipeg in *Curtain Time* (Boston, 1949), and Patrick B. O'Neill's "Regina's Golden Age of Theatre: Her Playhouses and Players (1903–1918)," *Saskatchewan History*, 28 (1975), 29–37. Eugene Tompkins and Quincy Kilby's *History of the Boston Theatre, 1854–1901* (Boston, 1908) is detailed and reliable, and Roger Meersman and Robert Boyer survey the history of Washington's National Theatre in "The National Theatre in Washington: Buildings and Audiences, 1835–1972," in *Records of the Columbia Historical Society of Washington, D.C., 1971–1972*, edited by F. C. Rosenberger (Washington, D.C., 1973), 190–242.

The ambitions and problems of independent regional theatres founded after World War II are foreshadowed in Norris Houghton's *Advance from Broadway* (New York, 1941), and taken up in several intelligent discussions in the 1960s. Martin Gottfried dispassionately assesses the values of conservative and experimental theatre in *A Theatre Divided: The Postwar American Stage* (Boston, 1967); Robert E. Gard, Marston Balch, and Pauline B. Temkin survey the state of commercial, community, and educational theatre in the United States in the 1960s in *Theatre in America: Appraisal and Challenge* (Madison, 1968); and Julius Novick considers the state of the professional theatre in America and Canada in *Beyond Broadway: The Quest for Permanent Theatres* (New York, 1968). Two successful regional theatres, perhaps typical of the new breed, are the Guthrie in Minneapolis and the Shaw at Niagara-on-the-Lake. Guthrie speaks of his efforts in Minneapolis in *A New Theatre* (New York, 1964), and Brian Doherty describes the Shaw Theatre in *Not Bloody Likely: The Shaw Festival, 1962–1973* (Toronto, 1974).

Touring by Foreign Stars and Companies

Henry Knepler's *The Gilded Stage: The Years of the Great International Actresses* (New York, 1968) is a good survey of the touring phenomenon in the United States, as reflected in visits by Rachel, Adelaide Ristori, Bernhardt,

and Duse. Patrick B. O'Neill's "The British Canadian Theatrical Organization Society and the Trans Canada Theatre Society," *Journal of Canadian
Studies*, 15 (1980), 56–67, is an important study of the Canadian reaction
to New York control of Canadian tours.

Sarah Bernhardt's tours of the United States and Canada have received
considerable attention. She writes about them herself in *Memories of My
Life* (New York, 1907), and Cornelia O. Skinner describes them in *Madame
Sarah* (Boston, 1967). First-hand accounts of being on tour with Bernhardt
are given by Grace Hortense Tower, "With Sarah Bernhardt on Her Tour in
California," *Theatre*, 6 (1906), 181–83, and Margaret Mower, "Touring à la
Bernhardt [1916–17]," *Theatre Arts*, 45 (1961), 68–71. Helena Modjeska's
American career is recalled in *Memories and Impressions of Helena Modjeska*
(New York, 1910), and assessed by Marion Moore Coleman in *Fair Rosaline:
The American Career of Helena Modjeska* (Cheshire, Conn., 1969). Linda
Hall's "Lillie Langtry and the American West," *Journal of Popular Culture*,
7 (1974), 873–81, covers Langtry's western tours; more comprehensive,
though not exhaustive, coverage is provided in Pierre Sichel's *The Jersey
Lily: The Story of the Fabulous Mrs. Langtry* (Englewood, N.J., 1958).
Jeanne Bordeaux' *Eleonora Duse: The Story of Her Life* (London, 1925)
gives only brief comment on the tours; fuller treatment is accorded Ellen
Terry's visits to North America by Roger Manvell in *Ellen Terry* (New York,
1968).

Of prominent European actors who toured North America, Tommaso
Salvini and Frank Benson are very reticent about their experiences, Salvini
in *Leaves from the Autobiography of Tommaso Salvini* (New York, 1893),
and Benson in *My Memoirs* (London, 1930). Johnston Forbes-Robertson is
more forthcoming in *A Player Under Three Reigns* (Toronto, 1925), and
generous coverage appears in *The Autobiography of Sir John Martin-
Harvey* (London, 1933).

The Art Theatre

The literature of and about the Art and Little Theatre movement in North
America is extensive. In Canada some of the incentive behind the movement
was nationalistic, a reaction against American influence as much as against
the commercialism of Broadway. In "Nationalism and Drama" in *The
Yearbook of the Arts in Canada 1928–29*, edited by Bertram Brooker
(Toronto, 1929), Merrill Denison refutes nationalism as a viable cultural
force, but other essayists advocate it. Bernard Sandwell protests against
American influence in "The Annexation of Our Stage," *Canadian Magazine*,
38 (1911), 22–26, and John Coulter looks to the achievements in Ireland as
an example for Canada in "The Canadian Theatre and the Irish Exemplar,"
Theatre Arts Monthly, 22 (1938) 503–509. A clear call to reject Broadway

commercialism is made by John Edward Hoare in "A Plea for a Canadian Theatre," *University Magazine*, 10 (1911), 239–53. The most influential of the Canadian Little Theatres was Hart House Theatre in Toronto, the history of which is outlined in Ian Montagnes' *An Uncommon Fellowship: The Story of Hart House* (Toronto, 1969). Also important was the Toronto Arts and Letters Club, described in Augustus Bridle's *The Story of the Club* (Toronto, 1945). Betty Lee's *Love and Whisky: The Story of the Dominion Drama Festival* (Toronto, 1973) is informative about the Little Theatres from across Canada which competed in the annual drama competition. Roy Mitchell's *Creative Theatre* (London, 1930) is important for understanding the ideas of one of the most imaginative directors Canada has produced. In Quebec the theories and achievements of Emile Legault are important. His article, "Le théâtre qu'il nous faut," *Amerique français*, 2 (1943), 27–35, and his autobiography, *Confidences* (Montreal, 1955), should be consulted. Also valuable are two books on Montreal's Théâtre du Nouveau Monde, Eloi de Grandmont's *Dix ans de théâtre au Nouveau Monde* (Montreal, 1961), and Louis Martin Tard's *Vingt ans de théâtre au Nouveau Monde* (Montreal, 1971).

For the Art and Little Theatre movement in the United States, Oliver M. Sayler's *Our American Theatre* (New York, 1923) and Clarence Arthur Perry's *The Work of the Little Theatres* (New York, 1933) are both worth consulting for the detailed information they include about numerous theatres and their repertoires. Persuasive theoretical stands are taken by Kenneth McGowan in several seminal works, including *The Theatre of Tomorrow* (New York, 1921), *Continental Stagecraft* (New York, 1922) (with Robert Edmond Jones), and *Footlights Across America* (New York, 1929). In *The New Movement in the Theatre* (New York, 1914) and *The Art Theatre* (New York, 1916), Sheldon Cheney offers a vigorous defense of noncommercial theatre. The massive contribution of George Pierce Baker is well analyzed by Wisner Payne Kinne in *George Pierce Baker and the American Theatre* (Cambridge, Mass., 1954), and the aims and achievements of Winthrop Ames are summarized by David Edward MacArthur in "Winthrop Ames: The Gentleman as Producer-Director," *Educational Theatre Journal*, 16 (1964), 349–59.

A number of individual theatres and theatre organizations opposed to commercialism merit special attention. Chicago's New Theatre is the subject of Victor Mapes's "An Art Theatre in Operation," *Theatre*, 7 (1907), 202–209, and James L. Highlander's "America's First Art Theatre," *Educational Theatre Journal*, 11 (1959), 285–90. John Perry's "The New Theatre," *Quarterly Journal of Speech*, 58 (1972), 322–26, comments on New York's New Theatre, while Boston's Toy Theatre, founded shortly after New York's New, is briefly discussed in two contemporary articles, Lauriston F. Bullard's "Boston's Toy Theatre," *Theatre*, 15 (1912), 84–86, and Robert Swasey's "The Toy Theatre of Boston," *New England Magazine*, 50 (1913),

351–52. Helen Deutsch and Stella Hannau give a thorough account of the Provincetown Players in *The Provincetown: A Story of the Theatre* (New York, 1931), and the Theatre Guild's importance has been recognized in several studies, including Walter Prichard Eaton's *The Theatre Guild: The First Ten Years* (New York, 1929), Lawrence Langer's *The Magic Curtain* (New York, 1951), Theresa Helburn's *A Wayward Quest* (Boston, 1960), and Roy S. Walden's *Vintage Years of the Theatre Guild, 1928–1939* (Cleveland, 1972). Finally, the Federal Theatre has also been well served by studies such as Willson Whitman's *Bread and Circuses: A Study of the Federal Theatre* (New York, 1937), the informed and substantial inside account by Hallie Flanagan, *Arena: The History of the Federal Theatre* (New York, 1940), Jane DeHart Mathews' *The Federal Theatre 1935–1939: Plays, Relief and Politics* (Princeton, 1967), and John O'Connor and Lorraine Brown's brief but well-illustrated survey, *Free, Adult, Uncensored: The Living History of the Federal Theatre Project* (Washington, 1978).

Index

Contributors

MARY M. BROWN is Assistant Dean in the Faculty of Arts and Associate Professor of English at the University of Western Ontario. She has published books and articles on nineteenth-century Canadian literature, and is one of several authors of a projected two-volume history of theatre in Ontario, commissioned by the Ontario Historical Studies Series. Professor Brown is currently writing a book on the Michigan, Ohio, and Canadian circuit of theatres controlled by C. J. Whitney of Detroit and Ambrose Small of Toronto between 1875 and 1919.

MARVIN CARLSON, formerly Professor of Theatre Arts at Cornell University, is now Professor of Theatre and Drama and Director of Graduate Studies at the University of Indiana. He is the author of articles on French, German, Italian, Scandinavian, and English theatre history and dramatic literature which have appeared in *Theatre Journal, Drama Review, Modern Drama, Theatre Survey, Scandinavian Studies*, and other journals. His books on theatre history include *The Theatre of the French Revolution, Goethe and the Theatre in Weimar*, and, most recently, *The Italian Stage from Goldoni to D'Annunzio*. Professor Carlson received a Guggenheim fellowship for the study of nineteenth-century French staging.

HELEN KRICH CHINOY is Professor of Theatre at Smith College. Among her widely known publications are *Actors on Acting* and *Directors on Directing*, both edited with Toby Cole, and *Reunion: A Self-Portrait of the Group Theatre*. Her forthcoming volume, *Women in American Theatre: Images, Careers, Movements*, edited with Linda Walsh Jenkins, is an illustrated anthology and sourcebook, the first of its kind on the subject of women's experience in American theatre. Professor Chinoy is an Associate Editor of *Theatre Journal* and serves on the Research Commission of the American Theatre Association, of which she was made a Fellow in 1980. She has also held the chair of the Research Committee of the American Society for Theatre Research, and is a member of the National Theatre Conference. Professor Chinoy has held fellowships from the American Association of University Women and the National Endowment for the Humanities.

L. W. CONOLLY, formerly Professor of English at the University of Alberta, is now Professor of Drama and Chairman of the Department at the University of Guelph, Ontario. Co-editor of *Essays in Theatre*, he has published articles in a wide variety of British, American, and Canadian journals, and his books include *The Censorship of English Drama 1737–1824*, *English Drama and Theatre 1800–1900: A Guide to Information Sources* (with J. P. Wearing), and *A Directory of British Theatre Research Resources in North America*. Professor Conolly was co-founder of *Nineteenth Century Theatre Research*, and now serves as advisory editor, a position he also holds with *Theatre History in Canada*. He is a former President of the Association for Canadian Theatre History and is currently a member of the executive committees of the American Society for Theatre Research and the International Federation for Theatre Research. Professor Conolly is currently working on a history of the English-speaking theatre in Canada.

ROBERTSON DAVIES, formerly Master of Massey College and Professor of English at the University of Toronto, is one of Canada's leading men of letters. Holder of several honorary degrees, Professor Davies received the Lorne Pierce Medal from the Royal Society of Canada in 1961 for his contributions to Canadian literature, and the Governor General's award for fiction in 1973. He was made a Companion of the Order of Canada in 1972. Professor Davies' plays and novels are widely known, and he has published a number of books and articles on Canadian and British theatre.

JEAN–CLÉO GODIN is Professor of French at the University of Montreal, and served as Chairman of his department from 1974 to 1977. He has published over twenty articles in American, French, and Canadian journals, and his books include *Henri Bosco, une poétique du mystère*, *Le Theatre québécois* (with Laurent Mailhot) and *Le Theatre québécois II*. In 1977 Professor Godin founded the Société d'histoire du théâtre du Québec. He is a member of the editorial board of *Theatre History in Canada* and director of the University of Montreal's Théâtrothèque, a documentation center which collects information and archival material pertinent to Quebec and French-Canadian theatre.

DOUGLAS McDERMOTT is Professor of Drama at California State College, Stanislaus, located in Turlock, California. His doctorate is from the University of Iowa, and he was previously on the faculty of the University of California, Davis. He has published articles and reviews in various journals and collections, and he is a member of the editorial board of *Theatre Survey*. Professor McDermott specializes in the history of the American provincial theatre.

RICHARD MOODY is Emeritus Professor of Theatre and Drama, University of Indiana. His most recent book is *From Corlear's Hook to Herald Square*, a study of Ned Harrigan, the nineteenth-century actor-playwright-lyricist-entrepreneur. Among Professor Moody's many other publications are *America Takes the Stage: Romanticism in American Drama and Theatre 1750–1900*, *Edwin Forrest: First Star of the American Stage*, *The Astor Place Riot*, *Dramas from the American Theatre 1762–1909*, and *Lillian Hellman, Playwright*. Professor Moody was on the founding boards of the Theatre Communications Group and the University Theatre Association. He also served for three years as a member of the Board of Trustees of the National Theatre Conference. Between 1958 and 1970 he was director of the University Theatre and was involved in the Brown County Playhouse expansion, the purchase of the Showboat Majestic, and the formation of the Indiana Theatre Company. Professor Moody has been a Guggenheim Fellow, a Senior Fellow of the National Endowment for the Humanities, and a Fellow of the American Theatre Association.

ANDREW PARKIN teaches English at the University of British Columbia. Editor of *The Canadian Journal of Irish Studies*, Professor Parkin has published widely on modern drama. His books include *The Dramatic Imagination of W. B. Yeats*, a study guide to Shaw's *Caesar and Cleopatra*, and *Stage One: A Canadian Scenebook*, which deals with the development of Canadian drama to 1972.

ARNOLD ROOD is Professor of Dramatic Art at Dowling College. He has also taught at Queens College, Hunter College, and Adelphi University. In addition to his academic theatre background, Professor Rood has had considerable professional experience with organizations such as Lemonade Opera and the Metropolitan Opera. From his extensive Gordon Craig collection, he has contributed to exhibitions at the New York Public Library, the Lincoln Center Museum of the Performing Arts, the British Theatre Museum, the Grolier Club, and the National Gallery of Canada. Professor Rood wrote the catalogue for the Lincoln Center exhibition, co-authored *Edward Gordon Craig: A Bibliography* for the Society for Theatre Research, and edited *Gordon Craig on Movement and Dance* for Dance Horizons. He is currently working on an iconography of Craig's designs and drawings as well as a book on Craig and Isadora Duncan.

ANN SADDLEMYER, formerly Director of the University of Toronto's Graduate Centre for the Study of Drama, is currently Professor of English in Victoria College, University of Toronto. A Fellow of the Royal Society of Canada, she has served as Chairman of the International Association for the Study of Anglo-Irish Literature, and as first President of the Association for

Canadian Theatre History. Author and editor of many articles and books on Yeats, Synge, Lady Gregory, and the Irish theatre, Professor Saddlemyer is co-editor of *Theatre History in Canada* and general editor of a projected two-volume history of theatre in Ontario. Her most recent book is *Theatre Business: The Correspondence of the First Abbey Theatre Directors*. Professor Saddlemyer has lectured extensively on modern drama and theatre history in Canada, the United States, France, and Ireland.

ROBERT K. SARLÓS teaches at the University of California, Davis, where he is also director of the doctoral program in theatre research. In articles, exhibitions, and lectures he has dealt with the Medieval stage (Valenciennes), Elizabethan theatre (First Blackfriars'), Baroque scenery (G. Galli Bibiena), American theatre, Hungarian drama, and research methodology. Professor Sarlós has staged a performance reconstruction of an English court masque, and his book on the Provincetown Players is soon to be published. He is Vice-President of the Woodland Opera House Board of Directors and serves on the editorial board of *Theatre Survey*.

MICHAEL J. SIDNELL is Professor of English and Drama at the University of Toronto, where he was, until recently, Director of the Graduate Centre for the Study of Drama. He has published many articles on Irish literature and theatre and is the co-editor of two volumes of Yeats's writings. He is currently writing the history of the (London) Group Theatre. Professor Sidnell has also directed many productions at the Hart House Theatre of the University of Toronto and elsewhere.

ROSS STUART teaches theatre at York University, Ontario, where he served for four years as Chairman of the Department of Fine Arts at Atkinson College, and for a year as Acting Chairman of the Department of Theatre. His doctoral dissertation for the Drama Centre at the University of Toronto was a stylistic analysis of productions on the open stage at the Festival Theatre, Stratford, Ontario. A founding editor of the *Canadian Theatre Review*, Professor Stuart has contributed articles to that journal as well as to *Books in Canada*, *Quill and Quire*, and *Quarry*. He wrote the sections on musical theatre and review for the forthcoming *Encyclopedia of Music in Canada*. Professor Stuart served as President of the Association for Canadian Theatre History from 1979 to 1981 and is a member of the editorial board of *Theatre History in Canada*.

DON B. WILMETH is Professor of Theatre Arts and English at Brown University, and Chairman of the Department of Theatre Arts. He is former book review editor of *Theatre Journal* and serves as advisory editor for *Nineteenth Century Theatre Research*. His books include *The American*

Stage to World War I, George Frederick Cooke: Machiavel of the Stage, American and English Popular Entertainment, The Language of American Popular Entertainment, and *Variety Entertainment and Outdoor Amusements: A Reference Guide.* Currently, Professor Wilmeth is co-editing selected plays by William Gillette and Augustin Daly for Cambridge University Press. He serves on the executive boards of the American Society for Theatre Research and the Theatre Library Association, and is on the board of trustees of the Society for the Advancement of Education.

ALAN WOODS teaches theatre at Ohio State University, where he serves as Director of the Theatre Research Institute and edits its journal, *Theatre Studies.* He chairs the American Theatre Association's Commission on Theatre Research, and he edited *Theatre Journal* from 1979 through 1980. His articles on nineteenth-century popular theatre have appeared in *Theatre Survey, Journal of Sports History, Educational Theatre Journal* and *Theatre Studies,* among other journals. While at the University of Southern California, Professor Woods helped create the Ethel Barrymore Performing Arts Collection.